WORKING IN
CHILDREN'S HOMES

LIVING AWAY FROM HOME: STUDIES IN RESIDENTIAL CARE

Other titles in the series

Farmer & Pollock — Caring for Sexually Abused and Abusing Children away from Home

Sinclair & Gibbs — Children's Homes: A Study in Diversity

Department of Health — Children Living away from Home: Messages from Research

Hills & Child — Evaluating Residential Child Care Training: Towards Qualified Leadership

Wade, Biehal, Clayden & Stein — Going Missing: Young People Absent from Care

Sinclair — Residential Care for Children: Literature Review

WORKING IN CHILDREN'S HOMES

Challenges and Complexities

Dorothy Whitaker
Lesley Archer
Leslie Hicks

JOHN WILEY & SONS

Chichester · New York · Weinheim · Brisbane · Singapore · Toronto

Other Wiley Editorial Offices

John Wiley & Sons, Inc., 605 Third Avenue,
New York, NY 10158-0012, USA

WILEY-VCH Verlag GmbH, Pappelallee 3,
D-69469 Weinheim, Germany

Jacaranda Wiley Ltd, 33 Park Road, Milton,
Queensland 4064, Australia

John Wiley & Sons (Asia) Pte Ltd, 2 Clementi Loop #02-01,
Jin Xing Distripark, Singapore 129809

John Wiley & Sons (Canada) Ltd, 22 Worcester Road,
Rexdale, Ontario M9W 1L1, Canada

British Library Cataloguing in Publication Data

A catalogue record for this book is available from the British Library

ISBN 0-471-97953-8

Typeset in 10/12pt Palatino by Dorwyn Ltd, Rowlands Castle, Hants
Printed and bound in Great Britain by Redwood Books Ltd, Trowbridge, Wilts
This book is printed on acid-free paper responsibly manufactured from sustainable
forestry, in which at least two trees are planted for each one used for paper production.

CONTENTS

About the authors vii
Preface ix
Acknowledgements xi
Foreword xiii
Abbreviations xiv

1   Focusing on staff groups 1

2   The Homes, and the circumstances of the young people 10

3   The range of tasks in day-to-day work 19

4   Rewards and stresses, ups and downs 31

5   Working with individual young people 47

6   Working with the mix of young people 66

7   Working with and being managed by the larger organisation.. 81

8   Working with people and organisations in wider networks ... 101

9   Maintaining viability as a staff team, in the face of change 120

10 Working purposefully 133

11 Building a picture of good practice 153

12 Characteristics of good practice 167

13 Factors which support or hinder good practice 179

14 Factors which influence outcomes for individual young
    people 195

15 The quality of Homes as care settings 208

16 General comments on the challenges and complexities which
    staff groups face in Children's Homes 223

References and further reading 238

Index 243

ABOUT THE AUTHORS

Dorothy Whitaker is Emeritus Professor of Social Work in the Department of Social Policy and Social Work at the University of York (England). She has had a long-term interest in group dynamics and group psychotherapy, more recently expanded to include the dynamics of organisations and of personal and organisational networks. She is co-author with Herbert A. Thelen of *Emotionality and Group Culture* (Stock and Thelen, 1958); with Morton A. Lieberman of *Psychotherapy through the Group Process* (Whitaker and Lieberman, 1964), which formally sets out the propositions of Group Focal Conflict theory, and she is author of *Using Groups to Help People* (1985), a book written as guidance for practitioners. She has published articles on aspects of therapeutic groups, diverse further applications of Group Focal Conflict theory, relationships between theories about groups and between theory and practice, research partnerships with service-providing organisations, and guidance for practitioners and managers in the helping professions wishing to undertake research on aspects of their own work. In recent years she has conducted research on the group care of vulnerable populations, collaborating with Lesley Archer on two projects on the quality of life in residential homes for the elderly, and with Dr Archer and Galvin Whitaker on a project on the group care of adults with learning difficulties.

Lesley Archer is a Senior Research Fellow in the Social Work Research and Development Unit at the University of York. Her recent work includes being part of the team preparing *Children Living away from Home: Messages from Research* for the Department of Health, which brings together the findings from 13 pieces of research. She is committed to the development of collaborative research with organisations in the helping professions. This includes helping social work professionals and managers to design and carry out their own research; working collaboratively with organisations on larger, externally commissioned pieces of research; and disseminating findings in ways that make a difference to the quality of life of client populations.

Leslie Hicks is a Research Fellow in Social Policy and Social Work based in the Social Work Research and Development Unit at the University of York. Her research and teaching interests are in health and social care. As well as pursuing a special interest in the care of children and young people who are looked after away from home, her recent work concerns living standards; gender, dependence and age; developing cultures of learning in workplace settings; and modelling, developing and training in interview skills for practitioners and researchers. She also has contributed to the *Children Living away from Home: Messages from Research* Overview publication.

PREFACE

The broad purpose of this book is to depict and seek to understand the task of working in Children's Homes as experienced by unit managers and residential care staff. We set out to understand how staff think about their work and what they do to fulfil their core task of looking after and benefiting the children and young people in their care. The rationale for adopting this particular focus is the common-sense appreciation that the manner in which staff members function is bound to have an impact on the experience of the children and young people.

The staff groups taking part in this research were working in Homes within the public sector in England. The Homes were supported and managed by Social Services Departments, located in local authorities. From 6 to 16 children and young people were looked after in the Homes, which were mainly located in residential areas. Care staff typically included a unit manager, senior care staff, and care workers. Domestics and cooks employed in some Homes also had daily contact with the young people.

Social Services Departments have many responsibilities other than those to do with Children's Homes. With respect to children and young people, each is also responsible for fostering; for maintaining an at-risk register for children, some of whom still live in their own homes; and for carrying out assessment and preventative work with children and families. Field social workers retain responsibility for all such children, wherever they are placed. Departments are also responsible for services for vulnerable adults, including elderly people in residential care or in their own homes, learning-disabled adults, and people with psychiatric disturbances.

The research on which this book is based was exploratory in character. We wished to be open to whatever staff members had to tell us and show us about their working lives. The research process was one of making opportunities for unit managers and members of staff to do this sharing. Part of our task as researchers was to become channels through which members of staff could make known to others, without direct experience of the work, their experiences, actions, thoughts and feelings as residential carers. Another part of our task was to order, organise and draw conclusions from the data that emerged. The research thus includes two perspectives—that of residential workers, and that of ourselves as researchers considering the meaning and import of what was being shared by members of care staff.

We believe that much of what was learned has relevance well beyond the contexts in which the research was carried out. In some instances, broader relevance cannot be assumed but can be tested.

What was learned carries implications for those selecting staff, for supervisors and consultants, for educators and trainers, for managers at different levels in organisations reponsible for residential care, for those in outside organisations which also work with children, for policy-makers, and for those providing direct care in Homes.

ACKNOWLEDGEMENTS

The research on which this book is based could not have been accomplished without the goodwill and cooperation of a number of local authority Social Services Departments in England, of unit managers of Children's Homes who agreed to be interviewed, and of the staff of six Children's Homes who allowed the researchers to visit and hold discussions in their Homes over a period of more than a year. It was through staff and unit managers who were doing direct work that the researchers were able to develop, over time, an understanding of the working lives of those who undertake the taxing responsibilities connected with looking after children and young people in residential settings. Managers in their larger organisations are also to be thanked, firstly for allowing us to access Homes and speak with care workers, and secondly for participating in coordination and dissemination activities.

For the phase of the research in which six Homes were visted regularly, the university-based researchers were joined by three people seconded from the participating authorities. The resulting 'Project Workers Team' took responsibility for making visits to Homes and in meeting monthly as a research team of six. Our thanks go to these three people for their assistance in the work itself and for helping to keep the authorities' perspectives in view. The research concentrated on staff, but we also got to know a number of the young people in the six Homes where ongoing contact was maintained, and we thank them for sharing their experiences with us.

The research, originally titled 'The prevailing cultures and staff dynamics in Children's Homes', would not have happened at all without financial support provided by the Department of Health. We are grateful for that support, and for the sustained interest shown by members of the Department of Health in the research itself, the write-up, and follow-on activities. The research was enriched through the establishment of a Department of Health Advisory Group who monitored the research and advised us on it throughout its three-year life. We thank all those involved: Dr Carolyn Davies, Norman Duncan, Ted Hillier, John Rowlands, Jane Scott, Graham Jarvis, and Valerie Brasse, all of the Department of Health, and scientific advisers Stella Morris, David Pottage, and John

Warwick. This group, as all its members will be aware, was invaluable in discussing learnings as they emerged in the course of the research, keeping in view the interests of the Department of Health, and assisting the researchers to think through an appropriate structure for a final research report, and subsequently, for this book.

We have been assisted throughout by our secretary, Janet Moore, who provided all necessary technical help and support for the research and for the various dissemination activities undertaken in the course of it and afterwards. Beyond this, she maintained a close interest in the work from start to finish, stayed continuously in touch with the researchers' needs (and often anticipated them), and was an invaluable member of the research team.

FOREWORD

We are pleased to have the opportunity to provide the foreword to this book, which is one of a series of publications which, we are sure, will prove to be a significant contribution to thinking in both the practice and management of the care of children who need to live away from home.

The group of studies about residential care was commissioned to address key concerns arising from public inquiries, such as the Utting (Children in the Public Care) and Pindown Inquiries, and to provide a balanced account of what life is like for children and staff in the majority of children's homes in the UK in the 1990s.

Twelve linked research studies were commissioned by the Department of Health in the period 1990–94 (a thirteenth—that of David Berridge and Isabelle Brodie—was not commissioned by the Department). These research studies came in the wake of the implementation of the Children Act 1989 and its Regulations and Guidance, which provided significant new safeguards for children living away from home. Additional government action to protect these children was taken following the publication of the reports 'Children in the Public Care', 'Accommodating Children', 'Another Kind of Home' and 'Choosing with Care', notably through the publications of the Support Force for Children's Residential Care and circulars issued by the relevant Departments of State. However, as Sir William Utting tells us in his second report 'People Like Us', published in 1997, providing safe and caring settings for children looked after away from home remains a significant challenge for the nineties.

This book, taken together with the overview publication, and the others in the series contains lessons for all those concerned with children and young people living away from home, who are the responsibility of all of us.

Carolyn Davies, *Department of Health*
Lesley Archer, *University of York*
Leslie Hicks, *University of York*
Mike Little, *Dartington Social Research Unit*
—Editors

ABBREVIATIONS

A&E	Accident and Emergency
CCETSW	Central Council for Education and Training in Social Work
CQSW	Certiciate of Qualification in Social Work
CRCCYP	Certificate in the Residential Care of Children and Young People
CSS	Certificate of Social Services
DipSW	Diploma in Social Work
DoH	Department of Health
DSS	Department of Social Security
EWO	Education Welfare Officer
FSW	Field Social Worker
GCSE	General Certificate of Secondary Education
GPs	General Practitioners
LA	Local Authority
LEA	Local Education Authority
NNEB	National Nursing Examining Board
SSD	Social Services Department
SSI	Social Services Inspectorate

FOCUSING ON STAFF GROUPS

FOCUSING ON STAFF GROUPS AND ASSOCIATED PURPOSES

The focus of the research on which this book is based was on staff in residential homes for children. We concentrated on 'ordinary' Homes, excluding those which provided services for learning-disabled children or were conducted as therapeutic communities. Our purposes were to understand what staff face, what they do, how they think about their work, how they feel about themselves and the children and others with whom they interact, how they function, and the consequences and outcomes of how they function.

The rationale for this focus and this set of purposes was to discover how staff function as this bears crucially on the experience of children and young people in residential care. Children's Homes are set up in order to look after and benefit children and young people who, for various reasons, cannot live with their own families. Members of staff are there to create a caring and growth-promoting environment within which each child can thrive and develop, and recover insofar as possible from consequences of adverse previous experiences. Despite an increasing emphasis (in England) on foster care, the experience of living in a residential home is a part of the care career of many young people. It therefore continues to be important to understand what practice *is*, in residential settings, and how good practice can be supported and sustained.

THE RESEARCH APPROACH APPROPRIATE TO THE PURPOSES

The purposes of the research made certain demands on research approach and design. They required getting close-in to what happens in Children's Homes, so as to understand what staff do (both inside the Home and in interactions with the outside world), and how they think and interact. This argued for an intensive, qualitative piece of research. For practical reasons, the research would then have to be relatively small scale. Since we wanted to understand how things change over time, at least part of the research would have to be longitudinal in character. Because some of what we sought to understand was bound to be complex in ways which could not be anticipated in the beginning, the research would necessarily be exploratory in character. We wanted what we learned to be relevant beyond the staff and Homes in the study. The sample of Homes and staff groups had to be big enough to avoid idio-syncratic findings, but not so big as to be unmanageable in practical terms. Data-collection methods would have to be such as to capture the special character of working in Children's Homes, and to get in touch with the complexity of such work. Data-analysis methods would have to preserve the detail of residential work, yet introduce order into what was likely to be a large mass of data.

We wanted the research to be a form of partnership between ourselves and the unit managers and staff who were to be the informants for the research. To this partnership, unit managers and staff of Homes would bring their practical experience. The researchers would contribute frame-works for tapping into this experience, and take responsibility for sum-marising and ordering what was heard and being learned. Sharing and dissemination to unit managers, residential care workers, and participat-ing organisations were to be a part of the work as it progressed.

While the perspectives of staff members were to be preserved and reported, the researchers would, in addition, bring to bear their own perspectives on what was being told to them and shown by staff. It was expected that staff perspectives and researcher perspectives would be consonant, in part, but also likely to differ in some respects, especially with regard to the meanings placed on events.

THE START-POINT IN THEORY

We predicted, before the research began, that ideas to do with 'culture' and 'group dynamics' would be relevant to the purposes we had in mind and the data likely to emerge. This was based on an awareness that staff make up a social group whose members share particular purposes, face a common task, and are in frequent interaction with one another. Such groups—of which a staff group is of course only one example—form characteristic cultures, and come to interact in characteristic ways.

We take 'culture' to refer to the values, norms, shared beliefs, assump-tions and expectations held by a social group, roles and role differentia-tion, and characteristic interactive patterns and styles. Thinking in terms of culture draws attention to the fact that some aspects of culture are clearly visible—for instance, rules, rituals, artefacts, and written statements of purpose or guidelines—while other features of culture are implicit and can only be deduced by observing consistencies and inconsistencies within the social group over time. Among the less visible features of a culture are implicit assumptions, expectations, and 'rules of interpretation', and those aspects of norms, beliefs, and values which are additional to (and possibly inconsistent with) those contained in documents and public declarations.

We have found the following definitions from the literature helpful:

> Culture includes (i) a shared language, which symbolises and categorises events; (ii) a shared way of perceiving and thinking about the world; (iii) agreed forms of non-verbal communications and social interaction, which makes cooperation possible; (iv) rules and conventions about what shall be done in different situations; (v) agreed moral and other values, and a system of religious and allied beliefs; (vi) technology and material culture.
>
> (Argyle, 1969, p. 78)

> Culture can now be defined as (a) a pattern of basic assumptions, (b) invented, discovered, or developed by a given group, (c) as it learns to cope with its problems of external adaptation and internal integration, (d) that has worked well enough to be considered valid and, therefore (e) is to be taught to new members as the (f) correct way to perceive, think, and feel in relation to those problems. (Schein, 1990b, p. 111)

Thinking of a social group in terms of its culture calls attention to possible homogeneity or heterogeneity within the group with respect, for example, to norms and shared assumptions about the internal and external world. It points to the potential usefulness of examining features of the culture in relation to the demands, opportunities and constraints of the group's particular environment. When distinctive social groups are in contact one with the other, conflicts and compatibilities may be thought of in terms of culture clash and culture consonance. Attention can be directed to cultural change over time, and to the phenomenon of cultural lag, when members of a social group cling to established features of their culture even when changes in the environment require adaptation and change. All of the above is relevant to both very large and quite small social units.

'Group dynamics' is a term applied to relatively small social groups where face-to-face contact occurs or can occur. Such groups develop a set of 'espoused' values, which members can express in words and which they say are characteristic of them. Observation reveals how espoused values are expressed in behaviour, and whether espoused values are consistent or inconsistent with 'values-in-action'. Through their interaction, over time, small face-to-face groups develop shared beliefs, wishes, and aspirations. They also develop shared concerns, preoccupations and fears. To survive, they need to find ways to maintain themselves as a group and to cope with features of their environment. To do this, they are likely to adopt customs and practices which support survival. Role differentiation usually occurs, with certain members taking on particular tasks and responsibilities essential to the group. To maintain internal stability, members establish behavioural norms, and views of the world (beliefs) which all members are expected to accept. There will also be ways of trying to control and influence those who deviate from the group's socially constructed norms and beliefs—by formal or informal rewards and punishments. Some survival tactics carry with them disadvantages to the social group. For example, a group might adopt the device of finding a common enemy, which binds them together but at the same time puts many of their members at risk, should overt conflict break out. As another example, members might identify a scapegoat from within their own membership, who can be blamed when things go wrong. Small social groups can develop cooperatively or collusively maintained psychological defences—for example, denial or rationalisation. These support cohesiveness and are advantageous in that regard, but have the disadvantage of being distorted perceptions of the 'real' reality. Ways in which small groups differ from one another include their particular goals and goal systems, degrees of cohesion and consensus, roles and role differentiation (both formal and informal), leadership and leadership styles, and characteristic ways of responding to conflict. Groups differ, too, in how they maintain the boundaries between themselves and other social groups with which they are in contact—some boundaries are rigidly maintained, some are more permeable. Group dynamics as a field of study also encompasses intergroup relationships.

'Culture' and 'group dynamics' are distinctive fields of study. Historically, they have different origins. The study of culture was embedded in the first instance in social and cultural anthropology, while group dynamics emerged from within social psychology and later also became important in clinical psychology. It is evident, however, that certain ideas and even certain terms appear in both. Common elements include, for example, norms, belief systems, and role differentiation. The idea that 'truth' is defined by consensus (through shared beliefs which are unchallenged within the social group) is accepted by both. Each also uses terms and ideas not ordinarily used by the other. For example, cultural anthropology points to legends, artefacts, and rituals, not ordinarily thought of as applying to small groups. Group dynamics calls attention to shared psychological defences and shared covert goals, not ordinarily applied to large social groups. Further thought, however, suggests that some of these ideas can cross over from one field to the other, if they are somewhat reformulated. For example, one does not usually think of a small group as being characterised by legends. Yet a small group, if it has existed for some time, may well have a fund of stories which refer back to events in its shared past and which function to maintain a sense of identity and continuity for the group.

Students of group dynamics are more likely to examine fine-grained interpersonal interactions in face-to-face group settings—who said what, what then followed, how a sequence of comments and interactions can build into a theme. Those examining cultures are more likely to be interested in large-scale cultural change, cultural diversity, contact and conflict between whole cultures. Yet small social units as well as large ones are seen as developing characteristic cultures; interpersonal and group interactions are acknowledged as building blocks of culture; it is understood that a sub-unit within some larger cultural entity may well be a small group in frequent face-to-face contact.

Our application of the set of ideas described above is to relatively small social groups composed of those who work as staff in a Children's Home. It is reasonable to suppose that such social groups, like others, will be describable in terms of prevailing beliefs, norms, expectations, assumptions and values, and that these will be expressed in customary practices, rules, and the like. It is reasonable to expect that the ways in which staff interact with one another and with others important to the Home's operations, will both express and shape their values, norms, assumptions, and so on. It is also reasonable to expect that some part of a staff group's shared beliefs and assumptions will be held implicitly—not put into words but yet powerfully influential. Finally, it is reasonable to expect that the environment, with its particular demands, opportunities and constraints, is significant in shaping the character of a staff group.

THE RESEARCH PLAN

The research was to be a three-year project. It was supported by the UK Department of Health, which also supported some follow-on work after the research had been completed. It was decided to divide the research into two parts. The first part would collect accounts of episodes encountered in practice from unit managers through in-depth, qualitative telephone interviews. The second part would be smaller in scale and longitudinal. In it, six of the Homes would be followed over a period of approximately one year, through visits made to each Home at intervals of about a month, and discussions with whole staff groups. We refer to the two parts of the research as 'Study 1' and 'Study 2'.

The Study 1 sample was to include 39 Homes—three from each of 13 authorities in England, excluding London. Of the 13 local authorities included in this research, six were metropolitan authorities and seven were county authorities.

Each unit manager was asked to fill in a 'Short Profile' of his or her Home, which asked for background information.

Study 1 was designed to collect experiences of unit managers, in order to understand what they faced at the 'cutting edge' of practice, and how they thought about and responded to difficult situations.

Each of 39 unit managers was asked to provide four accounts of challenging and difficult situations encountered in practice. Two of these were to be manageable in the end, with good outcomes; two were to be difficult to manage satisfactorily, with poor outcomes. The focus for the accounts was not restricted: it was made clear that an account could be about individual young people, groups of young people, or any other aspect of the work of the unit. The intention, it will be evident, was to concentrate on borderline situations at or near the limits of what a unit manager felt that he or she and the staff could handle or manage, given the nature of the situation and any constraints within which staff were operating.

In order to carry out Study 1, preparatory work was needed, and record-keeping procedures had to be devised. Key tasks were to acquire the necessary permissions; identify the Homes and the unit managers who would be asked to participate in Study 1; prepare a 'Short Profile' for collecting contextual information from participating unit managers; devise an interview schedule for use with each unit manager; and conduct a small pilot study before the main data collection began.

Study 1 was expected to yield 39×4, i.e. 156 accounts. In the event, interviews could not be conducted with one of the unit managers. Some unit managers produced more than the four accounts asked for. A few produced less. The interviews yielded 152 accounts of specific episodes and 50 or so more general comments about issues facing unit managers and Homes.

The data available through Study 1 were subjected to theme and content analysis procedures. The essentials of each account were first summarised so that the data were in a less bulky form. The researchers then identified (a) the focus of each account (e.g. individual young people, two or more (or all) of the young people in interaction, problems within the staff group, relationships with young people's families, relationships with the larger organisation, and so on), and (b) its theme (e.g. the needs of individual young people, violence or other emergencies, stresses experienced by staff, etc.). Accounts pertaining to particular foci and themes were brought together into sub-populations of accounts which were examined through content analysis procedures. Issues explored through Study 1 were: the tasks of staff; the needs and demands of individual young people; violence and threats of violence; the mix of young people in the Homes, and comings and goings of children and young people; internal staff dynamics; relationships with the larger organisation of which the Home is a part; and the wider networks relevant to young people and to Homes. Study 1 data were analysed on their own, but what was learned was held until Study 2 had been completed, so that the data from both studies could be combined and further analyses undertaken.

Study 2 was designed to provide understandings about what happens in Homes and how staff groups operate over a period of time. Monthly visits were made to each Home, usually lasting from one-and-a-half to two hours. Group discussions were held with as many members of staff as could be present.

Arrangements were made for keeping in close touch with the cooperating organisations as the work went on. This was done through a 'Project Workers' Team' and a 'Project Coordination Group'. The Project Workers' Team consisted of the three university-based researchers and three people from the field, seconded part time from each of the three participating authorities. The six members of the Project Workers' Team formed themselves into pairs, who visited a given Home together throughout the period of Study 2. All the project workers met as a full group once a month. The Project Coordination Group consisted of unit managers of each of the six Homes, another member of each residential staff, external managers from the participating Departments (usually line-managers and/or service managers), and members of the Project Workers Team. This group met at approximately five-month intervals.

Study 2 was divided into two phases. *Phase 1* consisted of two workshop meetings in each of the Homes. The aim was to establish a working relationship with each staff group and to begin to acquire substantive understandings. *Phase 2* consisted of the long series of visits to each of the Homes. It began by introducing an action research procedure (after Kurt Lewin), which we hoped would constitute a frame for group discussions and provide information about how staff functioned and thought about their work. Action research consists of a series of cycles, with each cycle having the following steps: identifying a specific, concrete goal; devising an action plan which seems likely to move a situation towards achieving the identified goal; carrying out the plan; and judging consequences and reflecting on what was learned. A further action research cycle then follows. (This model is described in more detail in Chapter 10.) The researchers provided 'minutes' of each visit, which were detailed process notes. These were distributed to members of staff and checked for accuracy during the subsequent visit. In the course of each visit, sharing occurred about what was happening with respect to the action research cycles, and staff members told the researchers about events which had occurred since the previous visit.

The data yielded by Study 2 were in some ways less tidy than the data yielded by Study 1. Study 1 produced discrete accounts which had a beginning, middle, and end. Study 2 data were a mix of anecdotes, references to current staff preoccupations, and observable interpersonal interactions—sometimes within the staff group and sometimes between staff and young people. The interruptions which occurred were in themselves illuminating and also constituted data. Chains of related events sometimes carried on over weeks or months. Study 2 allowed the researchers to be in touch with changes over time as they occurred, including stimuli for change which were often unexpected and frequent. As with Study 1, themes were identified, some but not all of which had also appeared in Study 1.

The data yielded by Study 1 were analysed first and separately, as described above. When Study 2 data became available, a revised set of themes was constructed which took into account what was learned through both studies. None of the Study 1 themes were discarded, for all proved to be relevant, but some were further differentiated. On the basis of the combined data, work in Children's Homes as purposeful action was added as a theme which deserved explicit attention. The researchers also perceived that the combined data could be used to explore issues to do with the quality of practice and outcomes, so this too was added. The key themes so identified were then further examined through content analysis procedures applied to both Study 1 and Study 2 data. Content analysis took different forms depending on the nature of the theme. These are detailed in the chapters to which they are relevant.

DISSEMINATION AND FOLLOW-ON ACTIVITIES

Two 'dissemination days' were designed and conducted—one for the unit managers who had participated in Study 1, and managers and others from their organisations; and one for staff and unit managers who had participated in Study 2, and other members of their organisations. Key findings were presented and opportunities were made for those present to comment on their relevance, or otherwise, to their own experience and work situation. The dissemination day for Study 2 included opportunities for people at different levels of the participating organisations to discuss together the implications of the research findings for actions they might wish to take. Though not part of the research itself, these dissemination days enhanced our understanding of what, among our findings, was experienced as important by those working in Children's Homes and those managing services.

After the research had been completed and written up, four forms of follow-on activity were undertaken. Firstly, further meetings were held with the organisations which had participated in Study 2. Participants included those working in the Homes and providing direct care, the unit manager, line managers, higher managers and other relevant people within the larger organisation such as field social workers, training officers, and councillors (i.e. elected members, since the organisations were in the public sector). The purpose was to communicate to such groups what had been learned through the research, to invite those present to consider the relevance of the findings to their own situation, and to create opportunities for them to give thought to actions they might take. Secondly, meetings were arranged with selected people from among those providing group care within the voluntary and private sectors in England. The purpose was to share findings and gain some understanding of their relevance to work being done outside the public sector. Thirdly, since the research was generating ideas for what needed to be included in a theoretical framework concerning residential child care practice, these were tested through discussions with a small number of researchers, practitioners, and administrators with experience of residential care. Fourthly, meetings were held with key members of the UK Department of Health and the Social Services Inspectorate to assist the researchers to select out from the range of findings those of particular interest to policy makers at national level.

2

THE HOMES, AND THE CIRCUMSTANCES OF THE YOUNG PEOPLE

THE HOMES IN STUDY 1

There were 39 Homes in Study 1. Information about numbers of young people and staff characteristics was received from 34 of the 39 unit managers, who returned a form sent to them titled 'Short Profile'.

Of these 34 Homes, the average number of young people currently in the units was 7.2, and the average number of beds was 8.7. One unit had no residents at the time of interview, having just re-opened after refurbishment and change of purpose; another was operating at more than capacity by the use of a 'put-you-up' bed in the lounge. Excluding the youngest child—a five-month-old baby who was in the care of a teenage mother—the average age of girls was 14 years. The average age of boys was 13.4 years. The upper age was 18 years. Of the total number of young people in the units, 44.5% were girls. All of the units catered for both sexes. Approximately 88% of the total young people were categorised by those completing the forms as being 'British white'.

Twelve of the 34 unit managers who responded were women and 22 were men. Their average age was 41.9 years. All worked full time. They had been in their posts for an average of 5.7 years but the range was very wide. The longest appointment was 19 years, and the shortest a matter of a month. The unit managers averaged 14.9 years' experience in residential child care. With the exception of three, all described their ethnic background as 'British white'. All but five unit managers held some form of qualification. These varied: four held the CQSW (Certificate of Qualification in Social Work) or equivalent (the DipSW, or Diploma in Social Work), nine the CSS (Certificate in Social Services), six the CSS and other qualifications, and ten a certificate, diploma, or an in-service training credential of some kind.

The average staff complement (all staff, including domestics) was 13.7 per unit. This included both full-time and part-time staff. The average number of female care staff, per staff group, was 6.3, and the average number of male care staff, per staff group, was 3.7. Of the total staff (all contracts), approximately 92% were categorised by those who completed the form as 'British white'.

Of the total of 467 staff (all posts) employed in the units, four held CQSW and/or DipSW qualifications; ten held CSS qualifications; nine held degrees; four held nursing qualifications; three held NNEB (National Nursing Examining Board) qualifications; and a total of 38 held credentials of some other form, including City and Guilds, CRCCYP (Certificate in the Residential Care of Children and Young People), and some in-service training.

Nine of the units did not have staff vacancies. The remaining 25 units had the equivalent of approximately 51 child care staff vacancies in total, or an average of 2.04. Some vacancies were for full-time posts and some were part-time. Some units were in the process of appointing staff. Many drew on relief staff or borrowed staff from other units to provide cover.

The majority of the units were situated in residential areas. Two had moved during the last five years, and 26 reported some significant change which affected their functioning. Eleven of those 26 reported changes in purpose and function, size, the ages of the young people looked after, or a shift in composition from being a single-sex to a mixed-sex Home. Fifteen units had experienced other changes, such as expanding their aftercare service, introducing an independence programme, and/or dealing with a larger number of damaged young people than previously.

THE HOMES IN STUDY 2

The Study 2 sample was a sub-set of the larger sample. Six Homes, two from each of three authorities which had participated in Study 1, were selected for the longitudinal study.

The authorities in which these Homes were located were: a metropolitan authority on the fringe of a very large city (a commuter area), a county which covered a large rural area but had one major city, and a county authority which included a number of small to medium-sized towns and a large number of villages. Brief descriptions of the Homes follow.

Home A was a purpose-built Children's Home located in a no-through road in a very large, well-kept housing estate on the outskirts of a metropolitan city. The house was larger than those on either side of it and across the road from it. The unit had a semi-independence flat attached to it. The unit, for six young people, was characterised by a rapid turnover of young people and changes in the staff group. Six months before the research began, and subsequently, the unit had significant problems with accommodating an adverse mixture of offenders and non-offenders. Staff included an acting unit manager, two seniors, four long-standing care staff (three of whom did not have permanent contracts), a part-time administrative assistant, and one full-time equivalent domestic.

Home B was located on the outskirts of a large city (a 20-minute bus ride from the centre) on a main arterial road. It was in a built-up area with several local shops nearby. The house itself was old, Victorian, and obviously not purpose-built. It was pleasantly furnished and had space for seven young people—mainly teenagers. There was a rapid turnover of young people, although the staff—eight care staff, a unit manager, and a domestic—had been stable for a long time.

Home C was situated on a very busy arterial road which forms part of a conurbation of a large city. It was in a dormitory town with a population of around 50,000. The Home was located on a local bus route and a metro station and shopping centre were nearby. The ten-bedded Home was set back from the main road and sandwiched between a small civic hall and a Victorian park with mature trees. The Home had been purpose-built in the early 1980s, but since then its purpose had changed, and at the start of the research it was designated as a Children's Resource Centre. The building had been divided in two approximately three years before the research began, and one half of the building was occupied by fieldwork teams. There was a garden with a lawn suitable for playing games. There were eight residential staff (including the unit manager), three domestic staff and two cooks.

Home D was situated in the 'stockbroker belt' of a large city and had provision for 16 young people. There was a small town nearby, with a railway station and shopping precinct. The Home was near to main transport links, and was on a local bus route. By road, it was about 30 minutes from the city centre. The Home was in an affluent area: houses in the vicinity were sold in the region of £250,000 and above. The house was built around 1860 as the home of a mill-owner, set at a distance from the disease and poverty of inner-city life. It was a large, impressive building, with extensive grounds, including glasshouses which were no longer in use. There was plenty of space for football and games, and inside the house there was a gym area. The annexe (presumably built as the lodge), was 50 metres from the front door of the Home. It housed offices for the resource manager, unit manager, and general administration, and included a conference room. There was a core of residential staff who had worked at the unit for some time, with some more recent staff. The total staff comprised 13 residential, three night waking, five domestics, and one secretary. The unit provided a structured environment and specialised in dealing with the most challenging young people in the authority. The unit's on-site educational provision had closed just prior to the start of the Study 2 visits. When the research meetings began, preparation for imminent changes was underway. There were plans to house this unit's young people in two new purpose-built units, and the original unit was to close.

Home E was located across the end of a cul-de-sac in a run-down council housing estate in a medium-sized town. It was a purpose-built house which had been redecorated by the staff just as the research began. Around the same time the Home had new bedding and curtains, and, for the first time, a dishwasher. At the beginning of the research, the Home had six resident teenagers (in practice older boys, with whom staff preferred to work) and had a unit manager, five 'permanent' care staff (two of these, neither of them seniors, were from the permanent pool register and on contracts to the SSD but not to the Home), and a domestic. One senior had been off sick since before the project began, but her temporary replacement was well known to the staff and regarded as part of the staff group.

Home F was a large stone-built house which included two bedrooms that were paid for by the family of the unit manager and sometimes used by them. This arrangement was left over from the time when the officer-in-charge and her family lived on the premises. The house was located in a village, on the edge of a small council development, and had views of rolling countryside. The female staff group (a unit manager, two seniors, three care staff, a domestic, and a part-time cook) had, with one exception, been together for four years at the beginning of the research. The group of six young people (two boys and four girls) varied in age from 11 to 17 years. This group had been more or less stable for about two years, and some young people had been living at the Home even longer. All the young people had been significantly abused, and were regarded by staff as emotionally demanding. Prior to this two-year period of stability, the Home had had a very difficult time. Young people who had behaved violently and had been sent from police custody, joined the group; others had been remanded as emergencies to the unit. These new admissions severely disrupted the work of the staff and the lives of the young people already there. In early 1993, in the wake of the Children Act, the Home was designated as a long-term unit. The group of young people in the Home was stabilised, and all were attending school or college.

CIRCUMSTANCES AND BACKGROUNDS OF THE YOUNG PEOPLE

We learned about the circumstances and backgrounds of the children and young people living in the Homes from unit managers interviewed for Study 1 and through the series of visits to Children's Homes in Study 2. In the course of Study 2 we met a number of the young people ourselves, since some came to Study 2 meetings and joined in discussions.

What we have to say should be considered indicative of the kinds of children and young people with whom staff groups worked. We did not conduct a systematic survey of the young people and are unable to report frequencies. Nor do we claim that the young people in our Homes are representative of young people in residence generally, though we have no reason to suppose they are not.

The young people we heard about, and came to know, differed with respect to the circumstances surrounding their coming to live in the Homes; their current state and behaviours; relationships with parents; and personal strengths and vulnerabilities.

Circumstances Surrounding Coming to Live in the Homes

Some young people came into residential care for a short period because of a family crisis that was expected to right itself—for example, mother was ill in hospital with no one available to look after the young person. There were no previous placements, and the young person gave no special cause for concern. Such young people were waiting for circumstances to change to allow them to return home. Others came into care because of loss of the key, caring parent, or both parents, through death, and no one remained in his or her family or personal network who could provide care. Such young people were likely to be in a state of acute grief upon first entering the Home. Some had made suicide attempts and were considered to be at risk of self-harm. The residential Home might be regarded as a way-station while fostering was sought, but sometimes living in the Home became a long-stay arrangement. In some cases, where a young person was difficult and disturbed and was living at home with one or both parents or with foster parents, the key carers needed a period of respite from the stresses of care and the young person was placed in the Home for a week or two for 'respite care'. Some young people came into residential care because the key, caring parent had rejected him or her and no longer wanted the child to live in the family. Rejection might occur because of the behaviour of the child, or because the parent had formed some new relationship which excluded the young person or turned him or her into an irritant from the parent's point of view. The young person was alienated from, or in conflict with, the parent, or still yearning for the parent and suffering acute and ongoing distress.

Some young people had been abused physically or sexually by a family member or someone closely connected with the family, and so came into care. In some cases the abuse took the form of repeated humiliation or neglect. The abuse might have occurred recently, or it might have started years before and was ongoing. Sometimes the trauma following from having been abused was severe, manifesting in a range of behaviour disorders, and problems with identity or self-esteem. Some young people came into residence because they were considered to be at risk, for example because of drug-taking or being involved in prostitution.

Some young people had been in one or another form of substitute care virtually all of their lives, or for very long periods. Their 'care career' included multiple placements in a succession of Children's Homes, foster homes, and occasional stays with own parent(s).

Some young people elected to come into residential care, because of dissatisfaction with home and family, quarrels with parents, or feeling to be unsupported or badly treated by parents. Sometimes material deprivation played a part. Such young people may have requested care themselves, or behaved at home or school in such a way that their parents requested care, or may have come into care after having accused a parent of abuse.

Some young people were referred to residence by legal processes, under Youth Justice and the Police and Criminal Justice Act procedures. In such instances neither the young person nor the parent(s) might wish the young person to be in care.

Of the above, the first two sets of circumstances were seen only occasionally in this research; the others more frequently.

The Emotional and Physical State of Young People Entering Homes

At the time they entered the Home some young people were in a satisfactory state—emotionally, physically and psychologically—apart from to-be-expected feelings associated with coming into residence. These young people settled down relatively quickly after the initial transition period. They attended school, and caused no problems inside or outside the Home. Such young people were usually considered good candidates for fostering. If fostering could be arranged, they soon left the Home. In some instances, fostering was not arranged for various reasons: either a suitable foster home could not be found, or a return to own home was still hoped for, or the young person rejected the idea. Such young people often became firmly settled in the Home, and wanted to stay until old enough for independent living.

Some young people were suffering the consequences of trauma—including physical or sexual abuse, or abandonment by parents. Some were fixed in a lifestyle which was disadvantageous to themselves. When they first arrived, they had been offending, away from school, sniffing, or on drugs. Some were prone to violence or self-harm, or were withdrawn. Such behaviour might continue for some time.

Young people showed a range of behavioural and emotional problems. Some displayed chaotic behaviour and poor impulse control, including proneness to harm others, destroy property, and make physical threats against others. They ran away, caused disturbances at school, were excluded from school, and/or harassed neighbours. Offending might or might not be a part of this. Other young people were fearful, for example, of going to school or at the prospect of leaving care, with signs of high dependency on the unit or the staff. Some were emotionally or socially isolated. They tended to withdraw from others or form only superficial relationships with others. Some experienced a sense of being lost, of having no one and having no future.

Some young people committed offences. This had usually started in the past and was often ongoing. A common offence was taking cars without the owner's permission, but more serious offences occurred—for example, burglary with intimidation. Some young people offended on their own, some offended together with other young people, and a few were associated with adult criminals.

Some young people were engaged in inappropriate sexual behaviour, which could take a number of forms: prostitution (both boys and girls, sometimes with some adult in the community arranging contacts); frequent active sexual behaviour on the part of girls with boys or men found in the community and, sometimes, one or more boys in the Home; sexual abuse of other, often younger, children, usually by boys; involvement with adults in pornographic activity; exhibitionistic sexual behaviour in public; or simply a tendency towards highly sexualised behaviour displayed in the most ordinary of everyday contexts.

Personal Characteristics

There were differences among young people in personal strength and degree of vulnerability. Some young people showed considerable personal strengths in the face of difficult home circumstances: they were competent, courageous, sensitive to others and showed a capacity for non-hostile humour. Some young people showed fewer personal resources: they were easily triggered into temper outbursts, or easily hurt, or took every opportunity to do harm to others. Some attacked members of staff, physically and verbally. Some such children seemed unaware of the hurt they caused to others, or else relished it. Some harmed themselves. Vulnerability could be associated with being learning disabled and often the butt of other children, or having poor social skills, or being developmentally disadvantaged because of earlier neglect or trauma. Some of those who had been abused had become abusers themselves.

Life Stage

The young people were either pre-teens or adolescents, though at times children younger than 10 were in residence. The age range was usually relatively narrow, but even so the young people living in a Home could be at different life stages. An 11-year-old, for example, is at a very different life stage from a 16-year-old who may well be looking towards leaving care and living independently. Staff members were aware that chronological age is not necessarily indicative of life stage. They would say 'he is a young 15', or 'she is only 12, but into drugs and sex'.

Relationships with Parents

Relationships with parents varied: a young person and a parent might be in an acute state of conflict (emotional or physical); a young person might have been rejected by a parent and still be grieving and hoping for acceptance. A young person might have been rejected by a parent or parents and now want nothing to do with them; a parent might be in and out of the child's life, for example through periods of being in prison or through leading a chaotic lifestyle. A parent might not be able to keep a child at home for reasons outside his or her control (such as illness or a severe physical handicap) but remain committed to the child and in frequent contact. A parent who had been rejected by a son or daughter might still be standing by, hoping for a time when the young person would become willing to return home.

'Career in Care' to Date

It was not unusual for the current placement in a residential Home to be the most recent of many, with further placements often likely to be in store. Young people experienced periods in residential care, foster care, and returns home which were followed by further out-of-home placements. It was not unusual for a child or young person to be moved from one foster placement to another, as each in turn broke down, or to return to residential care for shorter or longer periods of time between foster placements. Sometimes a child was returned to the same residential home in which he or she had been living previously, but often, a return to residential care meant entering a different facility.

Schooling

Schooling had often been interrupted not once but many times. Many young people were consequently behind in their education. It was not unusual for them to fear school or find it distasteful. Some were currently excluded from school or refused to attend school.

THE MIX OF YOUNG PEOPLE LIVING IN THE HOME

The mix or composition of children and young people was different at different times. In any current mix, some but not all of the life circumstances, forms of relationships with parents, personal strengths or vulnerabilities, etc., detailed above were represented.

Turnover took different forms. Some Homes were designated long-stay Homes and, for them, a young person who came at the age of 13 or 14 might remain until care-leaving age. In such Homes, a young person leaving and another entering were major events. Some Homes were long-stay but had an emergency bed, so the Home was likely to house a core of longer-stay people alongside a number of young people who came and went quite rapidly. Some Homes accepted young people for respite care for a week or two. Young people sometimes came and went within a short time. The composition might be stable for a period, and then major changes might occur quickly, with two or three new young people being admitted in a single week. These various patterns of admissions, transfers, and rates of throughput meant that, in many Homes, both young people and members of staff were frequently faced with new people and, of course, the newcomers found themselves in a similar position.

3

THE RANGE OF TASKS IN DAY-TO-DAY WORK

In Study 1, we did not place restrictions on the focus of the accounts asked for. We made it clear to unit managers that we were interested in anything they had to say about their work life. The accounts they provided often focused on individual children or on a number of children. Other accounts, however, had to do with the larger organisation, or with neighbours, or with problems within the staff group. It quickly became apparent that a wide range of tasks face unit managers or members of staff, and that demands on them can emerge suddenly and unexpectedly. This was confirmed by Study 2, which also showed that tasks often pile up in day-to-day work, requiring staff to manage the urgent, the important, and the routine, all at the same time, and to shift rapidly from one task to another.

REALITIES OF STAFF MEMBERS' WORKING LIVES

Categorising the tasks which face staff groups assists in seeing the range and character of tasks which they must undertake. However, categorisation can make working life appear to be more orderly and compartmentalised than it actually is. Thus to categorise both clarifies and obscures the realities of staff members' working lives. In order not to lose sight of what working life is about, we give two examples.

Example 1: The Events of a Single Weekend

This example was recorded by the researchers during a Study 2 visit. The unit manager and her staff described events which had occurred in the course of the previous weekend:

'Over the weekend, we [the unit manager and one of her staff] had to go to the hospital twice with an emergency. What happened was that Martin [a young person], when he was here [resident in the unit] before, used to go to G [a nearby

village], where Dave [an ex-resident] lives, to meet up with a group of friends, usually in the evenings. . . . [Last week Martin] came home with an injury—a black eye. He has not changed this habit [of going over to G], and in the five nights [since] he has been here, there have been two major incidents. [On Friday] his head was split open, needing [the skin] to be clipped. He said he was in a builder's yard and fell over messing about with a board. Then, he said [that] Dave slashed at him 'with a pen knife', though [to staff] it looks like, and at first he said, it was a Stanley knife. It is a deep wound, which needed 12 stitches, and he [also] has superficial cuts. The police are involved and this is a matter for Child Protection. His mother has withdrawn permission for him to go to G [the village], but he still says he is going and will tell us he is going somewhere different, so we can't stop him. He was frightened last night, and said the attack was not warranted. It has been a bad patch'.

One of the researchers asked about what [other] behaviour [by the young people] had made it bad. 'They were cheeky, lying to defend each other, throwing things at handover. . . . They begged us [two staff on duty] to take them out [on Saturday], which we did, but we had two flat tyres, and had to get [another member of staff] to come out to sort it out, found we had not taken diaries [to find the telephone number], and Lee [a young person] was in the river [having gone in without permission], Martin fell and split his wound open, and despite promising to "be good". When we got back at 10 to 10, there were high jinks upstairs: foul language, etc. When I [the unit manager] was doing the care plans at 11 p.m., I thought they had got out of the unit, but Martin had his bare backside out of the window . . . The police came to say there had been a complaint [from neighbours] that someone was peeing out of the window. Martin was on his high horse, and wouldn't go to his room. At 12.30 there were visiting girls outside. It was a crap night, with paperwork not getting finished till 1.30. Today we got new tyres.'

'Martin is unofficially off school: he came out at lunchtime. . . . Mark has left school [officially], and Lee has refused to go, because he says he was attacked by some youths there—two weeks ago he had to go to hospital. Donald, who is at school, told me he thinks Mr S [the headteacher] is working up to excluding him: when I saw the look on his face, I just walked away. . . . Gary has been assaulted by Mark and Peter after Gary told us that they had taken a substance on Sunday. . . . Maybe we wouldn't have felt so bad if we had taken it? [Laughter]. . . . Gary told us that Mark had offered something to Chris [who is 12], and Mark was bragging to D [the domestic], today that they had been "high" and that staff hadn't noticed. Of course staff had noticed, and we told the Emergency Duty Team last night, who said put it on a FAX for the social workers tomorrow. Social workers have not yet rung, so I [the unit manager] phoned my manager, who advised I ring the drugs squad, which I've done. We're still waiting for them [the drugs squad] to come. With the young people's permission, we searched the rooms, but we didn't know what we were looking for. S [a member of staff] knew *a bit more, and found a "bomb"—a home-made pipe for smoking "pot", which according to S takes the burn out of the smoker's throat. He also noticed that "rock falls" had burned the carpet—he seemed to know what he was talking about. We also found bits of paper, and torn [cardboard] packets which are used to stop the bits of materials getting into the mouth. Obviously the boys had had something: they ate strange things all day, Mark was sick and he wet the bed.'*

During the long weekend shift just described, the same two staff were on duty. They had to deal with five emergency incidents: a serious cut, a return to hospital next day to have the cut re-stitched, two flat tyres, young people behaving badly late at night, and an allegation of drug abuse. Staff had to involve other professionals in these emergencies: the Accident and Emergency Unit of the local hospital, two different sets of police, several members of their own Department (the Emergency Duty Team, Child Protection, the field social workers of the boys, and the person who managed their Home along with others in the area) and two other members of their own off-duty staff (one of whom was drafted in to look after young people in the Home, and another of whom helped to inflate their tyres). Neighbours, and the young people's parents were also involved. The staff on duty had to ascertain how the boy came by the cut, and the truth of the allegation that young people were taking drugs. They had sought the permission of the group, according to Departmental regulations, before conducting their search for evidence of the allegation of drug abuse. They had to comfort a badly frightened boy, settle a group of young people who were high on drugs and disturbing neighbours, and later help to clean up after one of the group was ill. They had to complete paperwork on everything that had happened in connection with these sets of incidents, and bring care plans up to date. On the Monday, one boy absented himself from school at lunchtime and another reported that he was likely to be excluded from school.

Example 2: The Events of a Single Morning During a Research Visit

During a three-hour morning meeting between the researchers and all but two of the staff in a Home where most of the young people were in school, the following events had to be dealt with by staff. The phone rang: it was Chris's father to say that he had cycled into town and would be arriving soon to see his daughter. Later, he arrived, was greeted, and offered a cup of tea. The doorbell rang: it was the GP calling to examine Jane, who had returned from hospital after having taken an overdose the previous day, and had spent the night not feeling too well. The member of staff on duty the previous night, who had called out the GP that morning, left the meeting to be present during the examination. She later reported back to the group that the GP had rung the hospital to check on their treatment, called the district nurse who would be there in 30 minutes to do a blood test, and thought Jane was suffering from a mild tummy bug. The researchers observed that Christmas decorations were up in the unit, and birthday cards for two of the young people. Staff described how they had celebrated with cakes and presents. In the previous week staff had held a children's meeting where the purchase of a parrot was hotly debated; there had been a meeting about the imminent fostering of one boy and a review at school for one of the others; all staff had come in one day to say goodbye to a girl who was leaving the unit to live with her family; and the unit manager had taken her to her family home many miles away. The previous day the unit manager had been requested during supervision to do a report on the last year in the unit for management. That night was to be the staff's Christmas party. Jane's key worker reminded everyone that full notes about Jane should be left for the relief staff who were covering the unit during the party.

During the three-hour period just described, when staff were occupied with the two researchers, there were three other visitors to the Home, two of whom were following up an emergency which had occurred the previous day. References were made to special events which had occurred in the previous week, all demanding staff time (two birthday celebrations, events connected with a young person leaving, and three meetings—one with the group of young people, one related to the fostering of one of the children, and one which sought to sort out the school problems of another child). An unexpected requirement for a major written report had been placed on the unit manager, and tasks connected with the forthcoming staff Christmas party had to be pursued.

MOVING FROM THE RAW DATA TO A CLASSIFICATION OF TASKS

Study 1 produced raw data in the form of descriptions provided by unit managers of episodes of practice. Study 2 provided raw data in the form of what was said during researchers visits to Homes and what researchers observed during visits.

All these data were 'mined' to show, firstly, who and what makes up the salient environment of staff groups—that is, the people and the organisations with whom they must work—and, secondly, the range of tasks which unit managers and staff groups must undertake. This 'mining' was done by a form of content analysis. For each episode which became available through the Study 1 interviews, the people or the organisations who were involved were identified, as were the task or tasks facing the unit manager or staff group. These—people and organisations on the one hand, and tasks on the other—could then be sorted into categories suggested by the data. Categorising involved fairly straightforward judgements on the part of the researcher. It was evident enough that episodes varied—concentrating on interacting with neighbours, or with several rowdy residents, or with a child and his school, or with the staff group, etc. It was also evident that, according to the episode, the task might be to calm down a couple of out-of-control adolescents, to heal the rift in a divided staff group, or to get a child back into school.

The data from Study 1 'told' the researchers those things that comprised the working world of staff groups. Five main categories proved adequate to contain the range of tasks undertaken. The relatively less orderly data from Study 2 was then checked against what was learned through Study 1. No further main categories were needed, though the detail of what was included within categories was expanded.

Depicting the Working World of Staff Groups in a 'Life Space' Diagram

The idea of 'life space' comes from the work of Kurt Lewin. He was interested in how people conceptualise their social world—who they see as being important in it, who they interact with, the assumptions they make about the motivations, intentions, and attitudes of those who populate their social world, and how they move or 'locomote' within it. Lewin emphasised that it is the individual's perceptions and assumptions which influence his or her behaviour. A person's social world, or life space, is defined from his or her point of view. It may not be fully congruent with how others perceive the person's significant environment. Inclusion or exclusion from the life space is up to the person concerned, as are the meanings placed on elements of it (Lewin, 1951, pp. 188–199; McDavid and Harari, 1968, pp. 32, 238).

This idea can be extended to social units. The members of a social unit function in the real world, but it is *their* real world. That which is a part of the real world for one social unit or organisation is different from that which is part of the real world for another. For the staff of a Children's Home, the real world includes its Department's policies on the deployment of care workers, the particular mix of young people with whom the staff is working at any one time, and so on. The 'working life space' includes that which is *salient* to staff experience.

That which is salient for any social unit, or class of social units, can be shown in a life space diagram. For the staff of a Children's Home, a generalised or *schematic* diagram is shown in Figure 1, which shows what lies within the working life space of a staff team *in general terms*. It does not represent specific realities at any given time because it shows all the spaces as more or less equal—more or less equally demanding of a staff group's attention and time. This is not the case in real life. Constant changes occur in what is prominent and urgent in the life space of a staff group, as one day or even one moment gives way to the next. All the areas within the life space remain important, but some become part of the background while others loom large, preoccupy a staff, and demand staff time and attention. One has to imagine that some of the areas within the overall life space expand and become enormous while others temporarily contract. One has to imagine, further, that variations in relative saliency within the life space occur virtually all the time.

Staff constantly attend to the different areas within their life space, interacting more actively with some and less with others, depending on circumstances. They have goals and intentions with respect to individuals and groups of individuals which are located in different areas of the life space.

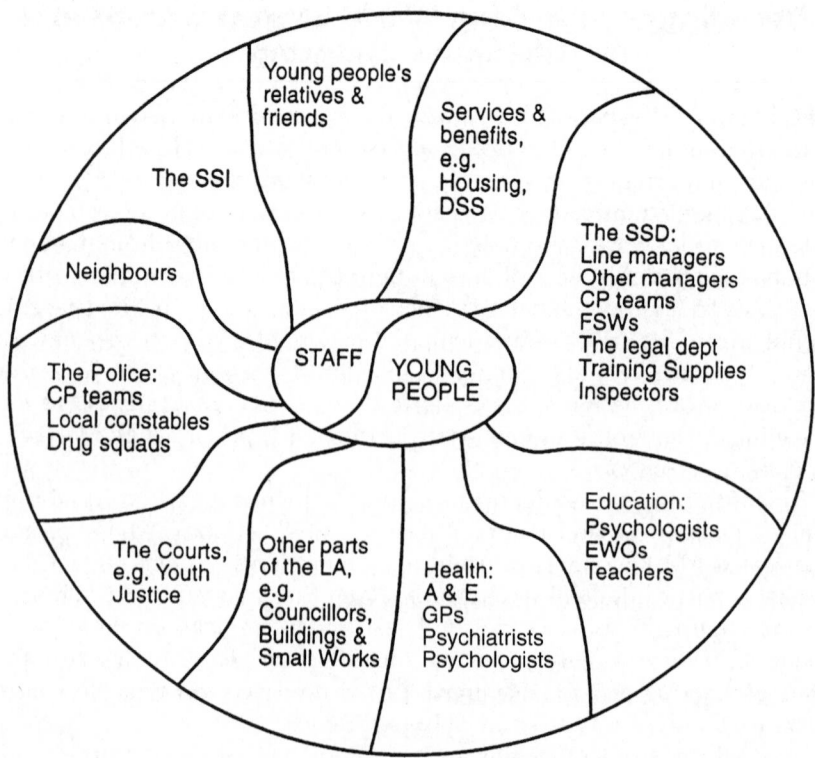

Figure 1 A schematic representation of the 'working life space' of the staff of a Children's Home

A Categorisation of the Tasks which Staff Groups Undertake

When content analysis was directed to identifying the range of tasks undertaken by staff groups, tasks fell into five broad areas, each containing a number of detailed sub-tasks. The broad areas were: working with individual young people; working with the group of young people; working with and being managed by the Social Services Department; working with people and organisations in the wider network; and surviving (maintaining viability) as a staff team which meets the needs of children.

Major task areas and the sub-tasks within each are shown in Table 1.

The physical location of each column in the table is not accidental. 'Surviving as a staff team which meets the needs of children' is placed in the centre, because the table is about the tasks which a *staff group* necessarily must undertake, and because we wished to show, spatially, the directions in which a staff must face when doing its work. The arrows which point to the left show tasks arising within the Home which staff members must address: working with the group of young people, and working with individual young people. The arrows which point to the right show tasks involved in working across the Home's boundaries with the outside world: working with and being managed by the Social Services Department; and working with people and organisations in the wider network.

Note that it would have been possible to describe tasks at a much more concrete level: 'get Eric off to school'; 'plan the meals and do the shopping'; 'write up the log'; 'attend a parents' evening at Jane's school'. It would also have been possible to describe tasks at a much more general level: 'promote and maintain good standards/methods of care which meet the individual physical, emotional, social and intellectual needs of young people'; assist in the maintenance of health and safety'. We chose a middle level of abstraction—one which would apply to all staff groups, and yet be near enough to concrete events to point to purposes and suggest operations.

Table 1 has the advantage of showing a very wide range of tasks in an orderly fashion. Its disadvantage is that it may suggest that tasks are discrete and situations static. That this is not the case has already been shown in the examples at the beginning of this chapter.

Working within Different Task Arenas at the Same Time

Within any single task noted in Table 1 there are a whole series of interrelated sub-tasks. Consider 'Admitting a young person, often under emergency conditions' as an instance of this: at the point when the

Table 1 The tasks of residential staff, all or many of which have to be accomplished within any given working shift

Working with the group of young people	Working with individual young people	Surviving as a staff team which meets the needs of children	Working with, and being managed by the Department	Working with others in the network
Managing the constant changes in the mix of young people	Admitting a young person, often under emergency conditions	Being part of and helping to build and maintain a staff team with an agreed value base, purpose, and function, through staff meetings, handovers, supervision, and working closely with other staff	Finding ways to convey the realities of caring for young people in the Home to the senior managers of the 'Looking After' system through line management and supervision systems	Liaison and co-operative work with each young person's individual network: family members, friends, voluntary visitors etc.
Encouraging supportive rather than destructive relationships in the group	Easing a young person's transition into the Unit			Liaison and co-operative work with local GPs and other Health professionals, especially in Accident and Emergency units at local hospitals, psychiatrists and psychologists, on behalf of individual young people
Avoiding harm-doing and keeping the group and individuals in it safe	Becoming a key worker to one or more individual young people; and being involved in work with other young people	Assessing, monitoring, and constantly updating own skills and knowledge base through informal and formal training and supervision	Carrying out SSD procedures and policies through regulations, following the rules and regime for the purposes and function of the Unit—being open to inspection of all of these—in the spirit as well as the letter, of the Children Act 1989	
Often dealing with abusers and abused; with contagious violence; drug and alcohol abuse; self-harm; and volatility, as well as the 'normal' developmental needs of a group of adolescents, with whom younger children are sometimes mixed	Assessing, planning, constantly reviewing, and replanning goals	Maintaining the viability of the unit, through being part of a changing rota, working shifts and overtime, and covering other staff (sometimes in other Units)		Establishing and maintaining relationships with local and special schools, EWOs, teachers, the Education Department, and educational psychologists on behalf of every young person
	Meeting a very damaged, often-abused young person's physical needs (for food, warmth, medical attention) educational needs, and emotional needs (for appropriate attachments)		Keeping and updating all paperwork relevant to the unit, so that it can be available at the reviews and planning meeting for each young person	
Encouraging constructive children's and young people's meetings		Accepting and supporting other staff (both new and relief)		Liaison and managing relationships with the police, Youth Justice and the Courts
Arranging holidays, outings, and celebrating birthdays, Christmas, and other festivals	Recognising triggers for and dealing with violence and mood swings, always in the best interests of the young person	Maintaining supplies, and the comfort, cleanliness, safety, and fabric of the building, within an agreed and audited budget	Following child protection procedures	Liaison and managing relationships with the neighbourhood where the Unit is located, often in the face of constant ups and downs in the way that the young people are regarded
Responding to moods and shifts in mood, and to crises	Encouraging constructive rather than harmful activities	Being alert to the possibility of allegation and physical harm, on the part of the young people or their relatives, and seeking to keep self, property, and colleagues safe when on duty	Liaison with each young person's field social worker, formally and informally, to exchange information, share planning, and to seek to work co-operatively	
Being aware of groups and sub-groups, bullying and alliances and recognising the changes in these over time	Keeping and updating both formal and informal records about a young person, both those to which access is permitted and those which are confidential			Representing Departmental Child Care policies in all interactions outside the Unit
Taking care not to respond in ways which could escalate difficult group situations	Protecting each young person from harm whatever its source	Being in touch with the constant and immediate changes within each shift, between one shift and the next, and with the fluctuations and oscillations which affect the whole unit over time	Through unit managers or deputies, being part of any consultation and information exchange processes with reference to Children's Services, and Departmental changes	
	Planning for and transferring a young person (and his/her educational/work needs) to another placement, home, or to independent living			

referral is made and usually during the referral telephone call, the young person's previous history and current state and needs have to be ascertained. Ideally a file detailing these should arrive with the young person, but often this is not the case. Staff may be reliant on information gained informally from different sources, or on what the member of staff taking the call was told by the referrer. Some information is essential right from the start, so if staff are not provided with it, they will need to search for it. It is, for example, important to know whether the young person has been abused or has been an abuser, especially if some of the young people have to share bedrooms.

Practical arrangements will have to be made, with respect to who will bring the child to the Home and who will admit the child. A bed may have to be stripped and re-made. If a member of the care staff has taken the referral phone call, the unit manager will have to be informed. Staff need to be provided with a medical consent form signed by the appropriate person, or if this has not been provided, they have to seek it. A new file will have to be set up. At the same time as engaging in administrative tasks connected with the new admission, members of staff will meanwhile be faced with a young person who might be frightened, or disoriented, or angry. Staff will need to do what they can to respond sensitively to the young person's mood and to how he or she initially behaves. They will need to make the young person welcome, assist him or her to get acquainted with the others and find a place in the group. Through observing the young person's behaviour and beginning to interact with him or her, members of staff launch into the process of understanding this particular unique person. They begin to build up a picture of the young person and form views about the sort of response which he or she particularly needs. More information will have to be sought, as soon as possible but often after the young person is already in the Home—for example, about the family, and about the field social worker's plans for the young person if a care plan is not available at the time of admission.

All of the work involved when admitting a young person to the unit must be undertaken at the same time as a number of others, which cannot be neglected. For example, someone has to deal with feeding young people coming home from school, or more likely with occupying those who have not been to school that day and who may be bored or fractious. An emergency situation with regard to some other child might need attention. A school might have to be contacted in connection with the exclusion of a young person. Responding to a demand from management for a report of some sort cannot be deferred for long. The person taking the referral might be preoccupied with other issues—perhaps the truth or otherwise of rumours about his or her job, or about a colleague currently suspended because of an allegation that is being investigated through Departmental procedures; or about a young person who has run away.

The admission of a child or young person is just one example. Each of the tasks included in Table 1 could be discussed in comparable terms, to show its complexity and its relation to other tasks.

How Tasks Pile Up

When members of staff come into work they will know about previously scheduled events, meetings and the like, but they cannot anticipate all that will face them. Every day of the year may well bring something new.

Residential care staff work shifts; other staff (domestics, cooks, administrators and unit managers) may 'on paper' work more regular hours. Care staff may begin their working day in the early morning or afternoon or evening. They may work for 10 hours and then go home, or do a sleep-in duty; or they may work for several days together and then be away from work for two or three days. The pattern of shifts and rotas varies from Home to Home, and may change. Staff may work regularly with others whom they know, or with relief staff whom they have never met before. Gaps in the rota occur which are unpredictable, when a member of staff is ill, when the Home is not fully staffed in the first place, or when an unplanned event occurs. A member of staff may work with one or more others, or (more rarely) may face a shift alone, although this is avoided as much as possible, on legal as well as practical grounds. Some young people may be in the house all day—every day for months at a time—or, more rarely, all may be in school during school terms. The young people in the Home may all be known to staff members coming on duty, or there may be young people who have arrived in the Home under emergency conditions while staff have been off duty.

As a staff member enters the building, all may be, on the surface, calm and quiet, or conditions may be very volatile. The mood of the group of young people, or even one of them, may determine the tenor of the working shift. Staff members have to get into tune with whatever is happening on any particular day very quickly.

Members of staff need to work with *all* the children and young people in the Home. Some present the 'ordinary' day-by-day difficulties expected of people at their life stage. Others are sad or disturbed and disturbing, still suffering the effects of recent losses or earlier trauma. With respect to these, staff have to contend with, understand, and respond to each young person's multiple problems.

The mixture of young people living together adds another dimension to the events of any shift. Staff on duty may be planning, or engaging in, some special event involving all or most of the young people. They might be faced with problems arising from the mix of young people: for example, an explosive episode which involves damage to property; or bullying. The behaviour of one young person may have an impact on another young person or the whole group. In some Homes the mix changes frequently.

Care staff often have one or two named children for whom each is responsible. However, each member of staff (including domestics and other ancillary staff) have to know and understand something of the needs and problems of every young person in the group, and how that young person fits into, and impacts on, the rest of the group.

All staff members have to face both inwards to the work which they do in the Home itself and outwards to the Department of which they are a part, under usual as well as unusual conditions. A domestic may need to be in contact with suppliers about dustbin bags, or a care worker may need to contact a field social worker about a particular young person, or a unit manager may need to liaise with his or her external line-manager about new policies devolving from higher management.

Additionally, staff groups face wider worlds: education (schools, and education welfare officers), health services (general practitioners; hospitals, especially accident and emergency departments), specialist services (psychologists and psychiatrists), the police (the local force, and the drug squad), the courts (Youth Justice, and those who are connected with the Police and Criminal Justice Act), the families of young people, neighbours, and the media.

Events have to be carefully documented in the Home's log and in a young person's file. Often, this has to be done late at night after a hard shift when the young people have gone to bed. Files for individual children have to be kept up-to-date, and sometimes duplicated so that confidential material can be kept separately. Every incident has to be carefully documented in a way that separates inference from fact. Additionally, staff have to communicate with one another and often have a day book to assist with this. Staff also have to talk to one another regularly at handover meetings (which may be daily), at regular staff meetings and more informally in order to maintain continuity of care, sustain teamwork, make plans, and take the work forward. Many events happen in any given shift which staff need to pass on to someone: a unit manager, a field social worker, or a colleague taking over from them.

Staff members have to face multiple demands on them arising from events both inside and outside the Home. They have to find time and space to stay in touch with those young people who are *not* making demands on them at a particular time, but who nevertheless need their attention and care.

Many of the tasks considered to be the responsibility of unit managers have to be within the competence of every other member of a Home's staff to some degree. In some Homes in Study 2, where rotas were stretched and the numbers of permanent staff were depleted, many tasks ordinarily undertaken by unit managers might become the responsibility of a more junior member of staff, or of relief staff, for a day or part of a day. Relatively new staff might take referrals or deal with line-managers, or support other staff through a difficult shift. Tasks ordinarily thought of as the province of care staff might be taken on by domestic staff—especially cooks and cleaners—with whom children interacted frequently.

Emergency situations occur and demands pile up, by chance or in consequence of things not going well, with one difficult situation leading to another. When crises occur, more contact is needed with the Department and with outside agencies. More paperwork ensues. Quick decisions have to be made as to which of the more routine tasks can be deferred.

Some tasks cannot be deferred. A six-monthly review for one child, set up weeks in advance and involving an interdisciplinary group of professionals and parents, cannot be set aside because the decorators have come at last, or because another young person has taken a drug overdose. Meals still have to be provided, young people welcomed home from school, an unexpected visit from a parent dealt with. A member of staff may have to stay on beyond the end of his or her shift, or off-duty staff may be called in. Staff have to continue to carry out tasks at different levels of complexity and importance whatever else is happening.

4

REWARDS AND STRESSES, UPS AND DOWNS

The accounts received from unit managers in Study 1 showed that unit managers and their staff members experience moments of great satisfaction and reward through their work, and also moments of great stress. Feelings of reward or of stress could be experienced with reference to any task area. Homes also had their ups and downs, which many unit managers referred to as 'good patches' and 'bad patches'.

Because of their evident importance, we decided to begin Study 2 by paying explicit attention to the themes of rewards and stresses, and good and bad patches. Two workshop meetings were held with each of the six staff groups. In the first of these, we asked the group: 'What is it like to work here?', 'What's rewarding?', 'What's tough?', 'What's easy?'. In the second workshop meeting we first asked whether, in the experience of those present, good and bad patches occurred. As expected, everyone said they did. We then put four questions to each of the staff groups: 'What is a good patch like?', 'What is a bad patch like?', 'What triggers a good patch?', 'What triggers a bad patch?'. Discussion was lively in all the workshop meetings.

More was learned about these issues in the approximately year-long series of visits to these same Homes. At the start of each visit, we asked 'What has happened since last time?', and then heard of difficulties, achievements, and crises.

THE DATA ANALYSIS PROCEDURE

The three main data sources were the interviews with unit managers in Study 1, the two workshop meetings in Study 2, and the long series of monthly visits to the Study 2 Homes.

Content analysis procedures were used to identify and order the information in these data sources relevant to the themes we were interested in. We began with the data most likely to hold relevant information in a concise form—the process notes for the workshop meetings held at the start of Study 2.

For each workshop meeting, successive points were first sorted into whether they pertained to 'reward' or to 'stress', or to 'good' and 'bad' patches. Sub-sorts were then undertaken. For example, with respect to reward and stress, a number of comments referred to pleasure at a young person's progress, and these were placed together; comments which referred to how helpful it was to have the support of colleagues were placed together; and so on. The data itself 'told' the researchers what the sub-categories were. Each 'bundle' of items was given a name or title which captured its essence.

There proved to be nine main sources of reward, and twelve main sources of stress. In addition to looking at sources, it was possible to examine such issues as how stressors can pile up and combine, how anxiety may be related to events which have not yet occurred but are anticipated, and how rewards can compensate for stress.

The investigation of 'good patches' and 'bad patches' showed a close relationship with rewards and stresses. Good patches, not surprisingly, tended to include experiences of reward, and bad patches experiences of stress. The framework which emerged consisted of the following: characteristics of a good patch; bad moments and difficult situations within a good patch; characteristics of a bad patch; good moments and good work within a bad patch; triggers for a bad patch; and events which can turn a bad patch around.

The remaining data—the Study 1 interviews and the Study 2 visits— were examined in the light of the frameworks which had been established. The idea had been to add to the frameworks if necessary, but they proved adequate for containing the data.

In the sections which follow, illustrations are either direct quotes from unit managers or members of staff, or summaries from researchers' notes.

Sources of Reward for Staff Members

Working together in a close, supportive staff team:

'[What is rewarding here is] the stimulation of all members of staff having their own opinions, yet working very closely together. The whole team (regardless of job title) is involved with the young people. The load is easier to bear because of the close team, who support one another. We all need it. The unit manager has loads of support from the team.'

'It helps to work in a team. You can turn to others. You don't have to say anything—others will be there. You don't need to ask. I feel that when I am on I don't need to ask. Feeling safe is important.'

Staff and young people spending time together as a group which enjoys shared experiences of both recreation and work:

'We feel we have created [an atmosphere] where we try hard to work as a team: us as a group [young people and staff] who, for example, go on holiday as a group.'

Working with and on behalf of the young people, and seeing them make gains and enjoy themselves:

'One of the most rewarding things is knowing that you've set a young person on the right tracks, or given them a new life, with another family, and you know that it's working, and that they're safe. I find that very rewarding, especially if I've been one of the main components in organising and setting that sort of thing up.'

'Even one who succeeds is worth it. D left 15 years ago and is now in Australia. There's a lad in the Royal Navy.'

'[It is rewarding] seeing lads move successfully through the semi-independence programme. We have had 16 lads through the semi-independence programme. It is rewarding when they achieve that. It is good when you bump into them on the street, a year or two later, and they speak with fondness of their time [here], and you see they are making headway, or [they] say, "I remember you when you used to say . . .".'

'I feel rewarded by one of the boys, that during the last two weeks has managed to stay out of what has been happening here, and has constantly tried. We are wanting him to stay and he has improved. He is a kid who has gone through the system, one unit after another, and now says he wants to be in one place where he can't walk out. It takes a while for them to realise they can progress.'

Planning special events and providing treats:

'Mark [a member of staff] is organising a mountain bike idea and remembers taking young people to Water World—in the rain with leggings and T-shirts on, and the young people still talk about it and staff see a different side to the young people.'

Feeling able to cope with whatever comes along: a sense of self-esteem, self-worth, and effectance (i.e. that what one does makes a difference):

'There's nothing better than coming on, and seeing that you've got a nice strong staff team, and knowing you can cope with anything that's going to happen. If your frame of mind's right, the rest of the team's frame's right, you look around . . . you know that there's nothing that can happen on that shift that can't be sorted out, it influences the kids, the atmosphere of the staff directly influences the kids.'

Feeling to be listened to by management, and respected by them; working under management structures which support the work:

The new procedures give people [young people and staff] the feeling they are listened to. Before the Area Children's Panel meetings, emergency placements used to cause problems—now most emergencies go elsewhere [if the child is likely to be in long-term care] and we only take 24-hour emergency placements. This relieves the young people [here] too. We feel a bit divorced from the EDT [Emergency Duty Team] now, and have limited contact.'

Feeling that there is something special about their Home, something which no other unit has or does:

'Something that we've got here that no other unit has, we don't just have a staff meeting, we have a senior meeting with Officer in Charge, deputy and team leaders prior to the staff meeting.'

'The kids attend the daily changeover meetings. Other Homes don't do that.'

Enjoying the variety of the work:

'What's interesting about residential work? There's never two days the same, you could never get bored.'

Appreciating having extra resources:

'[We were awarded] £1,700 to spend in two days, and had great fun spending every last penny.' '[The unit manager] wanted a dishwasher: she dreamt about it!' 'We spent £500 on three carpets—not the expensive kind, but what the kids chose, which won't last for ever. Three staff took four hours over the task and went to Texas, buying lamps, wicker chairs, shelves, etc., with coffee in the middle to swap notes.'

Sources of Stress for Staff Members

Experiencing fatigue and feeling emotionally drained:

'It is not hard physically, but mentally, especially as only two people are on at key times. Emotional demands are draining. The young people demand individual attention. Even when they're all in bed asleep, your mind is not relaxed, and you don't get proper sleep here.'

'Anyone who works a normal day gets a lunch break, but these staff don't, they don't get five minutes: it's constant, 24 hours. They're up in the night, they're

not getting their rest, and they've got to be up that next morning; they can't say "Well, I'll have a lie-in, I was up till 1 o'clock or whatever". They've still got to be up at that certain time to see those children off to school. They're with it 24 hours a day, they don't even get a break.'

Having to work with difficult mixes of young people; having no control over admissions, some of which are regarded as inappropriate; having no control over the mix of young people:

'No control over referrals. Having to have every kid who is referred. Staff can agree that they do not want a particular young person in, but we know what is going to happen at the end of it. The Department is cost-cutting. It's heads for beds at the moment. Unfortunately there is no talk or discussion about placements or about a vacancy. No consideration is given to the effects.'

'What affects us is the unpredictability. They can ring up with a referral. There is a placement officer, and all referrals come through her: to her from managers and social workers, and through her to Homes. She has no idea about what a Home is like. She should have some idea of the Homes, of the kids who get referred.'

'The mixture of offenders and non-offenders is impossible. This used to be a stable unit. We had three young people who got GCSEs [General Certificates of Secondary Education] last year and went to college. Inappropriate placements have been a bad influence on others. One boy, however, who we thought an inappropriate placement had shown a massive improvement, and then we got two others, and that boy went full circle, back to where he started. It's all down to beds: if a vacancy comes up here, regardless of the damage that will be done, it is filled and all our good work goes out of the window.'

Being at the receiving end of abuse from the young people; feeling that the young people and not the adults are in control; being disturbed by the attitudes displayed by the young people:

'There are verbal and physical attacks, discourtesy, and pointed lack of regard.'

'Goading and taunting has escalated to such a degree, it's constant, as soon as you walk through the door.'

Worrying about importing trouble:

Admission was sought, by management, for a girl who was known to be a friend of a girl already in the Home. They had previously offended together. Staff objected to admitting this girl, for fear that the two would resume their pattern of offending together, and perhaps draw others into similar behaviour. (Researcher's notes.)

Certain young people are well known to the staff of a Home: either they have lived in the Home earlier, or staff know about the havoc which has occurred in some other Home in the Authority where they have been resident. Staff are fearful of what will occur if the young person is admitted, and resist taking the young person in. They are, however, often overruled. (Researcher's notes.)

Being under-resourced; feeling reduced to merely being child-minders; not being able really to help the young people:

'This authority now has a policy of not sending young people out of the borough, to try and keep young people within their home environment and solve their problems locally. It will save an awful lot of money on outside placements. Unfortunately that money hasn't been channelled into or invested in us, the resources here. It means our job is more like child-minding than working with the child, we're just a holding place, and nothing gets to happen with these young people.'

'Because of shortage of staff, we're into a state of crisis management.

High staff turnover; losing support through the absence of senior staff or unit managers:

'We've lost all senior team leaders, in a matter of months. We've had to stop everything, pull together, to keep the place running and give an adequate service.'

'When the staff does get together, it's down to minor aspects, it's not a case of let's off-load, and what's worrying you, it's such a high turnover of staff comings and goings, at the moment we've all been saying right, let's make sure we keep a tight ship here.'

Feeling powerless:

'The young girls go out and staff do not know where they are. If you are on sleep-in duty, you don't sleep for worrying about them. You can't stop them going. The house itself, with four doors, and fire regulations which say one cannot lock them [from the inside], makes constraint impossible. In any case, as a staff group we are not into restraining them.'

'You can't stop them running away, and until you can stop them running away, you can't work with them.'

'Two years ago this was a stable unit. Over the last six months a stable group of young people has been replaced by emergencies, and remanded young offenders. Young people commit offenses and then are sent back here by the magistrates. Something ought to be done. These young people are under age and they re-offend again.'

'When staff feel to have no control and can do nothing—for example when they all abscond. Staff sit up and worry. We look at ourselves and blame ourselves for the event: could I have done it differently?'

Feeling uncertain as to whether a young person is in a risky situation or not:

'They offend and re-offend. They get out through the windows at night and we don't know where they are. How long do you wait before you inform the police?'

Worrying about young people not being in school because of being excluded or refusing school: the difficult task of getting them back into school, and the problem of what to do with them during the day:

'Five out of six of current residents are not in school, and we are trying to get them back. We ring schools or the Education Department and it takes months. The kids are drifting. Kids are lost in the system. We phone, chasing up schools, and the problem is repetitive. The majority of schools won't have them back, once they're excluded. If schools have a vacancy, they have to take them back, but they won't.'

[The telephone rang during a Study 2 visit.] 'That was the school—they said he'd just run through the playground, and is off. We'll give it some time, and get the police out, if necessary. We have got to try to get them back to school.'

'[When they are here all day] we give them school work, but it's hard to contain them and get them down to work. For some young people it is a crisis of confidence, a fear of going back, being behind and looking stupid. Underneath they're very insecure. They get used to being with us.'

'Once the habit of school is broken, they are on the road to nowhere.'

Feeling frightened for one's own physical safety, or the physical safety of some of the young people:

'A drunk and angry father turned up to see his son, and threatened to put the windows through.'

'Neighbours surrounded and threatened the unit manager with a beating, if he didn't stop a boy who was taking and driving away their cars. They also threatened to beat SSD [Social Services Department] managers at a meeting held later, to deal with their complaints.'

'The "minder" of a 16-year-old resident involved in a paedophile ring threatened all other young people in the unit if they told they were being abused by the 16-year-old.'

Thinking about the job all the time, even when off duty; worrying about colleagues:

'You're afraid of what's going to be happening when you've left. I had a week's leave and my choice was [whether] to phone every day, or not. I did not phone, but it caused me more stress and anxiety.'

'Most people here end up phoning up once they've got home, just to make sure that it's OK, what they've left behind. Are people all right? We did a trip out the other week. Bill managed to drop me off at home, because I'd stayed on and helped out, but I knew there was a problem in the minibus with the kids there. I was phoning him up at half past eleven, twelve o'clock at night, to make sure that things were OK, that he'd got back safe, and he was all right.'

Experiencing bad effects on home and family life:

'What's tough is having to phone up your wife, or your partner, and say I'm not going be home for another three or four hours, because I'm dealing with a situation. Or having to ask somebody else to do the phoning for you.'

'Having to answer the phone to wives, partners, husbands, whoever, who say, "Has he left yet, I'm a bit worried?". You say, "Well no, actually", and then you talk to them, because they've been worried.'

'With your own family, hobbies and social interests have flown out the window in your own private life, basically when you do have an evening off or an afternoon off, you're that bloody knackered, you just want to rest, to be really honest about it.'

Other sources of stress mentioned were poor relationships with neighbours; being in conflict or having poor relationships with managers or field social workers; residential homes having a bad press; inspections; having to integrate a new member of staff; dissatisfaction with the physical state of the building; a complaint or allegation hanging over the head of a member of staff; a system of relief staff which means that relief staff may be different every time, when it is known that the young people do not adjust easily to strangers.

How Stressors can Combine and have Lingering Effects

Listing stressors separately, as has just been done, conceals the fact that stressors often appear in combination, as shown in the following illustrations:

'DipSW [Diploma in Social Work], the Children Act, and the client group generally now has made it a very difficult working environment. People are off for DipSW training, there are staff shortages, and combined with the lack of resources, this makes the job we're doing more and more difficult, with the client group we've got. The client age group has dropped, but what we're getting through now is far more challenging, difficult young people.'

'It comes down to perception of what you expect from your work. I would suggest that we all expect to see some change in our young people in the time that they're here. We have a young person now where there isn't that change, and for us that is a source of frustration and a source of stress, because this young person is not changing, he's effecting change within the group in a negative way. . . .'

'This place is being used for young people who can't be dealt with elsewhere. A typical example: a young girl set fire to the building twice, was eventually moved to secure provision, they threw her out from there because her behaviour was challenging, and she was placed back here because there was no other secure provision at the time. As a consequence we had to double staff up on early and late shifts, which meant people working round the clock. The management wanted us to make sure that she didn't abscond or mutilate herself and we achieved that. We also had to cover ourselves and make sure that the way we did this was OK by senior management. Big expectations are put on us, we have to cope, and we get only limited recognition from senior management. They haven't got an inkling of what it's like to work a full day, and then not to go to sleep at all, to have to sit awake and then work another full day, and then probably work the next early shift as well.'

Sometimes a chain of events around a particularly difficult young person can go on over a long period of time, generating more or less continuous stress for a staff, with peak periods of high stress despite temporary let-ups and a degree of improvement. In Study 1, a unit manager told the following story:

A girl of 14 had left her foster family at Christmas last year [i.e. about 9 months previously] and came to us in February. She had made allegations of sexual abuse against the foster father. In April she started to send threatening letters to the foster carer, started to display angry behaviour, ran off a number of times, and once threw a brick through the foster carer's window. The police were involved a number of times. We arranged for some therapeutic input from a nearby centre which works with people who have been abused. After five or six weeks she started to feel a lot better about herself. She stopped sending the letters and she stopped phoning the foster carer. However, she gets herself worked up and gets out of control. She was on medication—a mild tranquilliser—which she takes every evening. What happens is that she gets very giddy, starts to laugh, not normally, but in a high-pitched way. This continues and then she starts to get quite aggressive and she can become quite threatening. She has smashed a great deal of the crockery. We have had five rooms smashed up this last week and she has been involved in every one. She is a young 14—more like an 11-year-old—but she is very big, weighs about 14 to 15 stone. This past weekend she was out with another girl and they came back with some air fresheners which they started to sniff. At one point there had been a barricading in one of the bedrooms and she had a knife with a seven-inch blade. She said she wasn't going to use it on a resident or a member of staff, but would use it on the police. She started to smash things, and picked up a large pan. The member of staff tried to talk to her and defend himself, and she picked up a piece of pot that she had smashed, lashed out at him and cut his hand open quite badly. I was called in. When I arrived she was unconscious on the floor of the kitchen and there was blood everywhere. I don't understand why she was unconscious but we called for an ambulance. The member of staff had seven stitches in his hand, and the girl said she couldn't remember anything and asked what she was doing in hospital. The impact on me is that I feel absolutely drained. Half the staff has been off and we have had one crisis after another over seven days. It has taken its toll on everybody.'

Difficulties which occurred in the past can continue to preoccupy a staff or a member of staff over long periods of time:

A unit manager reported that she still experienced distress over a series of events which had occurred several years previously. A girl who had proved uncontainable in the Home had been moved elsewhere. This girl's father made a total of something like 25 complaints against the unit manager over months and months, 'every one of which had to be investigated', with attendant stress for the whole staff, and 'mountains of extra paperwork'. (Researcher's notes.)

How Staff Members can Experience Anticipatory Anxiety

Staff members often become preoccupied with the possibility that an allegation of physical or sexual abuse might be made against them by a young person. They know from experience that young people who felt aggrieved, or were looking for a grievance, sometimes lodge a complaint against a member of staff, hooking the allegation onto something which staff regarded as an ordinary or even helpful interaction. Staff members also know that an allegation, once made, is very hard to recover from with reputation intact, even if the allegation is declared to be unproven after an investigation, and even if the young person retracts. Concern over the possibility of allegations was an ongoing preoccupation for many, amounting to a low-level state of persistent stress. It could lead staff members to avoid any sort of physical contact with a young person, including, for example, a goodbye kiss or hug, or a pat on the shoulder.

Another focus for worry about an event which had not yet occurred, but might, had to do with the possible closure of a Home, a change in its function, or the break-up of its staff. The prospect of such events sometimes reached a staff group through rumour, or through an article in the local press. A staff group might know that closure was being discussed but not know whether a decision had been reached or when it might be reached. Being in a state of uncertainty was distressing personally, and also created problems with respect to practice. For example, young people could not be prepared for being moved elsewhere as long as closure was still a matter of rumour, but staff members feared that by the time the decision was confirmed, there might be little time to arrange moves or prepare young people for them.

How Rewards can Compensate for Stress

'Here, everyone on the staff recognises everybody else's stresses; everybody thinks, "Well, I know exactly what you're feeling like, because I've felt like that"; everybody's experienced the same things within the unit; it's like you suddenly get a kick, "Oh God, I've never had a kick before, I've never had a spit in the face before, or I've never been told to F-off before, or I've never had to restrain somebody before and really got hurt". Or you might get somebody who has worked 50 hours in one week and they're really tired, and you say you know how they feel, because I've done it; we all muck in together.'

'Other staff are extremely important, because one can feel very isolated in this job. Management may not be aware [of what staff face] and they don't want to be aware, so it is important that one's own colleagues are aware.'

HOW REWARDS AND STRESSES RELATE TO UPS AND DOWNS

Experiences of reward and of stress are not distributed evenly over time. That is, it is not the case that every day or every week brings an even mix of rewards and stresses. Rather, a predominately good patch, characterised mainly by good morale and experiences of satisfaction and reward, may go on for some time, only to give way to a predominately bad patch. One member of staff said:

'It goes in cycles. Sometimes things are quiet, and then there is the other extreme—the roof gets ripped off. It appears like a snake.'

and he drew a wavy line in the air. This snake showed highs and lows occurring at regular intervals and reaching the same height or depth. In actuality, good and bad patches follow one another in a less orderly way, and different patterns occur in different Homes at different times. For example, a Home might have pulled itself out of a prolonged bad patch to a point where a predominantly good patch then persists for a long period, with only minor vacillations within it. Or a Home might suffer a sharp downturn but recover from it quickly. A Home might be thrown out of a good patch by some turn of events, and then experience a prolonged unsettled period before returning to a more favourable steady state. A bad patch could persist over months, with only minor and unsustained upturns. An event which triggered a downturn might be followed by further, knock-on events which lead to further downturns. In such a case the Home is in a downward spiral from which recovery may not be possible.

Some staff groups called attention to the fact that sometimes a Home could recover and restabilise after a relatively brief period of disruption, while sometimes it could not. A staff member with experience of both (that is, of recovering and not recovering) said:

'Usually when a new young person comes in you go through this bad patch but there's an end to it after about four weeks, not 17 or 19 weeks. . . . you can always see [the end], such as the young person rehabilitated and going back home, or the team pulling together, concentrating, setting out guidelines, and after about a fortnight, you're looking for stabilised behaviour.'

Difficult Situations within Good Patches, and Good Moments within Bad Patches

It was clear from what unit managers and staff said that a good patch is not without stress, and that disturbing events can occur. However, staff felt that if a problem situation surfaced during an otherwise good patch, it would be easier to handle.

'We have had a few hiccups [i.e. during this current good patch]. Max [a young person] equalled six weeks of trip-ups. The local garage man found him in his pyjamas and no shoes. He unsettled others. He had a one-to-one worker, who had never done a special before. He was a handful. He was determined to get back home. He didn't want control. At 10, he was a law to himself out till 3 a.m. We

tried to control him. He went to the toilet and was out through the window. You had to be there all the time with him. The group [of young people] helped to control him. If they had been unsettled, they would all have gone with him.'

'In a good patch there might be one or two difficult ones, but if the dynamics of the group [are favourable], it's easier to bring that person out of that.'

Members of staff could feel tired in a good patch as well as in a bad patch, but as one of them said, 'in a good patch you can be tired because of their [the young people's] bubble, but it is not such a bad kind of tiredness'.

There can be good moments and good work within a bad patch:

'Last night, when we eventually managed to get the house meeting going, quite a lot came from the house meeting, because of the discussion that took place. The young people were saying how they all felt and we were saying how we felt, so it was quite constructive. It was very late before we started, because of people being restrained here there and everywhere. And fortunately yesterday, Ben [member of staff] stayed on for an extra three and a half hours. Because two staff were dealing with one young person through there, and two staff were dealing with another young person upstairs, and that left the other seven young people, if Ben hadn't stayed, on their own, to their own devices.'

Triggers for, and Recovery from, a Bad Patch

The factor most frequently mentioned by staff groups as the trigger for a bad patch was a change towards a more difficult mix of young people:

'Four new residents moved in in two days. You can have five kids and it's OK. One more kid comes in and all of a sudden everything starts going downhill. All you need is one. There had been problems with solvent abusers—one lad came in with solvents.'

'We had people placed here on Section 47 assaults, 16-, 17-year-olds, serious offenders placed in a Children's Home: they were only placed here because there was nowhere else to put them. If you start putting that kind of kid in a place like this you've got potential problems, not so much for the staff team, but for the other kids, some of the kids we'd got here, the kids were frightened to death. We had sexual abusers, armed robbers (firearms). The Statement of Intent for this Home says that we'll take anybody. And if you're going to take anybody, you're going to take any kind of behaviour, and it's just how quick the staff team can get to grips with the new admissions and that's when you go through bad times, hard work, unpleasant times, bust-ups, fall-outs, confrontations, and it's how quick

we can get to grips with that. We can go on having no admissions and then, all of a sudden, in a week we'll have three admissions. Depending on the kind of young person we're getting in, that will directly relate to the environment that's created within the unit.'

'We've got some withdrawn damaged kids and some that show bizarre behaviour. Either the withdrawn ones shouldn't be here, or the other ones that are more aggressive and volatile shouldn't be here. It shouldn't be a mixture of both, it's not fair on the more vulnerable withdrawn ones.'

Another trigger for a bad patch was behaviour on the part of one young person who is or becomes particularly distressed or who breaks the group's norms:

'A young person hoping to go home and then it not happening can upset the whole unit.'

'A girl kept running off. The others felt that the rules were different for her than they were for them. They got so angry with her behaviour they poured a bucket of water over her. Her behaviour unsettled the others. They talked about how she should be punished and their punishments would have been much harsher than the staff's.'

A change in policy stemming from management, or a rumour about such, was sometimes reported as triggering a bad patch:

'A threat from outside makes the kids feel unsafe and threatened. During a three-month period when everyone was running away, it was because they felt it was safer outside the Home than inside. We had been told "You're closing". All you need is something like that. I think it showed in the kids.'

Staff shortages and newly imposed procedures also play a part:

'Staff shortages can lead a Home into a state of crisis management. It's certainly getting that way [i.e. towards crisis management]. It never used to be that way when we had a structure for cover and full complement of staff. At the moment we've got a vacancy for a deputy, a residential social worker vacancy, a waking night vacancy, and the cook is just about to retire.'

[A change in policy which required staff to fill out more forms than previously] 'makes staff work differently, and they can't give quality time to the young people, which is noticed by them.'

A change in how a staff group operates could sometimes lead to a shift from a good to a bad patch:

'You almost seem to have cycles, where you have a nice period and perhaps you let the reins out that little bit; it's very nice, very comfortable; then suddenly you can start to push the boundaries that little bit and you can get a little bit complacent or familiarity breeds contempt, and you find yourself all of a sudden in a situation again when you've got to bring back all the structure. You get new admissions in, they see that as the norm, and you generally pull in the reins.'

When offering explanations for what can turn a bad patch around, staff members again mentioned changes in the mix of young people more frequently than any other factor:

'[What helped was] losing the remands—as they went out the group began to stabilise.'

'There was a turning point over Christmas. We only had three residents. We got some new kids in. We all [staff and young people] started to look at things in a positive way—we took trips.'

'The Department said we had to have remanded young people, but it was too wide a banding. We all learned from it and have moved on. It is like Heaven now, more planning. We felt so isolated then, no Homes Officer. We suffered and the young people were abusing one another and there was no way out—just brick walls [from the Department].'

Some staff groups said that they needed a period of quiet in order to recover themselves. Supportive attitudes and behaviours on the part of management, if in place, were mentioned as likely to help a Home to emerge from a bad patch:

'[We need] a better management system which would do away with inappropriate placements and difficult mixes of young people, and help staff to feel fairly treated and respected.'

Some of the comments by staff members called attention to how a number of factors could interact with one another in influencing whether a patch is a good one or a bad one:

'The kind of patch you're in [good or bad] depends on the young people living here and the dynamics of the group, and that overlaps hand-in-hand with staff morale, and whether you've got the time to do things that we used to do in the past, and to operate in a way that we did in the past.'

'The good times and the bad times are very related to an unsettled or a settled client group. When you've got a settled client group you can do far more things

with them as a staff team than you can with an unsettled client group, because of the basic trust that you can give them. If you've got an unsettled client group, who can't be trusted to go out of the building, can't be trusted to do this or that, and you've got them within the building, basically what you're doing is a lot of containment, instead of actually doing things with them that they enjoy, you enjoy, and it has a knock-on effect.'

ARE GOOD AND BAD PATCHES INEVITABLE?

The researchers came to the view that a 'good patch' ought really to be described as a 'good-enough' patch, since it can include difficult times as well as easy ones, and disruptive young people as well as settled ones. Given the trauma that many of the young people have experienced, one could not expect it to be otherwise. However, in a good patch, staff feel that they are on top of the situation and have time to do the work, and they also feel supported by their management.

It is clear that it is desirable that good patches be sustained for as much of the time as possible, since both young people and staff are much more likely to benefit.

Bad patches nevertheless occur. Staff do what they can to turn a bad patch around but often feel helpless in the face of situations over which they have no control—a particularly difficult mix of young people, or lack of support from management, or rumours which threaten their survival. Staff members did not point specifically to their own skills in pulling out of a bad patch, but it is clear that skill plays a part. The staff member who referred to 'the team pulling together, concentrating, setting out guide-lines' was clearly pointing to a staff group's collective skills.

It became clear through examining sources of reward and stress, and sequences of good and bad parches, that it is unreasonable and simply not in line with the realities of the situation to expect good patches to characterise all Homes at all times. It is important to acknowledge that ups and downs are inevitable features of residential Homes for children and young people so that one does not expect the impossible, or immediately condemn a Home which is in a bad patch.

This is not to say that bad patches are not a matter for concern, especially if they persist over long periods of time or go from bad to worse in a downward spiral. In such cases, staff members and others in a service-providing department need to try to understand what may be occurring to prolong a bad patch for an inordinately long period or to make a bad situation worse. Only then can early and effective intervention occur.

5

WORKING WITH INDIVIDUAL YOUNG PEOPLE

In Chapter 3, five main task arenas were identified within which staff work. In this chapter and in Chapters 6, 7, 8, and 9, each task arena is examined more closely. This chapter looks at direct work with individual young people.

Many of the episodes described to us in Study 1, and reported or observed in Study 2, had to do with work or interactions with individual children or young people. These were extracted and formed into a sub-sample, which was then examined. Certain things stood out: 'work' occupied different periods of time—it could be very brief, or could extend over weeks or months. Staff groups worked towards particular goals—often to a number of goals at the same time for one child. Some work involved pre-planning and carefully working out intervention strategies. In contrast, some very effective work consisted in spontaneous responses to unexpected events and was intuitive in character. Goals were changed as circumstances changed. Work was greatly influenced by how long a child stayed in the Home. What was important for one child was unimportant for another. In short, work with individual children and young people was varied and complex.

To put order into complexity without at the same time oversimplifying, key themes needed to be identified. Those arrived at were: setting goals for individual young people; contexts, routes and approaches to working with individual young people; the 'fronts' on which work occurs; break-throughs, slow progress, setbacks and reversals; young people with whom members of staff feel they cannot work; constraints on work with individual young people; and how working with individual young people always occurs in the context of group living.

SETTING GOALS FOR INDIVIDUAL YOUNG PEOPLE

In the most general terms, staff seek to understand the situation and needs of each young person, direct their efforts towards what each young person needs and can accept, and adjust their efforts in the light of changing circumstances. This involves setting goals, based on as full an understanding of each young person as can be achieved.

Goals towards which staff members worked on behalf of a young person were often stated explicitly in care plans. However, these were often only a part of the picture—for example, the goal 'effect a reconciliation with mother' might be stated in a care plan, but additional goals might also be in place, such as 'build up his self-esteem'; 'stop him winding-up the others'. Further, staff might be pursuing sub-goals (or instrumental goals) related to the overall goal, such as 'support John's mother in attending the next review'. Not all goals were explicitly formulated. Goals were multiple, required constant readjustment, and included implicitly held as well as explicitly stated aims.

CONTEXTS, ROUTES AND APPROACHES TO WORKING WITH INDIVIDUAL YOUNG PEOPLE

When many instances of practice were looked at together, it became evident to the researchers that staff members adopt four main routes or avenues for such work. They work through (a) providing protected time for uninterrupted one-to-one discussions; (b) exchanging briefly with a young person during ordinary daily events; (c) working in and through groups of young people; and (d) working with others in the young person's network on his or her behalf. All of these routes are made use of, and in the best circumstances, work done in different contexts meshes together to the advantage of the young person concerned.

Protected Time for One-to-One Work

Staff members sometimes create opportunities for one-to-one contact, which they often refer to as 'quality time'. For example, they plan to have a bedtime chat, or arrange to take a young person shopping or out for a special treat. We did not hear of regularly scheduled therapeutic hours, and the care workers we came to know did not think of themselves as 'therapists', though some of their efforts amounted to providing therapeutic help. Sometimes a young person would 'engineer' one-to-one contact by, for example, coming down to the lounge after bedtime, seeking company or a mug of chocolate. Sometimes opportunities for one-to-one contact occurred in among day-to-day activities—for example, while escorting a young person to the dentist. Sometimes an event occurred which pointed to a need for one-to-one work—for example, an upset at school, or disappointment at a parent's broken promise. The young person might then be taken aside for a chat as soon as time permitted.

In some Homes it is understood that the person to work on a one-to-one basis is the young person's key worker, if he or she is available. It is also understood, however, that everyone needs to know each young person well enough to work directly with him or her when a situation calls for it, in the absence of the key worker. Some staff choose not to use a key worker system but make working with each young person a shared responsibility. In such cases there will be a 'link worker' rather than a 'key worker', who is responsible for maintaining contact with people and organisations outside the Home who are part of the young person's wider network.

Problems can arise if other young people become envious or resentful of the time taken for one-to-one work, or begin to see negative behaviour as the key to getting individual attention from members of staff. If one young person comes to be regarded by the others as 'the favourite', problems arise within the group of young people, and between the young people and staff.

Staff members who refer to one-to-one contact as 'quality time' are showing that they regard it highly and give it a central place. The research showed, however, that other forms of work in other contexts were also valuable.

Exchanging Briefly with a Young Person in the Course of Daily Events

The researchers were struck by the number of times that something quite simple and brief, which occurred in the course of day-to-day events, could contribute to a young person's welfare. For example:

On arriving at the Home for the first time, Margaret, a large and powerful 15-year-old, angrily hit at the wall in the front hall with her fists. A staff member said, 'Oh, don't do that; you'll hurt yourself!' (Researcher's notes.)

This took only seconds. The staff member expressed affection and concern rather than the fear or reprimand or reproach which Margaret may have expected. Many other examples could be provided: a 14-year-old was entrusted with painting the skirting boards in the dining room; the maturity of a 15-year-old was recognised when she was asked to accompany an 11-year-old to the dentist; a 12-year-old was complimented on her neat appearance; another 12-year-old who had resisted going to school for months, and had finally found the courage to attend, was warmly greeted by a staff member when he came home, and invited to tell about his day. 'Small' incidents such as these can make a big difference to the young people concerned, and their effects are cumulative.

Working in and through Groups of Young People

Another way of benefiting young people is to work through the dynamics of groups. Staff can devise activities for groups of young people which benefit many or most of them. They can make particular use of what is going on in a group of young people to benefit one individual. A discussion of the various ways in which this can be done is deferred until the next chapter, where 'working with the mix' is discussed.

WORKING WITH OTHERS ON THE YOUNG PERSON'S BEHALF

Not all of a staff group's efforts to benefit an individual young person occur face-to-face. For instance, staff work with schools to try to get an excluded young person re-admitted, or with parents to effect a reconciliation with the young person, or with members of a young person's extended family in an attempt to strengthen family support, or with field social workers in engaging in reviews and future planning, or with the police when a young person needs protection or control beyond that which the staff can provide.

This section gives an example of work done with and on behalf of a girl of 17, which shows how staff set and modified goals as circumstances changed, and how different forms of work were undertaken.

The time was soon coming when Rosie, 17, would have to leave care. She had two options: to live with an older sister in another part of the country, or to find a place of her own nearby where she could continue to have contact with the staff with whom she had lived for the past four years since her parents died. Rosie was also about to leave school and was interested in college but very fearful of it. She had serious ongoing problems with self-confidence. The staff set three goals: to assist Rosie to make a decision about her future living arrangements; to assist her to manage the transition to college; and to help her to become more self-confident. Work proceeded over a number of months.

Rosie decided she did not want to live with her sister but preferred sheltered accommodation nearby, so the staff and Rosie started to work towards this. Because Rosie was anxious about leaving the Home, the plan included provision for her to take Sunday dinner at the Home after she had left. The staff took every opportunity they could find, day by day, to boost Rosie's self-confidence. During this period, Rosie enrolled in college but was so overwhelmed by it on her first day that she refused to go back and became depressed and suicidal. She felt that she could not cope and did not want to leave the Home at all. The staff, with medical support, tried to bring her out of her depression by what they called 'tender, loving care'. During this period of crisis the staff said their aim was to 'keep her alive'. The goal of helping Rosie towards independent living was set aside for the time being. Staff were fearful that Rosie would make a suicide attempt, and therefore worked on a whole set of related and nested goals: getting the GP to take Rosie's emotional state seriously, making sure that Rosie did not have access to any pills other than those prescribed, informing staff members not on duty about Rosie's state that day and any significant events, dealing with the upset her depression caused for other young people in the Home, keeping Rosie's field social worker informed, communicating with the college about Rosie's absence and trying to keep the door open for her return, and informing Rosie's sister and inviting her to visit.

After several weeks, when Rosie had recovered somewhat, the unit manager asked for an appointment with Rosie's course tutor, and together they asked another student to meet her when she arrived back at college, and introduce her to others in the group. Rosie found that she and this girl had a lot in common. In the days which followed, they became friends. Rosie found that some of the pupils from her old school were also at college. She began to look more favourably on the idea of living with her sister. During this whole period the ongoing work with reference to self-esteem continued, with staff taking every opportunity to credit Rosie for her progress and her courage, for example in returning to college. Discussions about where Rosie might live in the future were resumed. A few weeks before her eighteenth birthday Rosie went to live with her sister. Because her sister lived some distance away, the plan to come back for Sunday dinners could not be carried out. However, Rosie was invited back to visit the Home several times and appeared to be doing well. She had applied for a job, and she and her sister intended to buy a car. (Researcher's summary.)

Work with Rosie extended over months. The goal of helping her to make the transition out of care was maintained and worked on alongside two further, related goals—helping her to enter college, and trying to increase her self-confidence. There was a period when these goals were put aside temporarily when a crisis occurred which changed staff priorities. Rosie's self-confidence plummeted when she found she could not cope with starting college. A serious depression followed, with suicidal thoughts. The staff's goal changed to 'keeping her alive'. If one follows this staff group's efforts over a period of time, one sees that staff were sensitive to Rosie s changing circumstances and feelings, and shifted their goals and their efforts accordingly. During the period when Rosie was in a state of crisis, staff monitored her closely. They worked with Rosie herself, Rosie's GP, her sister, her field social worker, and her course tutor at college. She was helped to make contact with others her own age who would be her fellow-pupils. At the same time staff had to work with other young people in the Home who were upset by Rosie's depression and suicidal thoughts.

What Rosie most needed, and what staff therefore focused on in their work with her, was different at different points in the sequence of events just described. Much of what they did could be described as 'working at the shifting frontier of Rosie's needs'. Working at the 'frontier of a young person's needs' is one of three 'fronts' at which work occurs. These 'fronts' are described next.

THREE 'FRONTS' ON WHICH WORK WITH INDIVIDUAL YOUNG PEOPLE OCCURS

When examining the work actually being done with individual young people, it became evident to the researchers that, whatever the detail of the goals and whatever the context or route utilised, staff efforts pointed in three main directions. We refer to these as 'fronts'. They are:

Containing and Controlling

Staff members aim to help each young person to lead a reasonably orderly life—getting to bed and getting up at a reasonable hour, being present for meals, attending school. They do this by establishing rules and creating customs for the group as a whole, intending that these will become norms which the whole group can accept.

Some young people, however, are prone to violent outbursts and destructive behaviour. They have temper tantrums, wreck their rooms, break windows and smash furniture, threaten others, make suicide attempts or otherwise harm themselves, are 'up on the roof', out all night, run away, commit offences, or harass neighbours.

Special efforts need to be made. Some children need constant monitoring, and can wear out a staff group. One 10-year-old, for example, repeatedly set fires. Others got out of control only from time to time, under provocation or when over-faced. Containing and controlling individual young people requires close attention to each one, and an appreciation of what might underlie behaviour regarded as unacceptable by staff. Staff members try to be sensitive to events which suggest that a young person is likely to be in a particularly vulnerable state, and to be available before a blow-up occurs. They try to notice and respond to early warning signs. If a young person does get out of control, staff try to stop the behaviour, if necessary by constraining the child physically. They will separate the out-of-control child physically from the others, provide a cooling-off period, and spend time with the young person individually. Many young people respond to this. The hope is that controls, at first imposed from the outside, will lead a young person to improve his or her self-control.

Some staff groups introduce a 'points' system in order to encourage acceptable behaviour. In such a system, a week is taken as a unit of time, and young people can earn personal 'points' by such behaviour as attending school, going to bed on time, and so on. At the end of the week their points are added up and can be turned into something which, from their point of view, is desirable. In some Homes, this is money, always given in addition to regular pocket money. In other Homes a young person can choose his or her own treat, from a range of treats on offer. Points systems which seem to work best include the proviso that points, once given, can never be lost because of subsequent unacceptable behaviour. Pocket money is always provided and is always independent of the points system.

It is generally understood in the world of child care that some ways of seeking to control young people are acceptable, while others are not. Spencer Millham and his colleagues, writing in 1981, listed the following as inappropriate controls: corporal punishment, transfer, group punishments, limitations on access to the outside world, public disapproval, secure rooms, and the use of drugs (Millham, Bullock, Hosie, & Haak, 1981). *The Children Act 1989 Guidance and Regulations, Volume 4, Residential Care*, lists the following as unacceptable: corporal punishment, deprivation of food and drink, restriction or refusal of visits/communications, requiring a child to wear distinctive or inappropriate clothing, withholding medication or medical or dental treatment, the use of accommodation to physically restrict the liberty of any child, intentional deprivation of sleep, and the imposition of fines (Section 1.91). In this research, we saw or heard about none of the above. Occasionally, there were references to attempts to 'ground' young people, or to forbid them to go to certain places where it was known that they got into trouble, but by and large staff did not limit access to the outside world unless young people were likely to be a risk to themselves or others, or when it was a court requirement.

A special comment should be made about transferring a child elsewhere. Children and young people are frequently transferred, for a variety of reasons. Is it ever done as a punishment? We heard of instances in which a young person was threatened with transfer if his behaviour did not improve. Transfer is sometimes used as a punishment although it is not named as such. A transfer may be arranged, for example, after a young person injured another child or (apparently) instigated an episode in which the fabric of the house is damaged. When a destructive episode occurs in the Home and someone is then moved elsewhere, it is the young person regarded as the guilty party who is likely to be moved.

Regarding secure rooms, these were not found in the Children's Homes we studied. However, young people are sometimes transferred to secure accommodation Homes. In every case in which we heard of this being done, it was for the safety of the child or of others, not as a punishment. Transfer to secure accommodation may nevertheless be perceived by some people, including sometimes the young person concerned, as a punishment.

In some instances, no effort on the part of staff to control a young person has the hoped-for result. The young person remains outside staff control, just as he or she had previously been out of parental control, or out of the foster carers' control, and/or out of the control of schools and of staff in other Children's Homes. A number of staff groups in this research made it clear that these persistently out-of-control young people were well known to care workers. Everyone knows them and is concerned about the destruction they bring in their wake. Sometimes such a young person was transferred elsewhere to relieve staff. Although no one exactly said so, it is seen to be someone else's turn to take on a particularly unmanageable child.

Where a young person cannot be contained or controlled or held in the Home, other forms of work cannot take place.

Working at the Frontier of the Young Person's Needs

This refers to trying to identify that which a child or young person most needs to achieve next in order for his or her life situation to improve. It refers to that which has not yet been achieved, or is not yet in place, but is still within the potential grasp of the young person. It has to do with the focus of the work, and the way that staff work with that young person.

Staff almost always try to find a focus—or sometimes several foci—to put in the forefront of their work. They develop a sense or an explicit understanding of what a particular young person needs most, at a particular time, and seek to work towards it. When staff members say, 'Every child is different', they mean that every child is different with respect to what is most important to him or her, then and there, and that every child needs to be worked with differently.

For one young person, what is most needed might be assistance in coping with a difficult, painful, recent transition:

A 12 year-old boy had been living abroad with his mother for most of his life. His mother felt she could no longer cope with him and put him on a plane with the intention that his father, from whom both mother and son had long been sepa-rated, would take over responsibility. The father, however, had developed a life-style which had no room in it for his son. The boy came into residential care. This boy was faced with the loss of his mother and her rejection of him, rejection from his father, and a new and unfamiliar living situation, all within a very short space of time. (Researcher's notes.)

For other young people, what was most needed might be assistance in returning to school after a period of having been excluded, or protection from self-harm, or extrication from association with adult criminals, or release from a drug habit, or help in recovering from a bereavement.

Sometimes what a child most needs (and which becomes the focus of the work) is tied to his or her life stage, or movements into or within substitute care. A young person nearing care-leaving age will need help in preparing for and managing the forthcoming transition. A young person of whatever age who has just been admitted to the Home will need help to settle in. These situation-specific needs are, however, almost al-ways connected with other needs related to more long-standing personal circumstances or personal characteristics—for example, almost life-long problems with self-esteem, or poor social skills, or a lifestyle which in-cludes offending.

Identifying what a child or young person most needs is, therefore, not always an easy matter. It may be possible to name an obvious need, such as 'needs help in returning to school', or 'needs to be prepared for inde-pendent living', but the further needs in which the easily-nameable one is embedded may be complex and harder to grasp.

One of the circumstances which can make the frontier of a young person's needs hard to grasp is that in which a young person's observable behaviour does not, or might not, match his or her likely underlying feelings. A child or young person might behave chaotically, or be quiet and untroublesome. In either case, strong feelings could underlie the behaviour but not be evident from the behaviour itself. The most visible thing about a chaotic young person is likely to be his or her unruly, destructive, and out-of-control behaviour. While it is easy to see that such a young person needs help in calming down and stopping the destructive behaviour, it is harder to get in touch with what might underlie the behaviour—possible feelings of despair, or hopelessness, or rage. A young person who, on the surface, appears calm, may be experiencing powerful distressing feelings inside. For example, such a young person might be profoundly confused about the reasons for having been rejected by a family, or might be worried about what the future might hold.

Staff judgements about what a child or young person needs may or may not be what the young person wants or prefers. A young person may agree with staff that it is important to get back to school, or get off drugs (if only he or she could see how to do it). On the other hand, a young person may wish to continue drug-taking, or resume a life of prostitution, or continue to stay away from school. Most staff members we got to know through this research understood that it was important to talk with a young person and seek his or her views, but they also knew that as responsible adults it was necessary for them to form their own views about what was most needed.

Seeking to Provide Reparative Experiences

The idea of working at the frontier of the young person's needs is useful—in fact, essential—but one also needs to think at another level. There is often a need for interpersonal experiences which could, over time, counteract or make up for the disadvantageous consequences of previous life experience. We have called these 'reparative experiences'. Related terms are 'corrective emotional experiences', 'disconfirming experiences', or 'crucial emotional experiences'.

Each of these terms carries a somewhat different connotation, and each contributes to an understanding of the processes involved. 'Reparative experiences' repair the consequences of earlier damage, and help a child or young person to discard behaviours or attitudes or feelings which, to him or her, are disadvantageous. The term 'corrective emotional experiences' is commonly used in psychotherapeutic work, and refers to much the same thing. Individuals are helped to get to a point where they no longer need previously well-established personal defences, self-perceptions, or characteristic expectations of and assumptions about others, all of which interfere with their own well-being and life goals. The term 'disconfirming experiences' is also used in therapeutic work. This refers to experiences which run counter to, or disconfirm, the beliefs and expectations which people have come to hold of themselves and others and which seem to them to be 'the way things are'. The term 'crucial experience' calls attention to the possibility that the process of achieving 'repair' or 'correction' may consist of a single significant event, often conspicuous and often experienced by carers and the person as a 'break-through'. Such events deserve being called 'crucial' even though much preparatory work has probably gone on, and follow-through will also be necessary.

Many young people in residential care carry with them, as burdensome baggage, feelings, attitudes, and characteristic behaviours which they would benefit from not having to live with. A young person may, for example, have come to believe that he or she must attack others because, if not, counter-attack will surely occur, or that the young person is not only unwanted by his or her parents but unworthy of being wanted by anyone, or that sexualised relationships are the only possible ones. Young people may have grown up under conditions in which ordinary progress through childhood—ordinary development—was virtually impossible. Such young people mistrust adults, with good reason, and cannot imagine having a sympathetic, caring relationship with an adult. They expect never to be given what they need, to the point that they either have given up trying, or are excessively demanding and impatient, finding it impossible to share with others or to wait for even a few minutes for anything they want. They so much expect never to be believed by adults that they keep an emotional distance, and avoid telling adults anything of importance to them. Many feel profoundly worthless—a feeling sometimes concealed by surface bravado. Some, especially girls, have become highly eroticised, unable to differentiate affectionate touching from sexualised touching. Many show little sign of being able to imagine how others might be feeling. They are often on a hair trigger, easily provoked into violence by such occurrences as having to wait ten minutes for a meal, or having been reprimanded by a teacher.

Such young people need not just one, but many repeated experiences to 'turn them around'—experiences which show them, for example, that adults really can be trusted, that they themselves are worthy individuals who deserve care and respect, and that they are competent and can develop more competence.

Reparative work can only occur over a period of time. Many exchanges in which a caring adult shows appreciation of a child with low esteem (for example) will be needed before internal feelings and associated behaviours begin to shift. There is typically a long build-up to a crucial event, or break-through, which then needs to be followed up to enable consolidated change to occur.

As a basis for reparative work, members of staff set goals on behalf of a young person. There are times when a goal, if named, is unlikely to make sense to the young person concerned. For example, a young person who is in a state of despair or hopelessness may see this as his or her natural condition rather than as something that can be worked on and recovered from. It would not occur to such a young person to define as a personal need 'to recover from a state of hopelessness' (or equivalent everyday language), but a staff member might do so. It follows that, with some young people, it may not be possible to discuss some of the goals towards which reparative work is directed, at least not until well into the process. Nor is it the case that staff always articulate what they are aiming for, in each step of their work.

Because reparative work requires time—months or years—it can only be undertaken, or undertaken with some chance of positive effects for the child, if the child stays in a Home long enough. Reparative work cannot easily be taken over by someone else, for it is embedded in personal relationships which take some time to develop. For this reason, the whole idea of reparative work cannot apply to very short-stay young people.

In addition to time, residential workers need certain understandings and practice skills. They need to develop an understanding, for any given young person, of the issue that needs repairing (or disconfirming, or correcting). They then need to be alert to opportunities in ordinary every-day contact to counter a young person's expectations, and to have a repertory of appropriate responses to draw upon.

In the interests of disconfirming a young person's entrenched expecta-tions, an adult carer tries to meet anger and threats with calmness rather than with retaliatory anger, the first signs of confiding with acceptance and understanding, unacceptable behaviour with an effort to understand why it is happening rather than with punishment, and so on. This occurs in part through words, but, importantly, also through tone of voice and behaviour.

Residential care workers do not necessarily think in terms of 'repara-tive' or 'disconfirming' or 'corrective' life experiences, but what they do for and with and in response to young people is often consistent with these ideas. For example, a member of staff who was sworn at by a 14-year-old girl and 'called every name', did not retaliate but told the girl that she would make some tea for them both. This defused the situation and bought them both time. Later, the staff member and the girl talked about what had led to such anger.

We are aware that this response, and other comparable ones, may be perceived by some as being 'soft' on young people. However, it is nearer to the reality to perceive that the staff member is carefully avoiding re-sponding to anger with anger or with punishment, which is what the young person expects, and knows all too well how to cope with. Instead, the member of staff responds with kindness and concern, which the young person does not expect and has had little experience of. This action is then followed up by an attempt to help the young person to understand his or her behaviour, and so get better control over it and have less need for it in the future. Being encouraged to look at one's own behaviour, what underlies it, and its consequences for self and others is not a soft option but a demanding and often painful one. It does not amount to condoning unacceptable behaviour.

It is important in all work of the kind described above that all staff on duty respond in consistent ways. Otherwise, the work being done by those members of staff who are sensitive to a young person's needs can be overturned by others, who behave differently. Planning meetings and review meetings therefore need to include explicit attention to what each young person is understood to need, and the associated response strategies. Communication needs to occur among all staff (including domestic workers) so that crucial work is not undermined.

HOW WORK ON THE THREE 'FRONTS' OFTEN GO TOGETHER

Containing and controlling, working at the frontier of the young person's needs and providing reparative experience often go together. In practice, two or all three of these fronts may well be worked on at the same time:

One lad had lived in a family and yet hadn't been living, really. He was 11 years old and he functioned like an 18-month-old. He ran like an 18-month-old. He began to realise he could be treated like a person. There were two sibs—just to see them walk, talk, feed themselves. . . . In a week he had learned to eat. After six months he could make tea. (Researcher's notes.)

It is clear that staff members were working at the frontier of these children's needs. These two siblings needed to develop basic skills in 'walking, talking, and feeding themselves' and that is what they were helped to do. In addition, when the staff member said of the 11-year-old, 'He began to realise he could be treated like a person', he was describing something which fits into the idea of recovering from the effects of earlier noxious experiences. One can infer that the boy had not previously been treated like a person. Perhaps he did not expect to be so treated, or perhaps he had no conception of what it was like to be treated as a person. Either way, he was now having experiences he had not had before, and 'he began to realise' it.

Behaviour on the part of a member of staff which is directed towards containing and controlling can at the same time constitute a reparative experience. As an example, a 13-year-old girl who is prevented by a member of staff from harming herself is being 'controlled', but may also be receiving the message that someone cares enough about her to stop her (an element in a reparative experience).

The following account was provided in written form by a member of staff for an in-service training programme. It is quoted verbatim, with his permission:

'A 14-year-old male resident had become very agitated and aggressive after some personal boundaries on my part had been reinforced. I had made my point and walked away from the young person concerned and stood in the doorway of the living room at the front of the house. He stormed through to the kitchen looking for me. He returned back down the hallway, shouting and swearing at me, his whole body language screamed aggression and he physically squared up to me. Here is the almost accidental part. I sat down on the floor against the wall opposite him. This totally disarmed him; it was an action which did not conform to his expectation of a situation like that and enabled me to turn a potentially explosive situation into something positive and constructive.'

In the researchers' view, the staff member was doing all of the following: he behaved in a way which forestalled violent behaviour, he disconfirmed the young person's expectation that violence will be met by counter-violence, and he opened the way for constructive discussion. Details are not provided as to the kind of constructive discussion which followed, but it would seem that in this episode, control, working at the frontier of the young person's needs, and reparative work, were all combined. This staff member's phrase, 'almost accidental' refers to the spontaneous character of his response. It is clear, however, that through reflecting on the episode later, as he did, he saw how the response made sense and was an instance of good practice.

Working at the frontier of a young person's needs can often be quite focused and circumscribed in terms of its goals, though such work still takes time. Providing reparative experiences always needs to occur and recur over long periods of time if it is to make a difference to a young person.

Slow Progress, Break-throughs, Setbacks and Reversals

Slow Progress

What is 'slow' and what is 'as fast as could be expected' is a matter of judgement and opinion. It is certainly the case that sometimes staff saw no effects from their efforts for long periods of time. Sometimes the psychological damage suffered by a young person is so profound and occurred so early that it takes months or longer of consistent loving care and intelligent attention to reach a child who has never learned to be responsive to or to trust adults.

Sometimes progress is slow (or even non-existent) because potentially useful work is not being done:

In an effort to prepare a 14-year-old boy for a return home, weekend visits were arranged. Each time he went home, this boy returned within hours, after having got into a physical fight with his mother. It had been assumed that the visits themselves would be adequate preparation, but this was proving not to be the case. (Researcher's notes.)

It can be hard to judge, in individual instances, whether continuing with a particular course of action will eventually produce results, or whether something else needs to be tried, and if so by whom—a member of the residential staff, or the young person's field social worker, or someone such as a family therapist.

Break-throughs

There are times when a young person who seemed to have been getting nowhere suddenly takes a giant step forward. This is, of course, pleasing to staff members and may also surprise them. Looking back, one can often see that important preparatory work had been going on which had gone unnoticed, but nevertheless paved the way for the break-through. This was the case for Kevin, the 'little frozen boy' described in Chapter 10.

Setbacks and Reversals

Staff members sometimes reported that a young person who had been progressing well suffered some setback, and was 'back to square one', or had seriously lost ground and was worse off than before. They saw such setbacks as being triggered by a range of events: for example, an upsetting encounter with a parent, or disturbances within the Home, or a quarrel with a teacher, or being overfaced by some new demand. The following are some examples:

A girl of 12 who had been attending school for two months after a six-month absence, declared that she would never go to school again, after feeling she had been treated unfairly by a teacher.

A boy of 14 who had run away frequently in the past but who had not done so for several months, took off with a friend from his previous school, whom he met by accident in the middle of the town.

Rosie, described earlier in this chapter, suffered a setback when she was over-faced by her first day at college. She was—temporarily—worse off than she had been for several years.

Sometimes a setback occurred because a decision was made which seemed right at the time, but led to unexpected and unwanted consequences:

The mother of a girl of 15 had asked, two years previously, that the girl be taken into care because she was taking drugs and was outside the mother's control. This girl, Ceci, was accommodated in a Children's Home, but when her drug-taking continued and she began to involve others, she was moved to secure accommodation. Over a period of about seven months Ceci was weaned from drugs and a decision was made at a review to return her to the Home. She returned, and soon reverted to drug-taking. It was decided at a further review meeting that the move out of secure accommodation had been premature and Ceci was returned there, staying for a further two months. She then returned to the Children's Home, and this time stayed off drugs. She was 16 by now, and was being helped by staff to prepare for independent living. Staff were enormously pleased by her progress and said she was 'going from strength to strength'. Ceci herself was pleased, and hopeful about her future. She planned to live on her own, but was in touch and on good terms with her mother and younger sister, saying, 'I know they'll always be there for me'. (Researcher's notes.)

As several of the examples show, a setback does not necessarily persist, and can be recovered from. However, members of staff can feel disappointed, inclined to self-blame, or vulnerable to criticisms from others when a setback occurs, and may feel angry if they feel it was caused by an unsympathetic parent or teacher, or triggered by the behaviour of one of the other young people in the Home.

YOUNG PEOPLE WITH WHOM STAFF FEEL THEY CANNOT WORK

Staff members sometimes take the view that a particular young person cannot be worked with in the setting of an 'ordinary' Children's Home:

A 15-year-old girl, who had had three foster placements in three months and had been assessed in another unit, was sent to a Children's Home even though all concerned, including those who referred her, felt that she should be placed in a specialist unit which could provide firmer control. During the few months that she was in the Home, she was arrested for public order offences four times, told another young person of having been abused in the past (but never disclosed this to staff), and behaved provokingly to other young people in the Home, to the point where a boy tried to strangle her. She told others that she heard voices. The unit manager and the staff felt powerless to help this girl and considered that the situation in the group of 10 young people was only just manageable whilst she was with them. Eventually, she was moved to a specialist unit.

A 14-year-old girl, Jo, was promiscuous. In the Home, Jo would get out at night through the windows and not return until the morning. She approached men in cars and took money from them in exchange for sex. She became involved with several men from the estate where the Home was located. Several times she was away for days at a time—no one knew where. She had sex with several younger boys in the Home. She was consistently defiant towards staff. The staff felt they could neither control her behaviour nor reach her in any way.

Edward, a 14-year-old boy, came into care because his parents considered him to be beyond control. He was stealing cars, involved with drugs, aggressive and threatening, and attacked adults. In the Home, this behaviour continued. The unit manager said, 'He would blatantly stand in front of you and sniff stuff—he made it quite obvious that he was a drug user; he wasn't prepared to modify his behaviour at all; he threatened adults; he threatened kids; he stole from us; his parents wouldn't have anything to do with him and he was just basically un-workable in this system.' The situation came to a head when Edward smashed up a visitor's car and threatened him with a knife. Charges were pressed. Staff felt that, 'He was a liability to everybody around him'. Edward was transferred to a facility accustomed to working with offenders. Shortly thereafter, he threatened suicide. Some time later his mother agreed to have him home. The unit manager considered that no change had occurred: 'That lad is still in the community, still doing everything he was doing prior to coming here.'

Although staff recognise that such young people need help, they are aware that little if any progress can be made in the current care context.

CONSTRAINTS ON WORK WITH INDIVIDUAL YOUNG PEOPLE

Situations sometimes arise where what is needed lies outside the skills of members of staff. For example, a 13-year-old boy who soils needs skilled therapeutic help; a girl of 10 has speech difficulties; a 14-year-old exhibits bizarre behaviour. In such circumstances staff seek outside help. Problems arise if outside help is hard to find, or there are delays, or the help does not continue for long enough.

A staff group who have been doing good work with a young person and are beginning to see good results can find that time runs out on them. The young person is transferred elsewhere at a time when staff consider that much more needs to be done, or before gains are consolidated. Perhaps fostering is to be tried, or the young person is transferred to another Children's Home nearer his or her own home. Sometimes staff members are happy about the move because they judge that the young person will be better off in the longer run. Sometimes, however, they are against the move for what seem to them to be good reasons, but report that they have no power to influence the decision. Sometimes staff would like to keep a 16-year-old with them for a longer period of time, on grounds that, whatever his or her chronological age, a further period in their care would be beneficial. If there is spare capacity in their unit, or no current demand for a bed, they may be able to do so, but if there is pressure on beds in their particular authority, they will be pressed to 'prepare him (or her) for independence'. Such premature transfers create problems for staff and young people. They also cause distress when staff feel that more could have been achieved, had the young person stayed with them longer.

All of the Homes which participated in this research were general-purpose Homes. None catered exclusively for children with learning difficulties, or were therapeutic communities or high-security facilities. Nevertheless some specialisation occurred—for example a Home might be designated a long-stay Home, or a Home for particularly difficult young people, or for young people remanded from the courts. Some general-purpose Homes included a physically separate sub-unit for preparing young people for independent living.

The nature of the specialised function carries with it particular boundaries within which staff work. For example, staff in a long-stay facility are in a position to bring up a child or young person from the time of admission—seeing him or her through, perhaps from early adolescence, to care-leaving age. With respect to a seriously damaged young person, staff could aspire to make up for the consequences of adverse earlier experiences and life circumstances and, hopefully, bring the young person to a better position to face adult life. They can engage in reparative work, as described above, which is impossible in a short-stay Home.

Short-stay Homes with a very rapid turnover of young people find themselves concentrating on helping young people to manage transitions.

A Home for young people remanded from the courts also tends to be relatively short-stay. The point of the work is to hold the young people in a safe and comfortable place while they await trial, and help them to face a court appearance and its consequences.

In all that has been said in this chapter, the focus has been on work with individual children or young people, and little has been said about concurrent events in the Home, with other children or with the group as a whole. This has been done to highlight the kind of work with individuals which can occur in Children's Homes, but it can convey a false impression because it de-emphasises the fact that work with individuals occurs in the context of group living. The next chapter moves on to examining working with the mix of young people who are resident at any particular time.

6

WORKING WITH THE MIX OF YOUNG PEOPLE

The term 'the mix' was used by many staff to refer to the composition of the child/young person group living in the Home at any one time. In Chapter 3, 'working with the mix of young people' was named as one of five task arenas.

In Children's Homes, the experience of both young people and staff members is crucially connected with the mix of young people in the Home, with the interactions which occur within the mix, and with how staff respond to them. As has already been seen in Chapter 4, staff members connect the mix of young people with 'good patches' and 'bad patches', and consider that the mix significantly influences the climate in the Home and the kinds of experiences which both staff and young people enjoy or endure. Changes in the mix were seen as a key factor in triggering bad patches or in assisting a Home to recover from them.

It is impossible to work in a Children's Home without responding to the mix of young people. Working with and through the young people as a group or in sub-groups is one of the practice routes by which individual young people come to benefit. Harm can also be done to individuals through what goes on within the mix. Staff try to maximise the positive potentials of group living and minimise the negative effects.

HOW THE THEME OF 'WORKING WITH THE MIX' WAS EXPLORED

Theme and content analysis methods were again employed. Episodes which, in one way or another, had to do with the mix, working with the mix, or the impact of the mix were gathered together and formed a sub-population of episodes. It was quickly apparent that episodes divided into group situations which have (a) positive, constructive consequences for the young people, or certain of them, and (b) group situations which have negative, damaging consequences for the young people, or certain of them. These were taken as two main clusters of situations. Forms of constructive or destructive interactions could be named and illustrated, and staff responses described.

GROUP SITUATIONS THAT HAVE POSITIVE, CONSTRUCTIVE CONSEQUENCES

The group of young people, together with the staff on duty, engage in some activity together in the Home which all enjoy:

'Staff do craft work and flip chart work with the young people, who love it. This is all life-skills work which boosts confidence. The unit manager asked for a flip chart for the staff team to do some group work. A member of staff starts off the topic and the girls take over. It has really brought out Sharon [one of the young people]. Now everybody is wanting to write on the board.'

'The group enjoys an evening devoted to "reverse role play", in which the young people become the staff and the staff become the young people. Everyone enjoys it, and both staff and young people end up understanding one another better.'

'All the staff and young people are preparing for a Christmas Fayre, to which they will invite neighbours.'

The staff and the young people go on outings together and all have a good time:

'Last year [in the summer] we hired a mini-bus and went out for day trips. The young people were so good—bar meals without nicking drinks. They went camping, including to Mary's Dad's farm and didn't swear, because he doesn't like it, and "helped" with the cattle—including the bull!'

Several members of staff and all the young people went on an outing to an adventure park, where all had a go at abseiling. Everyone had a good time, and one 13-year-old boy, in particular, could hardly stop talking about how many times he had abseiled up and down a cliff, with evident pride. (Researcher's notes.)

Regular residents meetings are held in which planning is done, complaints are aired, and conflicts are addressed:

Staff and young people together engage in planning—for example, of holidays and outings, evening activities, the purchase of new furniture, redecorating, etc. Such meetings also become the venue for discussing young people's complaints as they arise.

The young people support one another in behaviour seen as desirable by staff:

Jim and Brian have both been fearful of going to school, but they have become friends and now support one another in attending. (Researcher's notes.)

The group of young people help to contain an unruly newcomer:

When a newcomer helped himself to food meant for everyone s dinner, others told him, 'We don't do that here'. (Researcher's notes.)

Certain young people function as positive role models for others:

A young person who had come to appreciate the goodwill of the staff, showed through her behaviour that she could approach them without fear or worries. Through this, she offered a positive model to the more mistrustful young people in the group. (Researcher's notes.)

Certain young people, by their behaviour, assist staff members to maintain order:

'A very new resident was refusing to go to bed one night when the other young people had settled for the night. Kay, a female member of staff, was upstairs trying to deal with this situation. The unit manager was in the building, in the downstairs office. One of the young people came to fetch the unit manager, to stop the newcomer from "messing Kay about, as she's got to get up in the morning to get us up". Yet another resident told the one causing trouble to "just go to your bed and be quiet".'

Personal gains occur through vicarious experience: one young person hears about the experiences of certain others and benefits from it:

A young person with experience of living in secure accommodation described it to others so vividly [apparently enjoying the drama of it all] that others resolved never to put themselves in the position of being a candidate for transfer to secure accommodation. (Researcher's notes.)

Among the above, a special comment may be made about those activities which involve 'having a good time together', since good times might possibly be dismissed as being no more than that. Good times, such as those described, have a number of positive consequences. For example, they demonstrate to the young people that enjoyable times *can* be had with adults—important for young people whose experiences with adults have mostly been very negative. This, it may be noted, is an instance of a 'disconfirming' experience, as described in the preceding chapter. The difference is that, here, group interaction is the vehicle for disconfirming experiences which may be experienced by more than one young person at the same time. Often, an outing stretches the young people's skills and helps them to generate new ones—a source of pride and a boost to self-esteem. An outing may contain an opportunity to demonstrate physical courage, with the same consequence. Enhancing self-esteem is likely to be particularly important if the young person feels that he or she is a failure in other aspects of life—for example, at school. If the young people be-have well and are praised for it, this can be one small contribution to learning that good behaviour generates rewards. Having a good time together can contribute to a sense of belonging to a social group, which is again a valuable experience, especially if rare.

How Staff Strive to Maximise the Occurrence of Constructive Group Situations

Staff initiate group activities, or create customs and rituals within the Home, which provide opportunities for enjoyable social interaction, for sharing in planning, and for learning social and practical skills.

Social activities include outings and holidays, special celebrations, and within-Home customs around shared evening group activities, which might include games or working together to prepare a special bedtime snack.

In regularly scheduled residents' meetings, staff and young people share and plan together. They may plan social activities, or review rules and sanctions for maintaining order, or think out how to respond to some forthcoming special situation (such as how an invasion by decorators will be handled).

Some positive situations are not exactly planned but develop as staff members perceive opportunities arising in day-to-day living, and take advantage of them. Some of the most useful group interactions seem to occur in this way; for example, a few staff and some of the young people might be sitting around in the lounge, and after a favourite television programme finishes, the conversation drifts into a discussion about sex, or drug-taking, or what some of the young people dislike about school. The staff encourage sharing experiences and opinions, and assist the group to avoid blaming anyone, or making invidious comparisons. In such instances, staff have not initiated the discussion, but they take ad-vantage of it having arisen spontaneously.

Staff members can increase the value of positive group situations for individual young people by emphasising or 'underlining' what has occurred, and praising young people for handling some interactive situation well. Many examples could be cited: a staff member congratulates a young person for *not* imitating someone else's bad behaviour; or points out that a young person has faced, with courage, some encounter which he or she has previously found difficult; or acknowledges and praises some act of generosity.

GROUP SITUATIONS THAT HAVE NEGATIVE, DAMAGING CONSEQUENCES

Mass absconding or mass offending occurs. The whole group, or most of it, 'wrecked the place':

A boy of 13 complained to a member of staff that he was ready to leave on a planned outing, and that several others, who were not ready, ought to be left behind. When the member of staff said they would wait and that it would not be long, the boy became enraged, ran into the lounge and began to wreck it. He was soon joined by two others, and all three ran out of the building and began to break windows. In the end, all but two of the eight residents were involved in this episode of destruction, and the police were called. (Researcher's notes.)

Five of the young people were found by police at 5.00 a.m. in a stolen car. They had quietly climbed out of a window, and the member of staff who was sleeping-in did not know they were out of the house until the police rang. (Researcher's notes.)

A 16-year-old girl had left the Home to live in her own flat in the neighbourhood. Others repeatedly ran away to spend time in this flat, where they could engage in sniffing without interruption. (Researcher's notes.)

One young person, usually a newcomer, somehow 'contaminates' or 'corrupts' one or more of the others, who imitate the new young person and begin to behave as he (or she) does:

'We have an 8-year-old who has been imitating a disturbed 13-year-old. He did not behave this way before. Management describe the 13-year-old as receiving good quality care, yet he is having this impact on the 8-year-old. You could describe the 8-year-old as being abused by the care system. To say that the system is abusing that kid is right, because that lad wasn't like that until the other one came, and he's copied, that's where the abuse comes in, he's copied him, that's why the system is abusing him.'

'A newcomer refused to attend school. Other young people said, "If he is not attending school, why should we have to?" Soon three other young people refused to attend.'

One young person imitates the bad behaviour of another, after noticing that bad behaviour brings certain rewards:

'You get kids looking around the unit and thinking, "O.K., I'll pick that up and I'll throw it through the window, and then, and only then, you lot [staff] give me attention, you'll take me down to McDonald's, you'll give me what I want. That's the way to do it." I've seen it. In fairness to them, they are right. The only way they're going to get the quality time and attention out of us these days is by creating that sort of situation.'

One young person becomes the target of attack or the object of harassment by one or more others. The group divides into a number of 'villains' and a 'victim':

'We had a 16-year-old girl with special needs. She was 16 going on 8. The other kids reacted—they behaved differently to her because she was different. She wanted to be a part of the group, and gave them money, or sweets. She would have been picked on wherever she went. Her foster placement had broken down (and she came to us). Luckily we found her another foster placement.'

Virtually the whole group persecuted one boy, tying his clothes into knots, hiding his toothbrush, etc. (Researcher's notes.)

One young person provokes one or more others into attacking him:

A girl of 14 constantly taunted others, to the point where one of the older boys grabbed her and knocked her head against the wall. (Researcher's notes.)

Upon coming to live in the Home, Douglas, a boy of 12, immediately began accusing two older boys of bullying and attacking him. Staff indeed observed instances of violence towards Douglas, but realised that they occurred in response to Douglas 'telling' on the others. For example, Douglas told staff that a boy was keeping stolen goods in his room, and this boy pushed and kicked him, causing minor injuries. On another occasion Douglas told the staff who had set the fire alarm off, and later was attacked. (Researcher's notes.)

One young person (or more than one) becomes the victim of sexual abuse, on the part of another, usually older, young person:

Because it was all happening in secret, the staff of a Home did not at first realise that a 14-year-old boy was sexually abusing two younger boys. (Researcher's notes.)

The behaviour of one young person, which is outside the norms of the group, upsets the others, who complain to the staff and lose confidence in the staff being able to keep things under control:

A girl of 15 repeatedly was out at night and was known to be engaged in prostitution in the town. The other young people felt and said that the staff was failing the girl by not controlling her properly. (Researcher's notes.)

A pair of young people get into a special relationship with one another such that they support one another in behaviour considered unacceptable by staff:

Two boys, 14 and 15, committed offences together. They moved from taking cars without the owner's consent to burglary. On one occasion they were apprehended by the police and appeared in court, and then were remanded back to the Children's Home. They boasted of having got away with it. Other young people did not join in with them in offending, but were unsettled by these events. Staff were concerned that a bad example was being shown to the other young people. (Researcher's notes.)

A girl of 16 became sexually involved with a boy of 14, also living in the Home. The staff felt that the 14-year-old was being exploited by this older, sexually experienced girl. Matters became worse when the girl dropped the 14-year-old and took up with another boy in the Home, also younger. Conflict, envy and resentment spread through the group. (Researcher's notes.)

How Staff Strive to Minimise the Occurrence of Destructive Group and Interpersonal Situations

It is generally recognised that normal growing up is full of interactions with peers which lead to distress, hurt, anger, and envy. Adults cannot protect young people from hurtful experiences, nor should they wish to do so, altogether. Negative as well as positive experiences are material for learning about how to recognise and handle personal feelings, manage personal behaviour, and understand and respond to others.

Nevertheless, quite seriously destructive interactions can occur among young people. Parents, teachers, and others try to prevent or curtail these, or help young people deal with the aftermath. Residential staff do the same. They try to avoid bringing together the more difficult mixes of young people and to curtail full-blown destructive episodes. They try to avoid behaving in ways likely to escalate a difficult situation.

Trying to Avoid Mixes which Staff Predict will Create Serious Problems

Referrers sometimes want a particular young person to be admitted, but staff members are convinced that the admission would lead to a destructive and most probably unmanageable interpersonal or group situation. For example, staff did not want to admit an adolescent girl known to be at odds with a girl already living in the Home, and where the two girls were known to have got into physical fights involving injury. Another staff group did not want to admit a boy known to have associates in the adult criminal community, for fear of attracting adult criminals to the Home. Staff members reported that they had been pressed to re-admit a young person despite it being known that the young person had created havoc during a previous period of living in the same Home.

For the most part, when staff were faced with a young person whom they feared would create difficulties in the group, they made their protests known, but in the end gave in. This occurred in part because they had less power than the referrers making the decision, and in part because they themselves knew from experience that there had been times in the past when an admission had worked out well (or well enough) despite their reservations. For the sake of fairness, they were sometimes ready to accept a young person even though it felt risky to do so.

There were three circumstances in which a staff group might dig in its heels and struggle very hard to avoid admitting a young person: (1) direct experience with a young person who had been in the Home before—staff were very well aware of the problems that had occurred and were likely to occur again; (2) a staff group had firm evidence that admitting a particular young person would put others in the Home, and the Home itself, at risk; (3) a recent bad experience with, say, young offenders admitted to a general-purpose or even a long-stay Home, or particularly chaotic young people who were in transit and stayed only a few days but nevertheless left destruction of one kind or another in their wake. In such circumstances, memory of recent difficulties was acute, and staff not only wanted to avoid something similar happening, but felt the need for a period of relative calm so that all could recover.

As mentioned in the preceding chapter, sometimes a young person known to have particular difficulties was admitted because it was a staff group's 'turn' to take that person. There was sometimes an unspoken and not publicly acknowledged practice (or custom) to rotate such young people around the various Homes—to spread the load.

Noting and Responding to Early Warning Signs

Some staff members are particularly skilful at noting the early signs of disturbance. They find it hard to put into words just what they are detecting, but
make such comments as, 'You can tell something is brewing the minute you
walk in the door', or 'I can smell it'. Staff members who sense that something
is brewing will try to prevent it. They might temporarily separate potential
combatants, for example, by taking one shopping, sending two others to the
swimming pool, or simply taking one upstairs for a private chat. Or they
might involve the group in some energy-consuming activity, or invite all or
most of the group to engage in some cooperative activity.

Different staff groups had their favourite ways of responding, which
became customs to be resorted to when needed. In one Home, staff frequently involved the young people in making pancakes—a treat enjoyed
by all which involved not only cooperative effort but produced food
which everyone could eat and enjoy.

When successful management of a potentially difficult situation occurred, it was often by a combination of sensitive work on the part of the
staff combined with there being a mix of young people with sufficient
strengths to support staff efforts. Several of the examples presented earlier showed how some of the young people themselves behaved in ways
which supported staff in maintaining order. By the combined energies of
staff members and some young people, escalation was averted and a
widespread uproar prevented.

Avoiding Behaving in Ways Likely to Escalate a Difficult Situation

Adults can make things worse than they otherwise would be by not
acting soon enough or by behaving in some way which exacerbates a
difficult situation. For example, a staff member might not pick up early
warning signs of an impending 'explosion', and so allow a situation to
build up which might otherwise have been tamped down or dealt with in
its early stages:

*Staff were warned by a field social worker that Jim, one of their young people, had
had a very upsetting visit to his mother. The staff responded to this by taking Jim
and several others to an exciting theme park, with the idea in mind that this
would be a special treat for all of them but especially for Jim. Jim's visit home was
not mentioned, or discussed with him. Jim seemed to enjoy this treat, but came
home very excited, and could not settle for bed. Before morning came he had got
out of control, wrecked his room, and stirred up several others to join him in a
spate of window-breaking.* (Researcher's notes.)

The researchers considered that, although it was well meant, the treat intensified Jim's excitement. His needs would have been better served by a period of calm followed by the opportunity to talk about his visit home. On another occasion:

A girl had sworn at a member of staff, and another member of staff demanded that she apologise. She refused to do so, and she and the (second) staff member engaged in a shouting match which got more and more intense and ended up with the girl storming out of the house, to be gone overnight. The girl was at risk, and the episode left the others in an upset state. (Researcher's notes.)

Here, the staff member's behaviour had escalated the situation, where a calmer approach probably would not have. Moreover, since no one can 'make' another person apologise if they resist doing so, the staff member and the girl got into an adversarial relationship in which the girl was bound to win and the staff member was bound to lose.

When it is obvious that one young person is getting a great deal of staff attention, envy and resentment can build up in the others to the point where the 'favourite' is attacked, or complaints are made to the authority against the staff. It should be noted that if a young person is in a particularly upset state and needs special attention, this is often appreciated and tolerated by other young people. It is a different matter when, in the view of the young people, staff are paying special attention to one young person not because of that person's needs but because staff like him or her better: this is seen as unfairness or favouritism.

In sum, certain behaviours were highly likely to escalate a difficult situation: responding to aggression with counter-aggression; making demands on a child or young person which, for one reason or another, he or she is entirely incapable of meeting, and then insisting on conformity; getting into an adversarial position with a group of children such that only one side can 'win'; backing a child or several children into a corner from which there is no self-respecting way out. Many staff members have acquired skills at avoiding such situations. This is no small achievement when one considers that escalatory behaviours which set adults against children are commonplace in the larger culture.

Repairing the Consequences of Difficult or Explosive Group Situations

It would be wrong to give the impression that forestalling and curtailing difficult group situations is always possible. The following describes a situation which a staff group found unmanageable:

'New Year's Eve and New Year's Day were horrible: there were two new admissions and the place didn't feel like home. [The unit manager] objected to the referrals, to no avail. One of them was a young offender admitted from the cells for breaking curfew. The young people in the unit didn't dare say what they wanted on TV: the 15-year-old was terrifying. One of the new admissions is still in the unit (he sat in the chair all day shell-shocked, not talking to staff the first day), but the other went back next day, after getting out at night, breaking curfew, taking others with him and being up till 5 a.m. Staff are still recovering.'

As further examples, it is hard to see how a staff member could 'manage' two boys who quietly climbed out of windows at night and stole cars. It was hard to see how a staff group could 'manage' a hyperactive boy of 9 who set fires, behaved in a bizarre way, and was unpredictably violent, let alone how they could do this without devoting all their time and energy to this one child. An uproar, in which a number of young people are running around the house overturning furniture and breaking windows, can happen so suddenly that it is like an instant conflagration. The situation gets out of control so rapidly that it is hard even to register the sequence of events. If a number of young people are persecuting one particular girl or boy, this may happen in secret for some time before it comes to light. Inappropriate sexual contact between two or more young people in a Home more often than not happens in secret. By the time staff find out about it, the events have already occurred.

A number of staff used the terms 'mopping up', or 'damage limitation' to refer to what they do after a destructive episode has occurred. If an episode has involved all or most of the young people and has run its course or nearly run its course, staff try to pick up the pieces, restore order, and help those young people who have experienced particular distress. It was part of the practice wisdom of many staff to provide everyone with some breathing space and time to cool down after an uproar had occurred, and only then to sit down with those concerned to talk it out. Staff members might talk to young people individually, concentrating on those who show most distress. Or they might talk things over with the group of young people as a whole. Experienced staff said that they never tried to talk things out immediately, but always did something to reduce the emotional intensity first.

Sometimes the destructive event involves just a few of the young people rather than virtually all of them. For example:

A girl of 12 was regularly persecuted by a recently admitted boy, who stole and hid her things, called her names, and the like. He did not behave in this way towards anyone else. The girl was extremely distressed and kept asking: 'Why me?' (Researcher's notes.)

This girl, staff reported, had serious problems with self-esteem. Her life experience to date—with a mother who repeatedly entered and left her life—had left her convinced that she was intrinsically unlovable. It required very sensitive work with this girl, over a period of time, to help her to see that these episodes did not relate to her own intrinsic unacceptability. At the same time, the boy who was doing the bullying also needed to be understood—particularly with respect to how it was that he so needed to find someone to persecute. Further, if staff could figure out how he managed to single out a very vulnerable girl, they might become aware of the signals she may have been sending out which made her such an attractive target. Noting this could increase staff members' understanding of the girl, and suggest ways of helping her to avoid getting into such situations.

In another example of bullying:

A learning disabled boy was the target of bullying by most of the others. The staff spoke seriously to those who were doing the bullying, and at the same time worked with the boy being bullied, to help him to stand up for himself more effectively and avoid behaviour which invited bullying. Most of those doing the bullying desisted, but one boy carried on with it. After a time, others began to criticise him for his bullying behaviour, and he, too, stopped. (Researcher's notes.)

The way in which staff turned a distressing situation into learning involved assisting the boy who was being bullied to gain more control over his behaviour, and so reduced the likelihood of further episodes of bullying. Discussing matters with those doing the bullying improved the behaviour of most of them, presumably because being talked to 'seriously' undermined the dynamic of their having 'permission' to bully someone because 'everyone was doing it'. One boy was untouched by this and continued his bullying behaviour, but was subsequently influenced by the change in attitude in his peer group.

It will be clear that constructive use can be made of a destructive episode, when it is reviewed afterwards in an atmosphere of calm. When talking-through occurs, staff members encourage young people to review the event, share the feelings they had at various stages of it, and encourage particular young people to understand the part they played in the event, and the consequences of their behaviour for others. Potentially, everyone can gain, through learning that talking-through is possible and that difficult situations can be understood and managed. Individual young people can gain better control over what happens to them by perceiving the part they play in creating unwanted interpersonal situations. Sometimes staff help a young person to maintain some personal gain by naming it and giving them credit for it.

It must, however, be said that talking things through in a group requires the utmost skill and tact, for it is easy for both young people and members of staff to fall into placing blame, or re-igniting an explosive situation and thus forestalling learning. Members of staff need to be able to manage their own feelings and behaviour, perceive what is going on for the group and for the individuals in it, perceive how individual and group dynamics interconnect, be in touch with levels of tension in the group and in individuals, and 'manage' discussions within time limits. These are complex group management skills.

FAVOURABLE AND UNFAVOURABLE MIXES

A favourable or an unfavourable mix can be defined by its consequences, but this avoids asking and trying to answer the crucial questions: What *is* a favourable mix? What *is* an unfavourable mix?

Unfavourable mixes seem to take several forms. In one kind of unfavourable mix the young people are so diverse in their characteristic behaviour and their personal needs that some are bound to be threatening to others. There is little chance for the young people to form (or have the chance of forming) a mutually supportive group. In Chapter 4, when discussing bad patches, we reported staff feeling that one form of unfavourable mix included some insecure, hesitant, fearful young people and some others who angrily hit out at others and had little or no control over their destructive behaviour.

Too much diversity also makes it difficult for staff to establish a regime suitable to the range of young people they are trying to help. A regime which is firm enough to contain the unruly ones can be intimidating to the more fearful ones.

Another kind of difficult mix is one which includes young people who support one another in unacceptable behaviour directed towards others or who behave destructively towards one another. Carl and Paul committed offences together, provoked others together, and joined together in smashing up the house. Each supported and egged on the other. Marianne and Louise often got into physical fights with one another. Staff can sometimes deal with such problems but in some cases the behaviour is so entrenched that it is hard to influence.

Still another form of unfavourable mix is one in which the contagion of unacceptable behaviour is prone to spread through the whole group. Mass absconding or offending occurs, or all or most of the young people explode into an episode of breaking windows and otherwise damaging the house. In such situations there is often an identifiable instigator, who may be held to be to blame, without anyone recognising that the situation is more complex and that others played a part. The complexity of such situations is demonstrated by the fact that sometimes the others resist joining in with the behaviour of the instigator while at other times they do not. It is not the presence of an instigator which is the key factor, but that, plus how others respond.

In referring to favourable mixes, staff groups often say that things go well when the young people are a 'settled' group. They mean that the young people can be trusted to behave acceptably most of the time, that they can join with the staff in maintaining order, and that the staff and the young people can form into a coherent group and not be adversaries. In such a group, there may well be some disturbed, disruptive young people, but they do not trigger others into joining in with them.

'Settledness', we came to think, describes a mix of young people which includes strengths somewhere in the group composition, which assists a staff group to maintain control and which prevents destructive behaviour from spreading through the whole group. Such a group composition has the potential to be a secure base for the young people and a medium for experiences which heal. Chaotic and unruly children may be present, but others are resistant to their influence and sometimes help to control them.

To say that a favourable mix 'includes strengths somewhere in the group composition' does not necessarily mean that some young people are strong while others are not (though it could mean that), nor does it mean that a simple majority of more 'settled' young people needs to be present in the Home. The situation is more complex. Just one, or perhaps two, difficult, unruly young people can have a major negative effect on a Home. On the other hand, their behaviour might not spread throughout the whole group. It all depends on how the behaviour of the unruly ones 'touches' other young people—that is, how it connects with their own feelings, tendencies, and ambivalences—and how they behave in response to what they see and hear.

It will be clear that some forms of unfavourable mixes are easier to identify and to avoid than others. Two 'sworn enemies' are easier to identify than young people who appear to be in control of themselves most of the time but are yet vulnerable to imitating the bad behaviour of others because of internal, not very visible, ambivalences. Important features of the mix become evident only through experience with it. It follows that unfavourable mixes cannot always be avoided, but they often can be understood and worked with.

It is nevertheless the case that where there is a concentration of young people who have poor control over their own behaviour, as may be the case in almost any Children's Home at one time or another, difficult group situations are likely to arise. The really damaged young people with difficult behaviours, the people most likely to be associated with

problems for the group as a whole, present a problem for all those working in substitute care. Such young people have to be looked after somewhere. As Redl and Wineman put it, 'somebody in the framework of their
natural habitat has to survive with the [child's] symptoms as long as they
last' (Redl & Wineman, 1957, p. 70).

HOW CHANGES OCCUR OVER TIME IN A MIX OR IN HOW A MIX OPERATES

Sometimes the composition of the group of young people can be stable
but there is a change in the way the group operates. A change for the
better can occur as work with individual young people begins to show
results and they become more settled, less prone to violence, in better
control over their own behaviour, and better armed against being influenced by others. A change for the worse can occur in a stable group if
certain stressors appear—for example, a rumour that the Home is to be
closed, or illness within the staff, or when one young person becomes
especially distressed through a family crisis.

In the two chapters which follow, we turn to the environment with which
staff work outside the Home: in the first instance, the larger organisation,
and in the second instance the networks of individual young people and
of the Home.

7

WORKING WITH AND BEING MANAGED BY THE LARGER ORGANISATION

'Working with and being managed by the larger organisation'—in this case the Social Services Department—was mentioned in Chapter 3 as one of the five major task arenas for staff groups. This chapter focuses on staff interactions with those within the Department who are concerned with the residential care of children and young people. Theme and content analyses comparable to those used before were employed.

KEY FIGURES WITHIN THE LARGER ORGANISATION

The Children's Homes which participated in the research were located in the public sector, in Social Services Departments. The Homes were supported and managed by their Departments. These Departments were typically organised hierarchically. There was a unit manager for every Home, and several layers of management above the unit manager. There was an external line-manager, and, above him or her, middle and top managers, and the director. Councillors (people elected to be members of the county or metropolitan council) were sometimes influential. Though not officially in the management hierarchy, field social workers, responsible for the young people living in the Home, exercised certain management functions. Training officers also figure in the work life of staff groups, but less importantly as far as day-to-day operations with young people are concerned.

What is said here does not take into account the full range of tasks and responsibilities of line-managers, field social workers, or higher managers, which we are not in a position to comment upon. We emphasise here the experience of residential staffs as they come into contact with key people in the larger organisation, and are 'managed' by some of them.

Relationships with Line-managers and Higher Managers

The external line-manager is the link person between a residential staff group and higher management in the Department. He or she is expected to be aware of activities in the Home; to communicate Departmental policy to staff and see to it that policy is carried out; to communicate changes in policy to staff; to communicate staff needs, and staff reactions to policy, upwards; and to provide supervision and consultation—sometimes only to the unit manager and sometimes to the staff group as a whole. Staff members thus know their line-manager well and are usually in regular contact.

Staff groups usually have a much more remote relationship with higher management. They usually know who their significant higher managers are, by name and by role or title. Direct interaction does not often occur. In some cases 'higher management' seems to remain a somewhat ill-defined category of people, rather than differentiated individuals with different and nameable responsibilities.

Communication Problems

Staff sometimes feel that it is difficult to convey their viewpoints to line-managers and through them, to higher management. They may also feel that managers do not provide information soon enough.

'This week, not from our senior management, we read in the local paper that the unit that's supposed to be replacing this will probably be scrapped, because of lack of money. We've all read that in the paper. Wonderful to hear it from the paper, at the same time as Joe Public.'

'One of the kids read in the local paper that we are going to be closed. He said "did you know . . . ?" and we didn't. It was the first we had heard of it.' [Note: This proved to be incorrect—the kernel of truth in the press report was that management was considering changing the function of the Home—a possibility that was not communicated to the staff until much later, and which eventually did take place.]

When information is conveyed down the hierarchy at the early stages of an idea being formed, a line-manager is sometimes seen by staff to communicate uncertainties, as distinct from keeping staff informed of the progress of an idea or plan:

'He's [the line-manager] just created a lot of anxiety in my mind. He'd have been better off saying nothing until he'd got something concrete to say.'

The researchers came to appreciate that when a change is in prospect, the line-manager has a delicate decision to make as to when to inform the staff—avoiding being either 'too soon' or 'too late' with the news—a matter of perspective and judgement. The line-manager may also be under instructions from higher management not to pass information on to staff.

Communicating with external line-managers when the intention is to reach higher management is often viewed by staff as problematic. Staff sometimes expressed the view that they feel that they have to overstate their case in order to have it heard. This can become a tactic for 'dealing' with management.

'Previously . . . we've actually had [four extra] young people in. . . . We had to make sure it was reduced to more reasonable numbers, or the roof would have been off. [We] had to be blunt with management, use scare tactics, so that they would agree. But it meant there was no forward planning. They had to be scared into doing it, which is quite appalling really.'

Residential workers sometimes resort to stratagems to get their line-managers or service managers to take their point of view seriously:

'There are two ways of dealing with highlighting a problem [constructively dealing with the acknowledged problems, or letting things run to crisis point and forcing action]. The easiest thing in the world at the weekend, was where it got very fraught, six and a half years I've been in residential work, probably one of the worst afternoons I've had . . . a situation where we nearly lost control of the unit, where we had six, seven, 12- to 16-year-olds all irate; this was over this young kid that I was telling you about, this all came from that girl, snowballing. Which is the situation in a place like this, you've got to nip it in the bud, but really it would probably have been the best thing in the world for us to lose control of the unit: the kids are running round smashing things up, the papers down here [would say] "Kids run riot in Children's Home, why has this happened?" and all the rest of it. [And then it would be] Right, well we need to do this and we need to do that. But isn't it a pity when it has to get to that, instead of people acknowledging the problems that we've got, and actually dealing with it.'

Overstating a situation, or considering allowing it to develop to crisis point may be regarded as an 'effective' tactic, but it also makes staff vulnerable to being blamed for inadequate practice or for not acting soon enough.

From staff members' point of view, the question often is: Is the external line-manager 'one of us' or 'one of them'? At times, most usually when information is passed down the hierarchy, staff groups identify line-managers closely with their higher management system. At other times, staff want line-managers to identify with them and be *their* representatives when passing information upwards, or sideways to team managers or the Child Protection Team. This is reflected in the ways that staff describe their managers: sometimes line-managers are referred to as 'management'—in other words, in terms which do not distinguish between different levels of management. Such a conflation in perception of roles frequently raises difficulties for staff when communicating with the line-manager at an *individual* level—they find it hard to view their line-manager as being unequivocally free to represent their interests.

A Sense of being Supported, or Not, by External Line-managers and Higher Managers

Some unit managers and staff have close supportive and positive relationships with their line-managers:

'It hasn't always been plain sailing between my line-manager and me, but I think we understand each other pretty well now, and I do ask his advice, because I know that he will—he won't say "Well, you've got to do this, you've got to do that", he makes me look at things and he makes me see things for myself, which I find very useful.'

Other staff have mixed feelings about their line-managers:

A unit manager had written to a senior manager with reference to her need for another member of staff. After supervision with her line-manager she reported the line-manager had said 'There will be an answer'. The unit manager speculated, 'that means there will be no extra staff, or her [the line-manager's] response would have been different'. (Researcher's notes.)

Feeling to be supported by their line-managers is important for reducing stress and a sense of isolation in staff groups. If staff members feel supported, they feel they are more visible to others in the wider organisation.

Staff members need support and appreciation from higher managers, and sometimes get it, but often do not. It appears to be a rare event, much appreciated when it happens.

It is nice to know that you will get support from upper management when you need it. It sometimes feels like their attitude is, right, that's your unit, you get on with it, if you need support, look to the staff. Sometimes you want support from management, reassurance, and not always leave it to the officer-in-charge and the team leaders to support their team. Not just verbal reassurance, to be for the staff, not just for the young people. Acknowledgement, and also to offer the staff support in other ways. To be able to say if something goes wrong, not just how is the young person, but how are the staff as well. Sometimes it seems the attitude is forget the staff, you get paid to do that. They don't see what you're doing above and beyond the call of duty, because you're in this job because you care.'

Support from managers is particularly appreciated when an allegation is made against a member of staff:

'The service manager came down yesterday to go through an incident, a complaint against a member of staff. There was nothing found, it was all clean and no problem at all, but a complaint hanging over you causes anxiety: will I get the sack, will I get the mortgage paid, what's happening? It was nice of him to come down and spend an hour and a half just to go through the scenario and reassure everyone. It was an unusual thing for the service manager to do: the first time [I've known it].'

'At Christmas I was threatened by a lad who had a piece of wood and threatened to wrap it round my head. I took it off him, and the lad must have been upset by that, because a day later I was told not to go back into work. It was four days before I knew what the allegation was. I kicked up a stink and told them they were at fault and everything was pushed through in two weeks. . . .' (Said by a male member of staff.)

A female member of staff who had an incident alleged against her said:

'I refused to go back to the place which locked me out. I was interviewed by councillors and managers—a whole group—and had only one person to support me. My defence was that I wasn't there. I was on leave when it was supposed to have happened. I was not on duty. But afterwards I was only allowed to work [if I was] with a deputy, for two years, as if I was still being watched. It went on my record for five years, and I believe it's still there.'

A Sense of being Understood, or Not, by Line-managers and Higher Managers

Members of a residential staff group could feel that both their line-manager and higher managers underemphasised the importance placed by staff on the composition of their teams. A stable team, which brings with it opportunities for good internal communication and support from colleagues for day-to-day work, is important to residential workers.

Sometimes, this was made more difficult by a line-manager requesting that a member of staff cover for another team, or by managers somewhere higher up in the hierarchy operating a central pool of relief staff, resulting in different relief staff turning up at a Home at different times, often unknown to the staff or to the young people. One staff member said:

'It's come to the point where you really have to be selfish and basically say [I'm] not interested in other units, our priority is our staff team. It's not very nice when you see other units and other colleagues floundering with problems, because you like to offer skills, knowledge, expertise or whatever that you've got, but a part of you says no, that's down to management to sort it out, and of course you know it won't get sorted out . . . the stress factor here's enough for me to keep the lid on this, and if we start overlapping from other dimensions, it's going to cause loads of problems.'

Where units are frequently called upon to cover for each other, and staff are temporarily moved to fill in gaps as they occur in other Homes, line-managers can sometimes be regarded as using staff to solve their own 'problems'.

However, line-managers are more likely to be seen as being in touch with the realities of residential care than are higher managers:

'They [higher managers] leave us vulnerable, and they don't know how vulnerable we are.'

'[the hierarchy] still think of [us] as "the nice little Children's Home down on the park".'

'On the other hand, we don't want reassurance from them, because they don't know what they're on about, they haven't a clue.'

'Here, there's a lot of recognition from within your staff group and team, and that's more important than recognition from senior management. For example, one night when there was a fire, the support of the colleagues meant more than that of the resources manager, who sent a letter three weeks later to say "well done".'

The Impact of Decisions made by Middle Managers

Staff members report that they pay a price when decisions are made or new policies are introduced without taking the likely full consequences for care staff into account. For example:

'Somebody [in management] can say you can have X people [working a shift], and that involves you working two weekends out of three . . . the only way the

rotas will run successfully with the numbers you require on duty means that two weekends out of three you don't see your wife and kids, so it doesn't matter what happens, it all eventually filters down and by the time it gets to us, we're suffering.'

'We've had new memos round saying that there has got to be a permanent worker on every shift, but when you look, we've only got [two staff who are] full-time . . . you're hard pushed to find a permanent staff . . . [for every shift] . . . you bring permanent staff in from other units, even though this isn't their unit, they've got a permanent contract, so even though Elizabeth [long-standing relief] might know [our unit] better than the person we're bringing in, because that other person's got a full contract and Elizabeth hasn't, the other one would "sort of" be in charge. . . . [what happened was that] a councillor came in here for a visit and remarked that there were three relief workers on [and reported it]. Which shouldn't happen, I mean we agree it shouldn't happen, but, circumstances at the time, there was no choice.'

TENSIONS BETWEEN RESIDENTIAL WORKERS AND MANAGERS

Tensions around 'Appropriate' or 'Inappropriate' Placement

The term 'inappropriate placement' first appeared in Chapter 3, as one of the sources of stress for staff, and as a trigger for a 'bad patch'. It appeared again in Chapter 5, in the context of discussing young people with whom staff considered they could not work, and again in Chapter 6 when discussing hard-to-manage mixes of young people.

Here we return to this issue and discuss it in the context of staff opinions about differing views within Departments as to what constitutes an appropriate or an inappropriate placement.

'Inappropriate placement' is a short-hand term which staff members use to refer to any one of the following situations: (a) it is anticipated that the young person is a 'natural victim' who is bound to be bullied by others; (b) it is anticipated that the young person is in a very vulnerable state and that he or she could be helped within some compositions of young people, but not within the current one, where there is a preponderance of older, tougher, young people whose very presence he or she will find upsetting and distressing; (c) it is anticipated that the young person will be unmanageable in an ordinary Children's Home because of extremely challenging or disorganised behaviour; (d) it is known that there is a risk of a young person bringing threats on the Home or destructive behaviour from the adult criminal community; (e) the young person is known to have a pre-existing relationship with some young person already living in the Home, such that offending together or absconding together is likely to happen, or else, physically damaging encounters will occur.

Field social workers, those responsible for placements, or resource managers may not share staff views that a placement is inappropriate. Residential workers explained this disparity in several different ways: others are not as informed as the residential workers about the needs of the group of young people; or others assume that residential workers will be able to cope with any problems which arise (or would be able to cope if sufficiently skilled); or those responsible for placing a young person see an empty bed as a resource which must be used.

Staff members feel that external line-managers and others in the broader management system lack familiarity with the character and ethos of the units, and their current state, and are therefore not in a position to appreciate that a particular placement may be inappropriate. The gap between a staff group's view as to what is appropriate and what actually happens can be very wide.

'If you've got a fieldwork manager making an arbitrary decision as to where the best place is for the young person, how the hell does he or she know? They certainly never visit the units, they don't know what major services, what type of staff, the ethos of each unit, what it's pitched at, is it chaos and bedlam or is it relaxed and nice, and so I think they just make it up as they go along. That's probably unjust, but there's an element of truth in it.'

'For example, that little lad just come to the door there, nine years of age—what he needs is a lot of attention, what he responds to [a love and a cuddle], as we proved this morning, is a lot of, if he can get that, time and attention, otherwise, and unfortunately even with a staff team of say five and some evenings six staff, we struggle to be able to provide that for him. Consequently, he's mixing with kids that he just shouldn't be mixing with, offenders, he's being bullied, and a typical situation on Monday, as a consequence of two other kids bullying him, he wanted to leave the building and us having to say no, no, that's not acceptable, your safety, you know, we've got to stop you, and he just can't cope with that. There's one example of a very, very badly placed young person. . . . There are different reasons for this [inappropriate placements], sometimes it may just be that there are no other beds available in other units. With this particular young man, I tend to get the impression that it's more about the [field) social worker's understanding of what we actually do and the reason the unit exists. She tends to view him as being a very, very challenging young man, for example he has threatened his mother with a knife. Now that's fine, OK, for a 14-, 15-year-old, if he was going to be placed, you'd imagine that this would be the

most appropriate placement. And I think to a certain extent that's what she's focused in on, this young man who's obviously very aggressive, but she's not focused in on the fact that he's going to be in an environment which just isn't going to be conducive to his development. Or it's actually going to make things much worse. . . . And that's rather unfortunate. . . . [this young person is] short term—and we're now into, this is his second week. . . . and unfortunately, he's now in a situation where he wants to stay here, and he could actually be in care for another six or seven weeks. And whilst we think that he is more appropriate to moving, he's now in a position where he doesn't want to move. And it does make it more difficult. And he's going to experience more problems and more disruption. . . . We try and make it clear what we can, and what we can't [do], we will make it clear also we're working in partnership, so, we try and be as honest and as open as we can possibly be, what we can and what we can't do.'

Sometimes residential staff succeed in resisting a placement which they regard as inappropriate:

A young boy was referred for placement in the Home. He had been living in a unit some distance away, had become involved in gang warfare, where the gangs were involved in murders and drugs. He was attached to a gang and then changed allegiance. Because of this, there were adults who were now after him. They went into the unit in which he had been living with guns, and he had been in actual physical danger. The staff did not want this boy to come to them, as they saw this as merely transferring the problem: 'We are only a bus ride away', and bringing danger not only to the boy but to others in the Home. They felt that the boy should be placed out of the area altogether. Management had threatened to discipline the Home if they did not take this boy. Staff responded by seeking the support of two other Homes in the area, who agreed with their view. They had thus been able to tell management: 'You will have to discipline all three Homes because all three units are refusing to take him. It is not fair to the young people.' (Researcher's notes.)

In this situation, the staff of one Home relied heavily on the support of other units in order to establish bargaining power with management and to point out the implications of the request to place this young person.

Tensions around Staff Selection and Redeployment

The ways that staff members are selected and then assigned to one Home or another often left staff feeling that they had little or no control over the shape of their staff team. Also, individual staff sometimes felt stuck in their current posts because opportunities for promotion are limited.

Staff sometimes complained that selection procedures could be so rigid that prospective new members of staff did not find out enough about the job, and those doing the selection were prevented from being sufficiently informed about candidates. Some staff reported that selection policies have changed for the better:

Previously, everyone had to be asked the same questions because of equal opportunities. Applicants could not be invited around, so they could not develop an understanding of what they would be getting into. No references could be sought other than those provided. Now, candidates can be invited to the Home. Selectors can ask different candidates different questions, particularly helpful since follow-up within an interview is now possible. Selection panels can ask for additional references and they can even set a written test (to see if candidates have writing skills, and can comprehend what is set down on paper). (Researcher's notes.)

Staff also reported that managers sometimes appointed someone as a member of a care staff who was unqualified for the job, because they were responsible for redeploying that person *somewhere*:

Within the SSD there is a redeployment team whose task it is to find jobs for people who have lost their jobs because of the closure of Homes or who need to be found different jobs for health reasons. These people are inappropriately placed, in jobs for which their experience does not qualify them. For example, a driver/ handyman was found to be medically unfit because of a bad back and was made a residential social worker. A member of the waking night staff may be made a day residential social worker. In both instances the work they have done before is altogether different from the new task they have to take on. One can be lucky in that they work out, but there is always a risk. There is a three-month probationary period but a lot of damage can occur in three months. There are definite appointment procedures but these are bypassed. (Paraphrased from researcher's notes.)

Tensions around Internal Inspections

Departmental inspections can be time-consuming and the inspection process itself can have negative effects on the staff group:

A unit had been inspected prior to an SSI (Social Services Inspectorate—a national body) inspection scheduled to occur later in the year. The unit manager was given a pre-inspection pack and was asked to complete a 40-page document of details about the Home. He had three working days notice to do this. The inspectors had done things such as take the panels off the baths, criticised the number of cigarette butts in the flower border at the local bus stop which is nearby, and reported that there was a dirty fork in the kitchen drawer ('we've had one domestic for 12 weeks'). 'The thing is that if they'd have come at the end of last year they would have condemned the building.' The unit manager said that the visit only reports on what is happening on the days of the visit, there is no attempt to contextualise the inspection to 'see how far we've come'. (Researcher's notes.)

There can be disagreements between inspectors and staff in a Home about practice.

'I was appalled by one of the [internal] inspectors . . . he was not happy about school [attendance] and said he would drag the young people out of bed. We said, "You can't do that." He said, "Why not? If they don't go to school, they should have no breakfast." We said, "Denying food is against the Children Act." He said they should take breakfast between 7.30 and 8.00 a.m., or do without . . . I did not feel comfortable about his approach.'

Staff sometimes felt that an inspection report, because of its construction, did not convey fairly what the Home was like, or did not get to the heart of what they were doing.

Long delays in receiving inspection reports were difficult for staff:

'We had an excellent report on an unannounced (Departmental) inspection (which took place within the past month), but still have not heard the results of the other one (a Social Services Inspectorate inspection, a year earlier). We are very different now from what we were then.'

RELATIONSHIPS AND COMMUNICATION WITH FIELD SOCIAL WORKERS

A residential staff group's relationship with field social workers is exceedingly important for the young people in residential care, as there is overlap in responsibility and much room for differences of opinion and the possibility of working at cross purposes. The field social worker retains overall responsibility for a young person and may engage in ongoing work with him or her and/or the family. Residential staff are responsible for day-to-day care, and necessarily also work with the young person and his or her network. Field social workers cannot be in close or day-to-day touch with the young person. They often do not know about or take into account the composition of the current group of young people in a Home and how this necessarily influences day-by-day decisions about 'their' young person. Residential workers must of necessity work with and 'manage' young people in the context of a particular mix and rapidly changing group situations.

Who holds responsibility for what action is an important issue in staff members' relationships with field social workers. Decision-making responsibility, and the demarcation between field social workers' and residential workers' spheres of responsibility, is often ill-defined. Each holds different information about a particular young person. Case responsibility remains with field social workers, but what this means in practice is not always clear, or talked out. In these circumstances there is much room for conflicting views to arise as to what constitutes appropriate ways of working with individual young people.

Effective work, and the avoidance of tensions, relies on reciprocal communication—not always easy to achieve. A view not infrequently held by residential staff is captured in the following quote:

'There are two care plans on the go for each young person: the one that the field social worker draws up and the one that the residential staff formulate.'

Tensions arise when residential workers and field social workers appear to be working with separate goals in mind, and thereby differing priorities. The issue of 'who holds power', and who is responsible for what, becomes prominent:

A young person is due to stay with his mother for the weekend. Last minute changes mean that he now wants to stay with his grandmother. The young person is accommodated, and has his mother's agreement to staying with his gran. The situation has arisen out of office hours, when the field social worker is off-duty. The unit manager and staff of a unit are faced with making a decision which they hope the field social worker will support. They know that this kind of support depends on the nature of their relationship with the field social worker. (Researcher's notes.)

A unit manager reporting on a 13-year-old, in care since he was 4 or 5, said:

'There are only two planning meetings reported in the file since he was six, and one of those is ours. I have only met his field social worker once. I wonder if we have all the information? . . . We have been asking for a care plan since June [it was then November]. I have complained to my line-manager about him [the field social worker] but his line-manager still defends him, the only one who does. He . . . is not what [the boy] needs. [The field social worker] has told [the boy] he will get him a personal tutor because he doesn't like school. I told [the field social

worker] you need to work at wishes and feelings but also at what is best for young people.'

These examples convey residential workers' experience that their views carry less weight than do those of field social workers, and that the latter hold more power and have to be treated 'tactfully'. Where disagreement arises, staff come to feel that their views and judgements are not taken into account:

The staff of a Home, who favoured encouraging contact between a 14-year-old girl and her father, were in disagreement with the girl's field social worker, who regarded the contact as unwise. The situation was that the girl's alcoholic mother was not in a position to look after her at home; the girl's father was living a homosexual lifestyle elsewhere with a male partner. The girl wanted to live with her father. Her father did not want her to live with him and his friend, but was prepared to see her. The disagreement had to do with whether the contact with father would benefit the girl (the residential staff's view) or disturb her further by encouraging her to hope that father would eventually take her in, when it was clear that he would not (the field social worker's view). The field social worker's view prevailed. (Researcher's notes.)

A 15-year-old girl told her field social worker that another resident in the unit had forced her to take drugs. Later, she admitted that this was an attempt on her part to manoeuvre a return home. Her home situation was considered unsuitable: she had accused her mother's boyfriend of abuse, and had been abused by previous boyfriends of her mother. The field social worker placed her in a temporary foster placement overnight, but failed to inform the unit as to where she was. The unit had already reported her as missing to the police. (Researcher's notes.)

Situations where residential workers worked well *alongside* field social workers were described, but were often referred to in nostalgic tones, or contrasted with unsatisfactory situations.

A unit manager gave as an example of good practice a field social worker who, every three or four weeks for three or four hours, visited a 12-year-old boy who had earlier been beaten and tied to a chair by foster parents. This field social worker also made the unit staff feel good about the work they were doing with the boy, and collaborated with residential staff in helping the boy to see his records, and to plan how to deal with the boy's reactions when he saw them. The unit manager said that poor field social workers never turned up to see their residents, or else visited unannounced, or made appointments with young people they didn't keep, and left residential staff to pick up the pieces when young people felt let down. (Researcher's notes.)

Sometimes residential staff feel that their practice is being 'managed' by several different field social workers concurrently, or in rapid succession, when different field social workers are or become responsible for different young people living in the Home.

Residential staff also work with or are influenced by members of area teams other than field social workers, who make decisions which have an impact on the work of the Home.

A 14-year-old girl went from the unit into foster care. A few weeks later, the foster parents decided that they could not cope with her. The team manager rang the unit to ask if they had any beds, but did not say why he was asking. At the end of that day, the girl was brought back to the unit by a welfare officer (unknown to her) who had picked her up from school. The unit staff did not know she was coming. The girl's field social worker was on leave, the reason for the breakdown was unclear, and there could be no planning meeting for three days, because it was a weekend. Unit staff regarded moving the girl and the way that it was done as constituting unprofessional practice by the area team. (Researcher's notes.)

It is clear that, in this example, staff were placed in a poor position to work well with this girl, given the circumstances surrounding her return to the Home.

'BEING MANAGED' AND CARRYING OUT DEPARTMENTAL POLICIES AND PROCEDURES

There is consensus among those concerned with the residential care of children that Homes and staff groups need to be managed externally in order for good standards of care to be set and maintained. The way this works out in practice is summarised in the following key points.

In practice, it is the line-manager who occupies and embodies the external management role, and is the usual point of contact between a staff group and a Department's management system. The line-manager conveys news, especially about new policy decisions, to unit managers and staff. He or she occupies a lynch-pin position between a residential care staff and others in the organisational hierarchy.

The line-manager usually also takes on supervisory functions, either with the whole staff group or with the unit manager. He or she thus combines the functions of manager and supervisor. The following quotation, from the Central Council for Education and Training in Social Work, sums up the prevailing view about the importance of the line-manager in assuring standards:

> The importance of the role of professional support and line-management of group care units cannot be over-emphasized. . . . Research has confirmed the strong connection between the appropriate external management of group care practice and the ability of the staff to fulfil the complex tasks required of them. (Baldwin, 1990, quoted in CCETSW, 1992a, p. 22)

However, staff members can be reluctant to seek supervision from line-managers if this means exposing what might be regarded as weaknesses to someone who has power over promotion or contracts.

External line-managers sometimes fulfil their management and supervisory roles appropriately, and sometimes do not. For example, the researchers considered that a line-manager behaved appropriately when he clearly and explicitly informed a member of staff of the Department's investigatory procedures after an allegation had been made, and extended support without glossing over the seriousness of the situation. A line-manager who told a boy that he would be moved if his behaviour did not improve was clearly behaving inappropriately.

The external line-manager is located clearly within the Department's hierarchical structure, and the role itself is usually well-defined. However, in a very real sense, field social workers and those responsible for placements are also exercising a managerial role, especially with regard to the placement and subsequent movement of young people, In addition, field social workers 'manage' in the sense of holding onto certain decisions with respect to a young person while he or she is in residential care.

Decisions about staffing and staff selection, redeployment, and promotion are located within middle management. It is here also that procedures are established for lodging complaints and for the investigation of allegations made against members of staff.

Staff selection procedures can be a sore point for staff groups, especially where equal opportunities procedures are inflexibly applied, or unsuitable staff are placed in a Children's Home because managers are responsible for their redeployment.

Being the object of investigations when an allegation is made is a source of great stress for the accused person and the staff as a whole. A supportive attitude on the part of managers is much appreciated.

How rotas are worked out can present difficulties for staff. In theory, members of the residential staff work to rotas which they themselves devise and agree upon. In practice, rotas are influenced by management decisions, either directly or through knock-on effects. Staff members may end up working two weekends out of three, and/or very long hours.

To facilitate 'being managed', staff are required to follow Departmental and administrative procedures, e.g. keeping logs, devising care plans and updating them, recording all visitors to the Home, and reporting incidents to the Child Protection team. In general, staff see the need for such procedures, but sometimes experience problems related to the escalation of paperwork, which often has to be done late at night during sleep-in duty, because of the pressure of other tasks.

While staff groups accept the need for Departmental inspections, they can be time-consuming and can induce stress if not handled sensitively.

THE IMPACT OF MAJOR RESTRUCTURING AND CHANGES IN POLICY

From time to time higher managers restructure the Department in an attempt to deal with problems arising in the child care sector, or to achieve a better balance among the Department's many responsibilities. Restructuring may involve making Homes specialised, moving towards smaller Homes, or closing some Homes. Residential staff are not usually consulted about policy changes in a way which will inform decision-making.

Just occasionally an idea for restructuring comes from a unit manager, and negotiations then take place with management:

A Home which was a city-wide facility worked particularly with children who had been abused. There were no emergency admissions. This came about at the initiative of the unit manager and the staff, who saw a gap in the service, were prepared to fill it, and got agreement from management. (Researcher's notes.)

Negotiating with managers over such matters seems to require considerable skill and forethought. Sometimes such negotiations quickly become adversarial in character, and conflict can remain unresolved over some time.

Restructuring takes time and implementing new policies is subject to delays which staff find frustrating:

'Time and time again when that [an issue to do with reorganisation] is actually mentioned, and staff are of the opinion that something is supposed to happen at a specific point in time, then to be told, well, that it's going to go back, and be put back . . . you psychologically gear yourself up again, it's very deflating isn't it when it doesn't go ahead . . . you're on permanent standby [laughter] . . . like Fireball XL5! Red Alert!'

When staff are awaiting decisions and actions for which responsibility is located elsewhere in the SSD, they are placed in positions over which they have no control. They can do little but wait.

CUMULATIVE EFFECTS ON RESIDENTIAL STAFF

The problems and tensions referred to in this chapter can have a cumulative effect on staff, eroding morale over a period of time and leading to a pervasive sense of helplessness. Staff come to expect little of their management and may give up trying to have a say over their own work-life, or communicating their views, or objecting to decisions which they feel sure will have negative consequences, or defending courses of action which they are convinced are the right ones.

ARE RELATIONSHIPS BETWEEN RESIDENTIAL STAFF AND OTHERS IN THE ORGANISATION *FREQUENTLY* POOR?

Much more has been reported in this chapter about poor relationships than about good relationships. This is a reflection of what staff actually said and reported. The question arises as to whether this is in some way an artefact of the research or whether it is a fair representation of the actual comparative frequency of good and poor relationships, conflictual and non-conflictual encounters. It could be an artefact of the research if, for example, members of residential staff experienced the research as an opportunity to vent their complaints, and did not have the same need to report positive relationships.

The researchers came to the view that while the research *did* provide opportunities for members of staff to express complaints about management, it was also the case that poor relationships frequently existed. Each occurrence of a poor or problematic relationship is of concern since it has an impact on how staff function, on the experience of the young people, and on service delivery. If such occurrences become frequent, this is of particular concern. Some staff members summed up the impact in general terms:

'The people who are imposing the regimes under which we work, and the financial constraints under which we work, are so far removed from us, and so far removed from the reality of their decisions.'

'It worries me more than anything, that I'm part of an organisation that should be setting objectives and planning, and looking at things over a period of time, specialist functions and what we should be doing in the long term, short term, setting goals, and yet everything's just in drift. It just seems to be . . . it's quite frightening that you've got so many managers above you that have no experience of residential work, that they haven't a clue about some of the implications of

what they're saying and the effect that will have on motivation . . . the smooth running of the unit, staffing issues, timing, resources, I could go on and on. . . .'

Lack of consultation with residential staff, and/or failures and delays in providing information, is a theme which runs through many of the reported problem situations.

When staff members know that plans for changing children's services are in the offing, but are not consulted or informed about them, they can experience prolonged periods of uncertainty and helplessness, and special stress through knowing that managers are making decisions without being aware of the likely consequences for the running of the units.

Where middle managers' actions in relation to other units have potential to affect a particular unit, staff prefer to know about management actions and understand the reasons for them. For example, a manager may be attempting to provide a period of stability for a unit by protecting it from new admissions. This may well affect other units in the authority in terms of their own admissions. If staff come to know of this by chance, as distinct from playing an informed part in the wider problem solving, they find it hard to sympathise with either the position of the manager or the unit being protected. Instead, they see injustice.

It becomes important to try to understand what underlies and contributes to both good and problematic relationships between residential staff on the one hand, and managers and field social workers on the other hand. We turn to this next.

Sources of Tensions between Staff Groups and Management

Imbalances in the Location of Decision-making Power and Information

Managers and others who hold decision-making power over admissions and transfers often lack information which could usefully inform their decision-making. The information is held by care workers—for example, about the current state of the child or the work currently being done. Effective channels do not exist for that information to be conveyed to decision-makers, and/or care workers have no say in the decisions being made, so the imbalance persists. A similar imbalance, or gap, can be observed when new policies or procedures are handed down to residential care workers from managers. Care workers may have information or experience which suggests that the new policy or procedure will have additional consequences from those intended by management—

disadvantageous ones. Consultation, or prior indication that a change is impending, does not occur, so there is no way for the care workers' understandings to be brought to bear.

Lack of Clarity as to Jurisdiction

This was most clearly seen with respect to whether it was field social workers or residential workers who were responsible for work with families, or for day-to-day decisions concerning a child's contacts with parents and other relatives. Field social workers retained overall responsibility for a child and his or her family, but residential care workers necessarily had contact with families and were faced with day-to-day decisions concerning them. Where relationships between field social workers and residential care workers were good, and contact and discussion frequent, problems were minimal. However, sometimes conflict occurred, or the actions of one undid the actions of the other. Residential workers, who tended to have less status and power, could resent the actions of the field social workers but feel helpless to do anything about it.

Differences in Opinion about Priorities

Whoever in the organisation is responsible for receiving and acting on referrals may urgently need to find a bed—often, under emergency conditions. Their responsibility is discharged when a bed is found. In contrast, consider the situation of a care staff where a vacant bed actually exists in the Home. They may want to hold it for a young person who has just gone to a foster family, where the success of the placement is in doubt, and where the young person might need to return. Or, they might judge that the prospective admission will have an adverse effect on the children already in residence, or not fit into the existing composition. Conflict may ensue.

Conflict also sometimes occurs over whether a young person should remain in a Children's Home or be transferred elsewhere. Members of a residential staff may judge that there are good reasons why a particular child should stay, or go. Their reasons are based on such matters as the child's readiness to leave, or his or her need for a specialist facility. Decisions made by managers are more likely to have to do with practicalities (e.g. expense), or conformity to the organisation's rules and guidelines (e.g. it is best to place a child near to his or her own home).

Differing ideas about what is more important or less important to take into account when making decisions appear to be linked to conceptions of efficiency and effectiveness. Managers may consider it inefficient to hold empty beds, because to do so reveals a mismatch between demand and resources. They may consider it efficient to keep a young person in a Children's Home because to move him or her to a specialist facility would be more expensive. They may consider it efficient to discharge a young person when he or she reaches the age of 16 because a needed bed thereby becomes available. Residential staff are less concerned with efficiency as expressed in these terms—for example, spare capacity may be inefficient from management's point of view, but essential from the practitioner's point of view.

In the next chapter we look at another part of a staff group's external world—the wider networks, comprising both people and organisations, around each young person and around the Home.

8

WORKING WITH PEOPLE AND ORGANISATIONS IN WIDER NETWORKS

In Chapter 3 one of a staff group's five major task arenas was stated to be working with the wider network of people and organisations in the surrounding world—either the network surrounding each young person, or the network surrounding the Home. Here we explore in more detail how staff groups in Children's Homes operate with these networks. As before, episodes involving work with relatives, the police, schools, etc., as described by unit managers and members of staff, and/or observed by researchers, could be selected out and formed into a sub-sample. This could then be subjected to analysis to determine salient parts of a network and the kinds of interactions which occurred. Data were drawn from both Study 1 and Study 2. In Study 2, the character and focus of staffs' work with networks and network members could be followed over time, as they unfolded.

RELATIONSHIPS WITHIN A YOUNG PERSON'S NETWORK

Every young person is, of course, located within a unique personal network. Prior to being looked after away from home, this will include people in the 'informal' part of the network—one or two birth parents, perhaps a step-parent, siblings, other relatives, friends, school friends, neighbours, etc.—and other people who are located in the 'formal' part of the network—teachers, a general practitioner, sometimes the police, and others. When a child comes to the attention of the Social Services Department, a field social worker, at least, will enter the formal part of the network. Depending on the decisions then made, a fostering officer and foster parents may enter the child's network. If the young person enters residential care, care staff are added to the network, as well as the young people already living in the Home. Over time, the network of a young person living in residential care changes, both in terms of its membership, and in terms of relationships among network members. Some network members may drop out or become less important—for example, former school friends if the young person changes schools or drops out of school. New people may enter a network—for example, newly appointed residential care staff. The relationship between a young person and particular network members may shift, along with feelings and attitudes which the young person holds about them—as occurred for the 14-year-old who said of his parents: 'They didn't want me, and now I don't want them.' Changes may also occur in how network members feel about one another and in the attitudes they hold—for example, a teacher may begin to feel and think differently about care staff if a young person begins to present problems at school.

Operating in a Young Person's Network

Barry was now 14 and had been living in the same Children's Home on and off since he was a small child. When he was a little boy, Barry and his mother came to the attention of the Social Services Department because of his mother's mental health problems. A field social worker was assigned to work with the family, and Barry was placed in foster care. His first foster placement, and several subsequent ones, broke down. During an interval between one foster placement and the next he had lived at the same Home to which he later returned. He was soon fostered again and this, too, broke down after Barry had been violent to one of the foster parents' own children. He 'finally' came to the Home when he was 9.

From the age of 9 to 13, Barry's most recent foster parents continued to be in touch with him, and he paid visits to them. They were hostile to the residential staff, whose private view was that these foster parents experienced the placement breakdown as an indication of their failure (it had been their first experience of fostering) and felt that the key worker in the Home was succeeding where they had failed. At this point, when Barry was 13, two things happened: Barry's mother returned to live in the area; and plans were being made by Barry's field social worker (different from earlier ones) and a fostering officer to place him back with his most recent foster parents, who had requested this. The residential staff supported Barry's ongoing contact with the foster family but were not sure that another foster placement was right for him, or that if it were tried with these foster parents, it would work out this time. The foster parents were now caring for six children, all of them younger than Barry. Staff knew Barry was still very demanding of adults, and could be violent to younger children. The residential workers were mindful of the fact that Barry had taken a long time to recover from his feelings of hurt and rejection when his previous placement with this family had broken down. The staff kept their reservations to themselves, as Barry himself sometimes said he was eager to rejoin this foster family. (Staff thought that his eagerness was connected with a promised holiday in Florida.) Barry was being 'tried' with the foster parents through weekend visits.

When Barry heard that his own mother had returned to the area, he expressed a wish to see her. It had been many years since Barry had had contact with his mother. Staff worked to arrange a meeting at the Home and to take him to visit, but after he had seen his mother once, he refused to see her again. Visits to the prospective foster parents continued. The foster parents remained hostile to the staff—for example, they refused to come in for a cup of tea when they returned Barry to the Home. Staff felt hurt by this behaviour, but they continued to work towards the placement's success, and avoided being drawn into an acrimonious relationship with the foster parents.

No single example is likely to show all of the contact and all of the work which may be required when working with a young person's personal network on his or her behalf. In Barry's case, staff had contact with several field social workers, the fostering officer, the prospective foster parents (whom they had known for some years), and Barry's mother.

Working with Members of a Young Person's Network

Interacting and Working with Parents and Foster Parents

Few of the children and young people we heard about had no family at all. Sometimes contact had been lost but, for many, a degree of contact was maintained.

The Children Act 1989 made it a requirement that staff in Social Services Departments should seek to work in partnership with the parents of young people in their care, whether the young person was being accommodated or had been received into residence by the processes of law. Residential workers generally accept the importance of liaising and working with parents, and many said they made greater efforts now than before the Act came in. In practice, liaising with parents is sometimes a difficult task and a complex process.

Young people's relationships with a parent or parents varied, as already detailed in Chapter 2. Contact might be frequent or rare, child and parent might be estranged or still close, the relationship might be very conflict-ridden or less so, and more, or less, beneficial to the young person.

Members of residential staff have informal contact with parents when they come to visit or request that a child visits them. Sometimes trial visits home are arranged for a few hours or a weekend, and staff members may then become involved in helping the young person prepare for such visits and deal with the aftermath. Review meetings are potentially a more formal venue for contact with parents.

Parents are increasingly invited to attend review meetings, and the young person may also be present. The intention is to keep the parent informed and create opportunities to share in planning. Review meetings also offer opportunities for young person and parent to be in contact and look at the future together. Some such meetings function as intended, but difficulties are frequently encountered.

Some parents will not attend reviews. Others come, but do not remain. We were told by staff that some parents feel overfaced at the prospect of attending a review meeting, and much work needs to be done, either by a field social worker or a residential worker, to help them face and feel reasonably comfortable about such a meeting. Once a meeting begins, some parents remain silent and do not reveal the feelings which members of residential staff know they have. Now and then, a parent explodes, or behaves violently, or runs out of the meeting in fury or distress.

If the young person is also present at a review meeting, conflict can arise between child and parent. For example:

Sam had written things down on his review form which would be bound to hurt his mother. Conflict developed between the residential staff and the field social worker. The residential staff felt that what Sam had written down should not be brought into the meeting, but worked with elsewhere. The field social worker felt that it was important that the child's views should be heard. In the meeting, the mother was told what Sam had written. They got into an argument, and Sam ran out of the meeting, followed by staff who could not catch up with him. Staff did their best to comfort his very upset mother. Sam was reported to the police as missing. It was also found that Sam had taken another boy with him when he ran away, and together they had stolen a neighbour's motorcycle. (Researcher's notes.)

In this example, a procedure which could be defended in principle had unintended and unwanted consequences.

Sometimes there is lack of clarity as to whether the field social worker or a residential worker is responsible for outreach work with families in their own homes. A child's field social worker and residential workers may disagree as to the preferred direction for outreach work. Lack of clarity, or conflict, is often ongoing—problems do not get resolved. Discontinuity in outreach work may occur as a consequence of job changes.

Sometimes parents behave in ways which exacerbate conflict between a field social worker and residential workers. For example, a mother, in the service of getting her own needs met, may tell residential social workers that she trusts them but does not trust her field social worker, or vice versa.

Residential staff groups, mindful of the Children Act 1989, strive to keep in contact with parents and work with them. Sometimes they succeed. This is particularly likely to be the case when care workers and parents share the same goal—usually that of the child returning home and becoming reintegrated into the family. Sometimes working together meets obstacles. A parent may be volatile or violent, or rejecting and careless of the child, or behave so inconsistently that continuity of work and of shared effort is hard to maintain. Members of staff may nevertheless continue to try to keep parents involved and in the picture by, for example, maintaining contact by telephone if a parent does not respond to invitations to visit, and scrupulously keeping parents informed when their child is ill, or has done well at school or learned a new skill, or is in trouble with the police. Some parents come to value help and advice from the staff, and become, in effect, clients of a staff group. Others are consistently hostile.

Residential staff are often faced with having to make very difficult judgements in the matter of whether or not to continue to try, against the odds, to work together with parents, or even to encourage contact between parent and child. The Children Act 1989 emphasises partnership, but staff may doubt that this is in the best interests of a young person if he or she repeatedly experiences distress and dashed hopes after a contact with the parent, or wants nothing further to do with the parent and is in fact establishing new attachments.

In some cases, the mother's partner had abused the child and this led to the child being taken into care. In such instances, as long as the partner remained in the household, it was likely to be deemed inappropriate to return the child there.

Often, it is not only birth parents who are involved in a young person's personal and family network. Some young people have been fostered previously, often several times, and foster care may have alternated with admissions to residential care. Sometimes young people have been adopted and then rejected by adoptive families. In such circumstances, residential staff may be working with one or more sets of foster parents as well as birth parents or (more rarely) with adoptive parents.

Interacting and Working with Other Family Members

Other family members who may figure in a young person's network are grandparents, siblings, step-parents, or mother's partner. Staff may work towards a grandparent taking on parental responsibility for a young person, or may support a grandparent in being a link between a young person and his or her parent(s), and in this way assisting in a reconciliation. Staff members typically tried to build on existing strengths in the family or extended family, wherever they are to be found.

Brothers and sisters of young people in residence also come within the ambit of staff's work. Sibling relationships can be complex and problematic. Sometimes siblings are separated by being placed in different care settings. When this occurs residential staff and/or field social workers often try to help the siblings to stay in touch and maintain or develop supportive relationships. One 'chosen' child may remain at home, while other siblings are placed elsewhere. The 'chosen' child may be envied or resented.

A young person may aspire to be like an older brother or sister when adult carers consider that this is not in the child's best interests. A child may have to be protected from contact with an older sibling who has abused him or her in the past. On the other hand, a sibling can be an invaluable source of support, especially at the point where an adolescent is reaching care-leaving age.

Interacting with a Young Person's Friends

Young people's friends can be a mixed blessing. Sometimes they lead a young person into trouble—with drugs, with taking and driving away cars, burglary, or even into paedophile rings and prostitution. Sometimes they are helpful—for example, by assisting a young person at school. In one Home in the study, the researchers became acquainted with a young man in the neighbourhood almost as well as the children in the Home. Wayne was always around—having soup poured over him by one of the girls after an argument at the gate, telling another young person in the Home when a suspected paedophile's car was down the road and then phoning and being of assistance to the police. Staff seemed quite fond of Wayne, but shook their heads despairingly when he and one of their own young people went collecting for a non-existent charity late at night in the neighbourhood. In the same Home, problems often arose with ex-residents, particularly one who was no longer living in the Home, who regularly returned to break in and steal whatever he could. In another Home an ex-resident, who remained friends with the young people in the neighbourhood, regularly returned with a gang to terrorise the local shops.

Unit managers and staff told of 'safe houses' run by ex-residents of Children's Homes in their neighbourhoods. Here young people would congregate, drink alcohol, and become involved in sexual relationships, drugs, and crime, often when they should have been at school. In one instance it was the mother of one of the young people in care who was providing such a service to others. In another case it was a neighbour whom staff had spent much time supporting who gave runaways a bed and would deny their presence to the police who came to look for them.

A young person's outside friends might themselves need to be supported, or might be a source of danger to a young person. Staff members sometimes faced difficult decisions: if they became overly concerned about young people's friends, they might risk alienating their charges, but, on the other hand, if they did not intervene, they might leave young people at risk of exploitation.

Liaison and Cooperative Work with Health Professionals

In the course of our research, accidents and non-accidental injury of one child by another were often reported. Young people sometimes harmed themselves. Abuse, of one young person by another, could occur. Staff groups worked hard to prevent such occurrences or to deal with them quickly when they occurred. This typically involved work with the young people and with health professionals. There are limits to what staff can do and, over the three years of the study, several deaths occurred from overdosing or from an accident.

When a young person was first admitted to the Home an early task for staff would be to obtain a medical consent form, since without this document being signed a Home would not be able to seek medical help on behalf of the young person. It needed to be signed by a parent or guardian, or in some local authorities by senior management if parents refused to sign.

Homes were always in contact with general practitioners in situations where young people had overdosed, or already suffered from some chronic condition such as epilepsy or asthma. Part of the task with general practitioners had to be to assist them to understand the complex needs and behaviour of the young people to whom general practitioners were called out, or seen during surgery hours. Some staff members told us that they themselves were not allowed to administer any medication (even an aspirin) without a general practitioner's permission. Sometimes working with a general practitioner had to be done with great tact. A GP might be hostile when called out at night to administer a remedy which a family member could have bought at the local pharmacy. Some initially hostile general practitioners changed their views, and came to respect the staff and seek their opinions with regard to the needs of certain of the young people.

Visits to local hospitals were frequently mentioned. Often staff would have to take young people who had hurt themselves or been hurt by others into accident and emergency units. Young people who had over-dosed on large quantities of paracetamol had to be taken to hospital very quickly.

When one young person was injured by another, not only did local medical services need to be called upon, but Child Protection procedures had to be invoked. This included telling parents, field social workers and the Child Protection Team—the latter would include an independent social worker and the police. Often the Emergency Duty Team (EDT) would be the first to hear about such an injury, since such episodes frequently happened in the evening or late at night or over weekends, when staff in the Department, except for the EDT, were not available.

A difficult relationship sometimes existed between specialist units within the Health Service and the staff of Homes. Staff members some-times judged that a young person needed specialist psychiatric help, but this was often hard to arrange, or hard to arrange for quickly. If treatment was initiated, staff members often had no access to what was happening between the professional and the young person, apart from what the young person said. In a situation in which a young person was targeting a member of staff, it would have made sense for the member of staff and young person to be seen together by a therapist, but we were not told of this occurring.

Young people themselves could refuse psychiatric help at a time when all the adults around them judged that treatment might help. Staff mem-bers were then powerless to insist that a young person should attend an appointment.

Establishing and Maintaining Relationships with Education Services

Many young people living in Children's Homes who are between 13 and 15 years old have had a long history of problems with schools and school-ing, and bring these problems with them when they enter the Home.

Staff regard non-attendance at school, for whatever reason, as a major problem for the young person. Non-attendance also creates problems for staff groups, who then face a task for which they feel ill-equipped—namely, providing 'structured educational experiences' for excluded young people or school refusers. Staff say repeatedly, 'we are not teachers'. They also have the practical problem that once one or some of their young people are out of school, staff members do not have the uninterrupted space or time for necessary paperwork, for meetings con-ducted during school hours, or for household tasks which need to be done. A young person out of school is also likely to bring other members of his or her personal network into the arena of staff members' work—his or her field social worker, neighbourhood children who are also out of school, and in some cases the police.

What gets in the way of school attendance for young people are such things as: falling behind after a period of patchy attendance at school; being the butt of their peers if they attend; being in a state of such emotional turmoil that they have no energy for educational endeavour; being subject to outbursts of temper and loss of control, such that they are beyond being managed in the classroom; exhibiting bizarre behaviour; or taking drugs. Some residential staff feel that young people need time and space to adjust after some unsettling or traumatic experience (e.g. the move into care, or a suicide attempt) before returning to school. A young person may also feel a need to stay close to his or her current carers so that school has little appeal. Some young people have come to devalue school and see no point in attending.

A young person may be excluded from school temporarily or for a time-limited period or may be expelled. Once a young person has been excluded from school, even if temporarily, staff often find it very hard to get that young person back to school. Young people may have been told of conditions which they must meet in order to be accepted back, which further alienate them—for example, they may be required to apologise to a teacher, when they feel that they have not been in the wrong. The process of returning a young person to school requires somebody from within the Social Services Department to liaise with the school and the education authorities on the young person's behalf. This may be done by the young person's field social worker or by the key worker in the Home. Contact is likely to be needed with the school itself, the head or the year tutor, or perhaps the teacher(s) of the form(s) which the young person has been in, and the Education Welfare Officer. If the young person has been expelled, statementing is required. ('Statementing' refers to a statutory requirement placed on Education Departments to prepare a statement of a child's educational needs when he or she has been expelled from school. A decision may be made that the child return to the previous school, or be admitted to another school, or be educated by some special arrangement. Education Departments are then required to take action on the basis of the statement, and to be open to re-statementing when circumstances change.) Statementing always takes time. So does getting a young person back into a school after he or she has been excluded.

Some unit managers attributed the school's refusal to have some young people back to an increasing trend for schools to take independent status and/or to the need for a school's published statistics (about attendance and examination results) to place the school in a good light.

All of the above can lead to very long delays in young people's return to school—perhaps months, or a year or more.

Sometimes a Home Tutor became involved with the young person's education in the Home—for two hours or so, perhaps twice each week. Arranging for a Home Tutor takes time. The arrangement can then break down very rapidly, especially if the tutor is unaccustomed to working with unsettled or resistant young people. Sometimes a tutor's lesson is experienced by the young person as pointless and intrusive: we heard of one young girl, who was facing the prospect of her mother's release from prison, being asked to identify all the adjectives in a prose passage. She could not devote her full attention to this task.

A staff group may make special efforts when exclusions become a particular problem. In one Home where all the young people were out of school, staff appointed a schools' liaison officer from among their number, whose task it was to liaise daily with Education Welfare Officers and schools and keep key workers in the Home informed of progress for their young people. Later, support from the line-manager of this and several other Homes in the area led to one Education Welfare Officer taking on a bridging role between the Social Services and Education Departments. Such initiatives strengthen the network and its likely effectiveness. Even so, keeping some young people in school is extraordinarily difficult and sometimes cannot be managed. In one Home a member of staff said, 'When these young people get to 21, I wouldn't be surprised if they sued us for failing to get them their education. They have a right to it, and it is the law that they should go to school.'

Working with the Local Police, Specialist Branches of the Police, and the Courts

The police are fairly frequent visitors to many Homes. They are sometimes called out by staff to restore order, or they come because they have been called out by neighbours who take offence at young people's behaviour, or because some local crime is attributed to young people in the unit (who may or may not have committed the offence). Many young people resident in Homes get into, or are already in, trouble with the law, often for crimes of theft, especially of cars. We were also told of burglaries, burglary with intimidation, crimes against the person, arson and criminal damage, sometimes committed against the Home itself.

Young people might have to attend court hearings in connection with such offences, but other reasons for having to appear in court have to do with allegations of abuse which they have made against members of their own families. We were told of delays as long as 18 months, if much time was required to assemble evidence. Long delays generated problems. In the interval between the event necessitating a hearing and the hearing itself, much work may have been done with a young person and indeed with the family, and the whole situation may have changed. A young person who then has to appear in court is vividly reminded of an earlier, difficult period of his or her life, and finds the court appearance distressing. Some young people experience anticipatory stress during the entire interval, and anxieties typically peak as the date of a court hearing neared. Some young people put a brave or nonchalant face on it, but staff reported evidence of distress in the form of sleep disturbances or an upsurge in disruptive behaviour.

Some staff felt that the work they were trying to do with or on behalf of the young person was undermined by court judgements, which they regarded as too lenient in some cases and too harsh in others. We were told of a magistrate who told a young person who had behaved very violently to 'be a good lad and don't do it again'. The boy was sent back to the Home where he had done thousands of pounds worth of damage and physically abused several staff. He then boasted of his exploits and clearly felt he had got away with it. In another case, staff members suffered acute distress themselves on behalf of a boy who was taken into custody after sexually abusing a younger boy. Staff did not consider it inappropriate for him to be in custody. While there, however, he was constantly persecuted by others because of the nature of his offence. It was this which staff found painful to contemplate.

Some staff members felt that some magistrates and some police officers showed a lack of understanding of what Homes were for, about what they could achieve, and how they operated. Some magistrates reportedly believed that all young people were in care for crimes, or that staff of a Children's Home could maintain a curfew imposed on a young person. In another area, the local police evidently got tired of being called out to the Home. They told staff that they would no longer come out, if called, even though every previous call had been under agreed Child Protection procedures.

In some areas, the police were described as 'brilliant'—a local police officer came out at a moment's notice when a burglary of the Home was expected, and even when there were no special problems would call regularly for a cup of tea. He was known and respected by the young people. In other areas, tensions persisted between the residential staff and the local police, especially when residential staff tended to think of their charges as emotionally damaged young people who sometimes committed crimes, while police thought of them as young criminals.

Specialist police services, such as the Drugs Squad and those who are part of Child Protection units, were potentially of much benefit to staff in their task of keeping young people safe—for example, by alerting staff to the dangers of local child molesters, or drug dealers. However, proper police actions by such specialist units could on rare occasions put young people or staff or even the future of the Home at risk, as in one rather dramatic instance when a young person in a Home informed on local drug dealers and a police raid followed, which in turn brought such threats to the young person and the staff that the unit had to be moved.

STAFF MEMBERS AS PART OF EACH YOUNG PERSON'S NETWORK

Until now we have been discussing residential workers' efforts to work with a young person's personal network as if the work is done from some neutral standpoint. This is not usually the case. Unless a young person stays in a Home only for a very brief period (sometimes, literally, only overnight), staff members soon become part of a young person's personal network. A key worker or link worker will be given special responsibilities with respect to the young person, and may become especially important. Or, the young person may relate best to the unit manager, or find his or her favourite members of staff, who then become special. The relationship between staff members and individual young people moves from the 'formal' (which it is bound to be, at first) to the more personal, as closeness develops and as residential workers take on parental roles and responsibilities.

Residential staff must necessarily get close to their charges in order to be their new carers. They are in a different position from field social workers, who may see the young person and/or the family at intervals and usually at scheduled times. When a member of staff is on duty he or she is often in contact with a young person for hours on end. If a child or young person is in a particularly distressed state, staff members may stay with him or her literally 24 hours a day.

Staff members special position in a young person's personal network means that they must in some sense become 'parents'. However, they must also be mindful to work in ways which do not alienate the young person from his or her own parent(s). They may also need to support parents. It can be a delicate task to avoid stirring up envy or resentment in a parent unnecessarily, if this can be done, and also to work with such feelings if and when they arise.

Residential workers have feelings of their own about other network members or events occurring in the network. For example:

A residential worker attending a review heard the mother of a 10-year-old say that she did not want him to return home, and observed the boy's distress. The worker said afterward, in angry tones, that she would never attend a review again—'Someone else can do it.'

A member of staff had to control her angry feelings when she observed the hurt which a 13-year-old girl experienced when her mother failed to keep her promise to visit.

Interacting and Working with the Network around the Home

The Home itself is located within a network of people and organisations which remain important parts of its environment as young people come and go. This network usually includes local schools, the police, neighbours, people and units within the Social Services Department, other departments in the local authority, and elected members. Ongoing efforts are directed towards *keeping the network 'healthy'*—that is, keeping its members knowledgeable about the Home and its work and aspirations, and receptive to its needs. In some cases, the same people or organisations are part of the networks of particular young people, but whether or not this is the case, they remain important to the Home and to the staff.

Working with and Maintaining Relationships with Neighbours

Neighbours are always a part of a Home's environment. Relationships with neighbours are sometimes excellent, sometimes not, but are always at risk of deteriorating if there are disturbances in or around the Home, or if neighbours suspect the Home's young people of having committed local crimes.

Assuming that the young people living in the Home were responsible for local crimes was not unusual. One member of staff said:

'It's always our kids. Whatever it is, it's always our kids. I know they're not angels, but it isn't always our kids.'

A new Home was prevented, by neighbourhood opposition, from being constructed, and literally 'never got off the ground'. Another Home lived under the constant threat of closure for a long time—neighbours had succeeded in closing the Home once already, and the staff considered that they knew that they could do it again. Regular meetings were held with these neighbours, which were attended by senior staff from the Department and councillors. Placements of young people had to be made with an eye to the impact on the neighbourhood, especially after two young people admitted as emergencies committed a burglary nearby. Yet these same neighbours could also be very supportive—attending coffee evenings, and praising staff members when things were in a more settled state.

The staff of many Homes work very hard to maintain good relationships with neighbours. They may arrange coffee evenings, or plan something special at Christmas to which neighbours are invited. They take opportunities which arise in the course of day-to-day living to be friendly, reassuring and supportive.

Working with Other Departments within the Larger Organisation and with Local Authority Councillors

Staff members have to operate with their own legal department in the local authority, either directly when a complaint is made against them or when a young person in their care has to attend court, or indirectly when the legal department interprets the law for the Social Services Department. As an example of the latter, we were told by some unit managers that, when the Children Act 1989 first came into operation, their legal departments told them that they must not stop children and young people leaving the Home even when they were potentially putting themselves at risk. This left staff unclear as to what was, in fact, permissible. In some Social Services Departments this was quickly rectified but in others conflict persisted, fuelled by incompatibilities between what residential staff judged to be best practice and what they were told they could and could not do by the legal department via their own managers.

However, it was not the legal department, but Supplies and Small Works which were frequently criticised by staff and unit managers who took part in this research. Staff spent immense amounts of time trying to give young people choice in their lives, and to make the unit comfortable. This could be undermined very quickly: by the arrival of a full set of institutional bedding (all exactly the same), and beds complete with waterproof mattresses; or a set of china cups and saucers (with rosebuds on it), which young people quickly broke; or the need to order half a dozen teaspoons through Supplies (at a £5 delivery charge and a month's delay) when they could be purchased down the street for £2. Generally, staff had to keep close records of every item in the Home. These were checked annually. In one Home, staff were not allowed to 'count' the mugs they bought themselves to replace the despised flowered china, and so appeared to be under-stocked.

Decisions about supplies were sometimes the outcome of a cost-cutting exercise undertaken at a high level in the authority:

In one local authority a decision was made that all food would be supplied centrally from a lorry once a week. This may have saved some money, but it undermined the staff's efforts to prepare young people for independent living by encouraging them to do daily shopping and choosing what would be prepared for tea. Staff disliked the lorry turning up when they were trying to make the Home more acceptable to the neighbours by avoiding the Home looking conspicuously 'institutional'. (Researcher's notes.)

In general, staff considered support services to be out of touch with what Homes were like and what staff members were trying to accomplish:

' "Support services" is a contradiction in terms.'

'This is a reflection of support services in general . . . one of the showers at [a unit where the member of staff had previously worked] was actually broken . . . and 10 children had to use one shower. If I looked at the diary at how many times we had been in contact with specific support services, and then at what was actually happening, I could almost guarantee there would have been at least 12 entries over six weeks.'

   Staff worked with other parts of their authorities from time to time, for example Housing Services when young people left care, or Environmental Health which inspected Homes regularly. Rules differed, and had to be learned: in one Home, staff had to keep back bits of all the food served to young people for regular inspection, while in another all surplus food had to be disposed of 20 minutes after a meal. Regulations about health and safety, especially those pertaining to fire risks, could lead to a more institutionalised appearance in a small Home than staff preferred. Fire alarms and hoses were frequently misused when a group of young people were 'playing up'. Staff, since they recognised the need for fire prevention equipment, felt that they had to live with some of the undesired consequences.
   In some authorities elected members (of the local authority council) paid regular monthly visits to the Home, and were mostly experienced as supportive. Sometimes staff wished they would not *always* arrive when the staff were trying to prepare a meal and young people were milling about. Staff saw elected members potentially as allies when the neighbourhood was trying to get the unit closed.
   Bureaucratic delays could undermine good intentions:

In one Home an elected member was appalled by the decoration of the rooms upstairs and insisted that they be redone. The Social Services Department responded, but could only make a limited amount of money available. This was

not sufficient to pay for the work to be done by the contractors directly em-
ployed within the authority, who had to be used to carry out such work. Staff
knew they could get a local man to do it cheaper, but this could not be done.
Staff and young people, working together, solved the problem by stripping the
rooms themselves, which cut the potential costs considerably. However prob-
lems still remained, in that the kinds of wallpaper available to choose from were
never intended for adolescents, and staff knew that if what was offered was put
up, the young people would vandalise it. Negotiations took place over weeks,
and by the time agreement was reached, the Home was told it would have to
wait several more weeks, since, by then, the money that had been promised had
been spent elsewhere and would not be available until the next budget. (Researcher's notes)

Maintaining Good Relationships with Local Schools

Staff make a point of working towards good relationships with local
schools whether or not problems exist with respect to any of their young
people. They attend parents' meetings and get to know teachers and
headteachers. This can stand them in good stead when problems *do* arise,
for they are already known to the school staff, and have established a
cordial relationship with them.

Being Inspected

In addition to inspections mounted by the Social Services Department,
described in the previous chapter, staff and Homes are inspected by their
authority's Health and Safety, and Health and Hygiene departments, and
by the (national) Social Services Inspectorate. Such inspections are accepted as necessary though they can cause anxiety. With regard to external inspections, staff appreciate fairness, that inspectors realise that lapses
from ideal standards might be outside staff control, that progress from
any previous inspection has been noted, and quick feedback.

Staff Groups and the General Public

Staff members often said that there is a need to educate the general
public about what Homes do and what they are for. Many members of
staff wanted people in the larger community to feel more responsible for
and sympathetic to the children and young people in the Home, rather
than blaming them for all that went wrong in the neighbourhood. Some
members of staff sought to educate the general public about the young
people—for example when they met acquaintances in their own local
pubs. Sometimes they found it hard to admit what their jobs were and

where they worked, especially if there had been a local or national scandal about the abuse of children, or when young people in local authority care had committed crimes which had been reported in the press or on television. They were concerned that neighbours and members of the community might assume that all Homes harbour 'young thugs'.

Staff were aware that negative attitudes among members of the general public, including neighbours, are fuelled by press reports of scandals, which support assumptions that young people in care are criminal, or crazy, or both, or that staff members are abusive.

CULTURAL CONSONANCES AND DISSONANCES BETWEEN STAFF GROUPS AND OUTSIDE ORGANISATIONS

In Chapter 1 we predicted that ideas to do with 'culture' and 'group dynamics' would prove relevant to the data likely to emerge. When examining relationships between a staff group and network members, some of the concepts related to culture have explanatory power. Outside organisations with which a staff group interacts are, like the staff group itself, social groups whose members share particular purposes and face a common task. This point is obvious when one thinks of schools, or of the police. Such social groups form characteristic cultures of their own, in response to demands from their environments and their need to function as an internally coherent group. (See especially the quotation from Schein on page 3.) Elements of adjacent cultures may be either consonant or dissonant. Given our interest in staff groups in Children's Homes, this can be restated by saying that certain features of the culture of a Children's Home may be consonant or dissonant with cultural features of other organisations within their working 'life space'.

Where there is consonance, this may hardly be noticed—staff groups simply know that it is possible and easy to work together. Where tensions occur, these are of course noted, and may lead to frustration, exasperation, or working at cross purposes. We suggest that such tensions can be understood in terms of cultural dissonance.

Consider relationships with schools as an example: where conflict or feelings of tension occur between the staff of a Home and of a school, it virtually always has to do with young people in the Home being excluded from school. School exclusion follows some behaviour on the part of a young person considered unacceptable by the school—fighting, or disrupting a class, or challenging/attacking teachers or other pupils, or embarrassing teachers or the headteacher in the presence of visitors.

Features of cultures which seem useful in understanding the tensions which then arise have to do with values, goals and goal systems, norms, procedures and routines.

The staff of Children's Homes and of schools value education, so in this respect they are in agreement. A school will strive to establish and enforce certain norms, which have to do with such matters as regular attendance, and order in the classroom, which support the school's mission of providing education. Staff of Homes have no quarrel with this, for not only do they see such norms from the school's point of view, but a staff group tries to establish comparable norms within the Home as an aid towards establishing an orderly and secure living environment for the young people.

There are, however, differences between schools and Children's Homes with respect to goals and goal systems, which prove to be crucial. A key goal for residential child care staff is to keep each young person in school. The school is concerned to support the learning of all of its pupils. If a young person behaves unacceptably in school, this interferes with the school's goal of supporting the learning of pupils in general. Exclusion is within the school's powers, and may be used to support this goal. Excluding a young person from school may thus solve a problem for the school, but it creates one for the staff of a Home, for it interferes with one of the staff's goals, i.e. to ensure that opportunities for education for each young person are maintained.

A further point is that both the staff of a Home and the staff of a school necessarily strive to retain a good reputation with their own larger organisations. This is necessary in order for them to maintain viability. For the staff of a Home, this means keeping young people in school: it is not unusual for a staff group to be considered to be failing in meeting their responsibilities if a number of young people are not at school. For a school, maintaining a good reputation includes maintaining good examination results, a good reputation in the community, and becoming or continuing to be a school to which many parents wish to send their children.

The occurrence of tension is not surprising. The school has the power to exclude a young person. In practice it is the school which decides whether a young person will be re-admitted or not, although the Education Department *can* overrule a school. The staff of a Children's Home may be held responsible for keeping its young people in school but they are without power to make this happen. Both the young people themselves, who may not want to attend school, and school personnel have more power over whether a young person attends school or not, and can act more directly than can the staff of a Home.

Schools, of course, are just one of the outside organisations with which staff must interact. With regard to relationships with the police we have seen conflict arise when different meanings are placed on a young person's offending behaviour. With regard to the Health Service, we have seen conflict arise when members of the Health Service hold to their own codes of confidentiality when residential staff feel they need more information, or where the rules under which staff have to operate lead them to seek medical advice for reasons which general practitioners regard as trivial. With regard to the juvenile justice system, staff members were sometimes dismayed when magistrates did not penalise persistent young offenders and sent them back to the Home.

Working across organisational boundaries becomes easier and more effective when personal relationships become established and contact is maintained over time, for example, with police officers, or with teachers. Ongoing communication helps members of different organisations to understand one another's behaviour better, and the pressures and constraints under which each operates.

In this and in the three preceding chapters the emphasis has been on what staff do in various spheres of their work. The next chapter turns attention to a task which is essential for effective work to take place in all other spheres—that of maintaining viability as a staff team.

9

MAINTAINING VIABILITY AS A STAFF TEAM, IN THE FACE OF CHANGE

A further important task area for residential staff, as named in Chapter 3, has to do with 'surviving as a staff team which meets the needs of children'. This way of putting it emphasises that while survival is important, surviving as a team at the expense of the children is not acceptable, as it would violate a shared norm and expectation held by on-the-ground workers, managers, and policy-makers alike. Surviving as a viable team is a necessary condition for doing good work in all other spheres of staff activity.

TEAM-BUILDING AND MAINTENANCE IN THE FACE OF CHANGE

'Viable', by dictionary definition, means 'capable of living; able to maintain a separate existence'. 'Viability' is defined as 'capacity for living; ability to live under certain conditions' (*Shorter Oxford English Dictionary*, third edition, 1955). By these definitions, a Children's Home is viable if it can continue to exist as a care-providing unit within its environment, and in the face of changes in its internal and external environment.

In Children's Homes, as in other work settings, a working group is often referred to as a team. This analogy, drawn from the world of sport, is not a bad one, as the members of a football team, for instance, work towards a common goal, understand the rules of the game, occupy different positions within the team, and take action, each in his own way, towards achieving the shared goal. It is obvious enough that a staff group, like any team, needs to be more than an aggregation of people who happen to be in the same place at the same time, if it is to achieve its goals.

Maintaining viability needs more or less constant attention on the part of a staff group. In broad terms, staff maintain viability by discussion, and by working together. Some examples follow which show ways in which this is done.

Examples of Creating a Viable Staff Group

A unit manager took up his post in a Children's Home which had a stable staff but had been without a unit manager for 18 months

The Home in which this unit manager had previously worked, also as unit manager, had been closed for financial reasons and the staff dispersed. Because he was being redeployed, he was not interviewed for his new post. He had heard, through gossip, that his new staff suspected that there were reasons other than financial ones for his previous Home being closed, and were uncertain about his competence.

The unit manager decided to hold an open staff meeting—that is, one with no agenda. After a slow start, during which he provided some factual information about his previous Home, someone asked him if he had wanted to come (to the present Home), to which he replied, 'Yes'. The staff then asked him his views about sanctions, about bedtimes, about means of controlling young people. In response to this he asked the staff what they did now, and why? Staff and the new unit manager exchanged information about what each was accustomed to. The unit manager said that he himself felt relieved by the end of this meeting, and that the atmosphere had lightened. After this, there were further staff meetings, with agendas. Staff concerns, for example about training, were aired, and new goals were set and new procedures worked out.

The device of using an open staff meeting is not without stress for all concerned. Despite this, the staff took the opportunity, firstly, to test the new unit manager's commitment to them and, after that, to seek out his views, especially about ways of controlling young people and maintaining order. The unit manager did not immediately express his views, but, instead, tried to elicit theirs. Staff members might have experienced this as a form of withholding on the part of the unit manager, but in fact it led to an exchange of views. The unit manager and staff were, in effect, testing out their likely compatibility. They were sufficiently reassured on this point to begin to work together.

A new staff group was formed which was composed of two sub-groups: four people who had been staff members of the Home for some time, and newcomers consisting of a new unit manager and six of his staff

who had been moved from a resource centre—a different kind of facility

The unit manager considered that the two groups of staff had different experiences, with different kinds of children, and were accustomed to different ways of working, and that those from the Resource Centre were seen by the others as intruders.

Frequent staff meetings were held at first—three or four times a week, on different issues—sometimes on specific children. Differences between the two sub-groups, particularly with respect to the task, and the situations encountered in their previous work setting were aired and shared. For those from the Resource Centre the emphasis had been on containing young people on remand, dealing with local pressures from neighbours, and running a tight regime. For those from the Children's Home the emphasis had been on trying to establish a home-like atmosphere with less stringent rules, and creating more of a 'family' atmosphere. In the course of these meetings, house rules, etc. were discussed. Over a period of two or three months, the two groups reached an accommodation with one another. The staff which had come from the Resource Centre could see that, in the new setting, rules could be somewhat relaxed. The staff which had been there all along felt less threatened by the newcomers. (Researcher's notes.)

During the frequently-held staff meetings on specific issues, this unit manager acknowledged the special skills and experiences of both sub-units of staff—staff from the Resource Centre as having special knowledge of and experience of dealing with more difficult children; and existing staff's experience of operating 'a normal type of family home' and establishing a home-like atmosphere. He, together with a senior member of staff, used the vehicle of sharing experience, and of facilitating discussion of such matters as basic house rules, attitudes about the young people's friends coming round, plans for specific children, etc. The unit manager evidently was able to avoid being seen by the 'old' staff as siding with his own staff against them.

When a large Home was divided into two smaller ones both of the resulting staff groups had to adapt to losing some of their members and forming themselves into a functioning staff in new environments

A member of staff who was moving to the new facility said of those who were remaining behind:

'They have created a new identity for themselves. It's not that they have remained as C ——, and we have created a new identity for L ——. They aren't C —— any more. Yes, they are in the same building, but they've created a completely separate identity and a different atmosphere within the unit, when you go there

it's not just a scaled-down C —— ; it's like a new unit in itself, in the old building.'

One of those who remained in the old premises with a (now) smaller number of young people and a smaller staff group said:

'The atmosphere's obviously completely different, it's much calmer, generally it makes it much easier to work with the young people; some of the kids that we've had here I felt sure created more problems in the old environment. We took 16 kids then, had less time, there was more pressure for them, obviously they react to the environment as well. I think it's been much much smoother and much easier; it's certainly easier to do your job now.'

Those who had moved to a new facility found that the smaller size of the house, the different physical layout, and the smaller number of staff both allowed and required them to operate differently from before:

'[In this smaller Home] it was claustrophobic at first, [but] there is more privacy here—the kids have got their own rooms.'

'You can work in a more therapeutic way here because of the smaller environment.'

Because staff numbers were smaller and there could not always be a senior on duty, staff members felt they had to do more thinking for themselves, through not always having access to a senior.

In this example, once the major change had occurred further changes occurred in its wake for both the resulting staff groups. There was a period of unsettledness followed by a re-established sense of stability which, in both cases, involved some shifts in outlook and practices.

A new unit manager joined a stable staff, bringing along with him both his good reputation and assumptions based on experiences in another unit

Staff were very pleased about this appointment: 'He's brilliant with kids.' The new unit manager declared his intention to work shifts alongside the staff, as a way of getting to know them. Staff were pleased with this, for in their view the new unit manager was showing his commitment to the Home, the young people, and themselves. All was promising, but even so, several incidents occurred early on which showed the need for all concerned to talk things out. One of these is described:

The kids take drinks to bed, and do not bring the cups back down—'there are cups all over'. The new unit manager wrote on the board: 'No more drinks.' Staff thought that this was not a good idea—the kids needed to be able to take drinks up with them at bedtime. Someone said, 'We took it to him. That was the first thing we talked through.' The unit manager said that where he came from, bedtime was at 10.30, and there were definite rules. He accepted a more flexible approach to bedtimes. A member of staff said, 'We get in, we discuss everything.' (Researcher's notes.)

This staff group and the new unit manager were positively disposed towards one another. Their styles were basically compatible in that all were prepared to discuss matters openly, including issues around which disagreement had occurred. Differences became evident early on, which needed to be resolved, stemming from the unit manager's different experiences in another Home, and the fact that he was entering a staff group which was new to him. Open and frank discussions dealt with these matters. This was in line with the culture already in place in the Home. The basic compatibility between unit manager and staff facilitated coping with initial problems.

Failure to Create a Viable Staff Team

A unit manager described ongoing incompatibility within a staff group, unresolved after two and a half years

A unit manager and deputy unit manager had come to a Home to take over its management two and a half years previously. There was a management team of four, with 12 residential social workers and 10 children. Some of the staff had been there for some time; others had joined recently. Those who had been in the Home for some time were not happy. There had been an ongoing morale problem, with high sickness rates, and the previous unit manager 'had just given up'. The new management team secured a residential week and the whole staff went. Much was aired and the situation improved, but the problems were not altogether dealt with. The unit manager put this down to the presence of three members of staff who 'are not suited or don't want to work here'. In his opinion these staff were unable to make relationships with the young people. Two of them had requested transfers. He said, 'We are working on two fronts. The first is to try to work with the whole staff, get things out in the open and improve relationships amongst the people who are here. The second is to try to assist the people who are not managing the job to acknowledge this and to go elsewhere.' The situation remained unresolved.

This staff group was clearly in a protracted and ongoing state of failure to gel, though it is hard to ascertain from the above description exactly what had been going on which had prevented an earlier resolution. For example, the researchers did not know the grounds on which the unit manager considered some members of staff unsuitable, or why transfers had not already been arranged for those who had requested them.

A permanent member of staff described ongoing instability in a Home

'When people are doing relief work and they come in a shift here, a shift there . . . for the next week, it's totally different. You never know quite who you are working with, and it makes your job that much harder. [If] you know who you're working with, you know the way that they work, and they know the way that you work, and the shift can run far more smoothly. It's far easier. Because you know what to expect from that person as a member of staff in any situation that arises—what their strengths are, what their weaknesses are, how they re going to approach it, and knowing that makes a shift easier. Because you really know.'

This staff group was very fragmented, in the sense of having only a tiny core, with heavy reliance on relief staff or short-contract staff. Such a staff group has very little chance of establishing itself as viable, especially if fragmentation persists for many months.

HOW A TEAM RECOVERS FROM A PERIOD OF LOW MORALE

Recovery, when it occurs, tends to follow from some new event which re-instills hope and/or releases energy for the task. The event might be a change in the composition of the group of young people within the Home, or the appointment of additional staff which makes up for previous staff shortages, or information which clarifies the future of the unit following a period of uncertainty or rumour, or the departure of one or two members of staff.

In the absence of some such event, it is hard for staff members to recover through their own efforts and in the face of some ongoing stressful situation. Just occasionally, a staff member will say 'we pulled ourselves together'.

When managers were aware that a staff group was in a state of poor morale, fragmentation, or internal conflict, a special team-building event or exercise might be provided. Staff members go away together as a group for a few days, with an outside 'facilitator'. Members of staff reported mixed reactions to these. One member of staff referred to a team-building event arranged by an authority in which he had previously worked, which had been interrupted:

'We did "including" and "excluding" exercises . . . [and we discussed] how do you get to that situation where people get to know each other better? There are exercises, there are games, but what happened was somebody was ill who was going to do the team-building. We actually spent a week in the unit decorating it, putting new curtains up, going out and buying stuff, going out en masse, all six of us there on eight hour shifts all day, every day, working together. We found out far more about each other than we did on any bloody exercise afterwards. It broke down all the barriers. . . . You got to know people's strengths and weaknesses, and in every team you work to people's strengths and weaknesses.'

A staff member from a different Home described a very successful team-building event, which had, like the previous example, occurred in an authority in which she had previously worked:

'I went to a 3-day event in S ——— . The external person ran it during the day and then we were in a hotel and they did a music workshop till nine, maybe ten o'clock, and then we socialised. It was good because the music workshop un-wound you after (the events of the day). . . . It was a very dysfunctional staff team. It was three days. By the time you went home you were on your knees, but it was brilliant. . . . People actually felt safe to say what they were unhappy about because she was a good trainer that made sure it never got out of hand. . . . She was encouraging us to do a lot of positives, so it wasn't all negatives.'

Others reported negative experiences:

'I've gone on these courses where people have come back and resigned. Just opted out.'

'I've heard of team-building exercises that have only lasted a few hours, they've been blown apart by the person that was running it. They've been too personal right from the word go. It has just blown it to bits.'

Such events range from the effective to the disastrous, depending largely on the skills of the consultant or trainer. A good facilitator encourages mutual exploration but does not force it and does not allow things to get out of hand. In our experience (extra to this research) a skilled facilitator does not introduce games or exercises without due attention to the likely consequences of doing so, and without built-in safeguards. It is as simple, and as difficult, as that.

MAINTAINING VIABILITY IN THE FACE OF STAFF CHANGES

When new people join an existing staff group, all concerned direct efforts to incorporating newcomers in a way which does not threaten the integrity or the basic character of the team.

Care staff rarely play a part in appointing new members of staff, though unit managers may. Unit managers and staff sometimes expressed very clear and definite views as to what sort of person was likely to be a satisfactory member of staff, and what questions needed to be asked in job interviews. An acting unit manager said:

'We need to know how they deal with confrontations, how they work as part of a team, how they see their role, what they do in their own private lives. . . . Their basic tool is their own personality. They need to be confident, have a good self-esteem, be open to new ideas. They have to have a full life themselves, and not just go home and watch TV. . . . We ask people how they cope with stress—what strategies they use. They need to be physically fit.'

When it comes to inducting new members of staff, long-term members of staff said:

'Inductions for the new staff have to be organised. The staff need time to gel and find out a little bit about each other. Taking time to do that is important, unless you want chaos.'

'New staff have come in, looked at how things are done, and the way we do things here, and picked it up and got on with it, and picked it up very well.'

Two members of staff said of their experiences when newly joining the team:

'The best advice given to me was to watch, not to feel pressurised into getting involved in anything if you didn't feel you were ready, but to actually sit and watch.'

'. . . and what you've got to do is suspend whatever agenda you've been working with, and then watch—watch the different way that the consistency is applied. We each have a different way of creating our own authority in any situation, and generally some people are laid back, some people are very forceful all the time, and somewhere in between are other people, and it's very difficult at first. But I think it's good that you do that—you bring stuff with you and then share it with people and hopefully others will pick from me what I do, and I will pick up from them. I learn every day from the people I work with.'

Induction clearly involves both formal and informal processes and is a two-way matter. Both existing staff and new staff contribute to the process of integrating a new person into a team. It is not just a matter of the new person accepting all of the existing ways of going on which characterise a team, for sometimes the new member influences the existing staff group.

Sometimes the attempt to integrate a new person fails:

We've had one or two people come into the group that have left after a short period because they just haven't fitted in. They are few and far between, people that have joined and haven't stopped that long. They tend not to stop for very long if—you can tell straight away if they're not going to fit in.' Another member of staff continued, saying that new staff had to be able to accept frank open criticism about themselves.

This comment and others like it suggest that both existing members of staff and newcomers engage in a testing-out process which eventuates in some new staff staying, and some going. New staff who stay have found a way to 'fit in'—in other words, the viability of the staff group and indeed their viability as individuals has been maintained. New staff members who do not stay have not found a way to fit in. They are right to leave, on two counts: firstly, they maintain their personal viability by leaving a working environment that has proved, for them, to be unmanageable; and, secondly, by their leaving, the viability of the staff group as a whole is maintained.

STRESS MANAGEMENT AS A CONTRIBUTION TO MAINTAINING VIABILITY AND STABILITY

As shown in Chapter 4, the task of caring for children and young people in a group setting can be highly rewarding and it can also generate high levels of stress. High stress and low morale go together, as do low stress and higher morale.

Stress is a part of the job, as staff universally acknowledged. A viable staff will have found ways of coping with stress which stand them in good stead, except, perhaps, under unusually extreme conditions. Prolonged periods of high stress/low morale are a matter for concern. They interfere with the well-being of staff and, in consequence, with the work they can do with and on behalf of the young people. Prolonged periods of low morale lead to a demoralised staff group whose members lose heart and motivation for the task. Staff members become weary. The job becomes just a job, and staff members fall into doing the minimum. Their state of stress becomes a preoccupation. High stress in staff also communicates itself to the young people, who cannot feel secure if members of staff do not feel secure. In contrast, a staff group with high morale remains energetic. Staff members retain their keenness to understand each young person, to be alert to day-to-day opportunities to benefit young people, and to be creative in their work.

We will not repeat here all of the sources of stress—for this, see Chapter 4. Here, we consider what staff do when stress builds up.

First and foremost, they turn to one another for support. Staff emphasised how important it was to them to be a part of a strong team. It was clear that a strong staff group could be a cushion against stress, and provide emotional support when stress levels were high.

Members of staff can become very sensitive to moods and atmospheres and to colleagues' needs for special support:

'I can walk into work and I know people will pick up on [my mood]. Jay will say to me "Are you all right? Are you tired?" I can spot Carol a mile off if she comes in and is not quite right. I can see right away. It's just knowing people well, the people that you work with.'

'If you were in an eight hour a day job, you could hide, couldn't you? But if you've got your shift and then you've got your sleep-in you can't keep it to yourself all that time, so it does come out. And people do recognise it. And again, there's loads of protection there, if they know you're vulnerable, they'll give you that extra space you want.'

Staff members also become very sensitive to what sort of behaviour actually constitutes support for particular colleagues:

A relatively new member of staff had been attacked physically by a 13-year-old girl who kicked and scratched her. She was quite distressed, and later expressed her appreciation of her colleagues, saying that the way they responded to her was just right. What they did exactly fitted her usual ways of dealing with stress: she did not know how the staff knew to do this, but they did. She went on to say that when something stressful happens she does not like people crowding around, but, rather, needs space in which to recover herself, only then appreciating the opportunity to talk to others. She had not described this personal preference to her colleagues, but they had sensed it. (Researcher's notes.)

Staff members in one Home described how they were in the habit of writing little notes of appreciation to one another. (Researcher's notes.)

Members of staff also turn to people in their personal lives from whom they can generally expect emotional support. This seemed to work well for some and not for others. Some felt that they should not dump their problems on family members or personal friends, thus leading them to feel upset as well. Some members of staff say that their partners would insist that they quit their jobs if they knew all of what goes on.

In response to certain kinds of crises, members of staff may turn to external line-managers—for example, for support when young people have made allegations of mistreatment against them. Members of staff expect line-managers to be understanding and not blaming while an investigation is going on, and to function as a buffer between the accused staff member and higher managers. If this kind of support is not forth-coming, anger and bitterness may follow.

A member of staff may express resentment towards a line-manager who is not immediately available when a crisis blows up in the Home—whether or not the expectation of immediate availability is realistic. Sometimes members of staff conceal problems experienced at work from external managers. They fear that seeking support from anyone outside their unit will be seen as a sign of weakness. Signs of burn-out may be concealed, in case they be taken as indications of inadequacy. For similar reasons, counsellors whom the organisation makes available to members of staff may not be used.

While staff members do support, protect, and reassure one another, they also put limits on the protection they provide to one another, if they feel that some serious standard of behaviour has been breached. The following refers to such an instance:

'[I've] been in the other circumstance where somebody was completely out of order, absolutely completely out of order, and the sense of loss that I felt, and other people felt, because we couldn't support that person who we'd worked very closely with, but he'd done something completely and totally stupid and was out of a job, and we all felt like a vacuum, because we couldn't support him, and that was a really difficult one to get through, because you want to support him and then you see the stupidity that was used, instead of judgement, and you're lost. Your instinct is to support that person, but you can't.'

This quote shows vividly how a member of staff can be torn between wanting to support a colleague but at the same time being quite unable to do so. To offer support would violate his or her own personal code of conduct and that of the staff group.

RESPONSES TO UNUSUALLY HIGH LEVELS OF STRESS

If stress levels outrun an individual staff member's capacity to cope, he or she may take sick leave, or continue to come to work but withdraw from interaction as much as possible, or blame the young person whose behaviour has led to distress. Some members of staff leave their jobs after particularly stressful incidents. It is not so very unusual for a staff group to have one or several staff members away, ill with stress. This has a knock-on effect on others because the Home is either short-staffed or must make do with relief staff who may not know the Home or the young people. More stress ensues, and threats to viability multiply.

If stress levels outrun a staff group's capacity to cope, the staff as a whole may resort to undesirable forms of shared defence. For example, we were told of a situation where the young people got out of control and staff on duty withdrew into the office, leaving the young people unsupervised. A staff group might build up a shared sense of resentment—against the young people who are making life so difficult, or against members of their own organisation whom they consider responsible for allowing stressful situations to occur, through placing young people inappropriately. While defensive responses are understandable (staff members have to find *some* way to survive in the workplace) they are also dysfunctional because they get in the way of fulfilling the primary task.

When Special Attention Needs to be Paid to a Staff Group

The need to build or maintain the viability of a staff team as a working group comes especially to the fore when some change occurs which disturbs a previous equilibrium. These include:

- A reconstituted staff group: a core group of staff stays together and is joined by a number of others who are strangers to the core staff and to one another.
- A reconstituted staff group: two groups of staff, each of which has previously worked together as part of an established team elsewhere, are brought together to form a new team.
- A new unit manager joins a well-established staff group.
- A staff group, for various reasons, loses three or four members within a short time, may have to deal with an interval of being short-staffed, and sooner or later faces the task of absorbing new members of staff.
- A large, previously integrated staff is divided into two parts, to become the staff teams in two smaller Homes.
- A Home changes its function and the existing staff group has to accommodate to this change.

- There is ongoing incompatibility among members of staff, with respect to what the task is understood to be, and desirable and acceptable ways of working.
- New young people are admitted who are especially disturbed and disturbing, and very demanding of staff time.
- Behaviour on the part of one or more young people adversely influences the attitudes and behaviour of neighbours and other members of the community towards the Home. In extreme instances the Home comes under threat, is attacked, or closed.

These are all instances of 'precipitating events' (or 'perturbations', or 'triggers for change'). Periods of disequilibrium follow, some of which may be quite prolonged. Staff recover sooner or later (sometimes much later) from most such periods of disequilibrium, usually in consequence of some further change in the environment. Sometimes external managers take action. They might disperse the staff group, or in extreme instances close the Home. They sometimes offer external consultation to help a staff group 'get outside itself' and take a fresh look at its situation. Sometimes managers provide a 'rest' by deferring new admissions for a period of time.

Sometimes it is not the staff group which needs to 'get outside itself' and take a fresh look, but the staff group plus external managers, when both play a part in keeping an unsatisfactory situation in place, or where both contribute to a downward spiral.

10

WORKING PURPOSEFULLY

THE PROCESS OF SETTING GOALS, MAKING PLANS, TAKING ACTION, AND REFLECTING ON CONSEQUENCES

In the preceding five chapters, goals and the actions associated with them have been referred to many times in the contexts, successively, of staff groups working with individual young people, working with the mix, working within the larger organisation, working within wider networks on behalf of young people, and working to maintain the viability of the staff group. In these five arenas of work, staff groups often identified particular goals and sought to achieve them through making plans and taking action. In other words, they identified purposes and sought to achieve them.

In this chapter we examine the processes involved in purposeful work in Children's Homes, whatever the arena in which the work is carried out. We have based our approach on the thinking of Kurt Lewin about action research, and have made particular use of the idea of successive 'action research cycles' (see Lewin, 1951).

It was part of the research design for Study 2 to introduce the idea of action research cycles to staff groups, as an aid to improving their practice. When this was done, as will be seen, staff groups sometimes made use of the model as intended, but sometimes did not. When they did not, this struck us at first as 'failure'. However, we soon saw that these apparent 'failures' proved invaluable for understanding what actually happens in the real world of residential child care practice with regard to purposeful work. The failures of action research, as much as the successes, revealed much about what happens when staff groups actually engage in, or try to engage in, purposeful activity. To convey what actually happened and what was learned, Lewin's action research model is described in more detail.

KURT LEWIN AND ACTION RESEARCH

Kurt Lewin devised the term 'action research' to refer to a range of research strategies which had in common studying and interacting with people operating in the real world in their ordinary ways (not in the experimental laboratory) with the intention of assisting them to effect positive change in, for example, social attitudes or characteristic behaviours. Action research evolved over the years through the work of Lewin himself and many of his students and colleagues. It was applied to diverse social problems including, notably, prejudice against minority groups.

In one of his last published papers, Lewin put forward a diagram which he titled 'Planning, fact-finding, and execution (Newcomb & Hartley, 1947, pp. 330–344). This diagram is much like the one shown in Figure 2. Lewin's diagram shows three elements: 'reconnaissance of goals and means'; 'decisions about 1' (i.e. the first step), and 'action step'. A new cycle then begins with 'reconnaissance of results', and the same steps follow.

When communicating the idea of action research to staff, we named four steps identifying a goal (first taking a reading of a situation); devising an action plan; acting on the plan; and evaluating the outcomes and consequences. These steps are shown in Figure 2 and described in a handout provided to staff, reproduced on pages 151–2.

When using the action research model as a template for understanding what actually happens in practice, we spelled the model out further, into six successive steps. Thus, an action research cycle includes the following: (1) taking a reading of a situation as it exists; (2) identifying a specific, concrete goal; (3) devising an action plan which seems likely to move a situation towards achieving the identified goal; (4) carrying out the plan during an agreed-upon implementation period; (5) reflecting on consequences (with respect to whether the goal was achieved or not, or partially achieved), and reflecting on the usefulness and appropriateness of the plan and on any unanticipated processes or outcomes; and (6) initiating another action research cycle (which may be related to the original goal or to a different goal).

The steps just described resemble planning and decision-making in everyday life—planning a holiday, or trying to get a child to be more helpful around the house, or acquiring a motor skill. The difference is that in everyday life successive steps are often collapsed in one's thinking, or some steps remain implicit, or are skipped over. It is possible to say, for example, 'My plan is to improve my piano-playing', without particularly

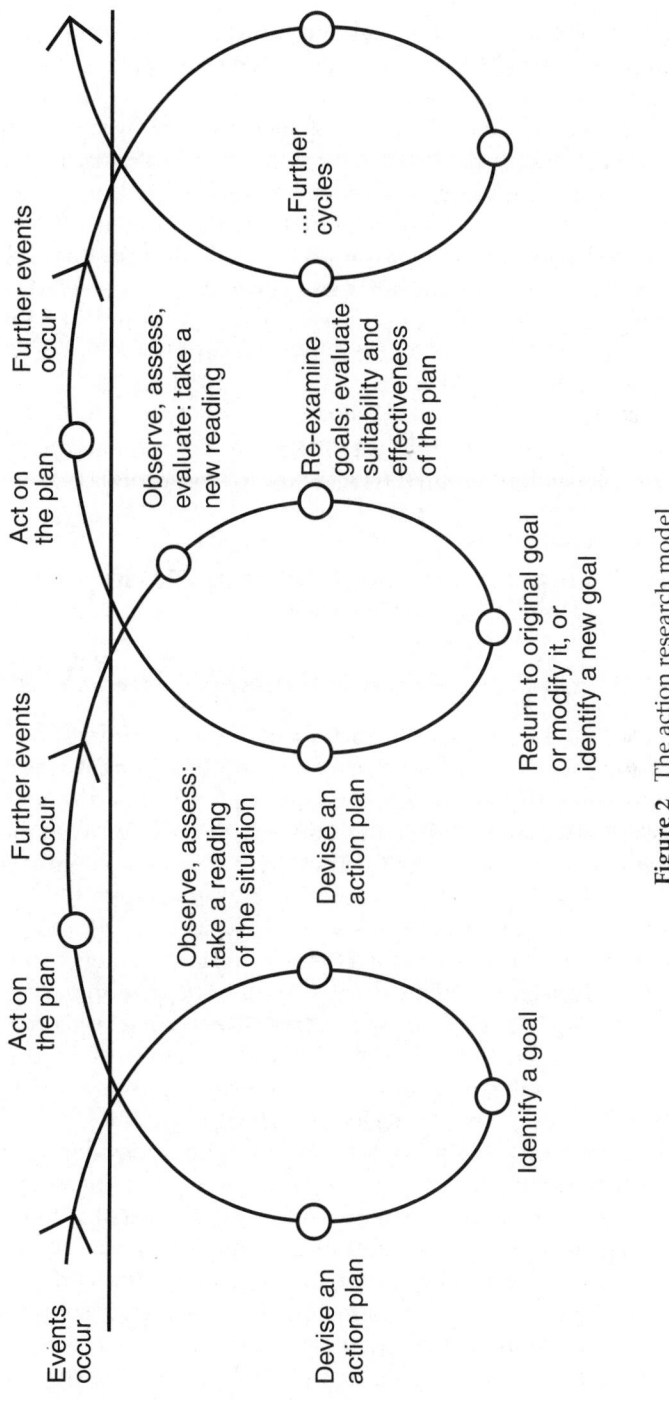

Figure 2 The action research model

realising that one has stated a goal and not described a plan. The plan, which might be 'practise regularly' is assumed or implied. If a plan works as intended, one is pleased, and does not necessarily pay much attention to what made the plan effective. If the goal is not achieved, one might say or think 'Well, back to the drawing-board', which means, in action research terms, that one holds to the same goal as before but realises that a new plan has to be devised since the first one did not have the expected effect. Or, one might decide to abandon the goal. Rough and ready planning of this kind is adequate for many everyday purposes. However, more explicit attention to goal-setting, planning and action-taking processes can pay off when goals are more complex, or alternative routes towards achieving them seem to have equal claims, or the full consequences of putting a plan into action cannot easily be anticipated ahead of time. It was on these grounds that it was considered potentially useful to introduce the action research framework to staff groups.

Introducing the Action Research Model to Staff Groups

Initial Responses of Staff to the Action Research Idea

At the end of the second visit to each of the Study 2 Homes, the idea of action research was introduced and a handout describing it was given to each member of staff. All of the staff groups understood the action research model and could see its connections with much of what they were doing in any case. At the start of the third visit, the researchers asked staff to give thought to the goal they would like to pursue first.

Four of the six staff groups responded by identifying one or more goals. They described in clear terms the underlying problems and history associated with each of their selected goals. The preliminary work of 'taking a reading' had already been done. Some of the goals referred to specific young people. Others were: a reward system to be used with the whole group of young people; more training for the staff; preparing a Statement of Purpose for their Home; getting a number of the young people back into school; getting locks fitted to bedroom doors; and preparing a brochure to be used as a 'welcome' for new young people.

Some of the goals that were named—especially those relating to individual young people—had already been specified as part of staff's ongoing work. Some were already in the pipeline, with staff taking the opportunity to reactivate them. Some emerged afresh. In some cases the goal was an old familiar one, but a new plan was worked out. For example, school attendance is a recurring problem in Children's Homes.

When one staff group named as a goal 'encouraging young people back to school', this was not a new goal, but the devised plan (to interview the young people individually to ascertain what lay behind non-attendance) had not previously been tried.

Two of the staff groups in Study 2 did not set goals when invited to do so. What got in the way? When the action research model was introduced to one of these staff groups it quickly became apparent that they were preoccupied with a problem which seemed to them intractable, and that it was hard for them to think about anything else. There was no real energy for 'taking a reading' with regard to anything else facing them. The situation which preoccupied them was discussed at length, but mainly took the form of telling the story and ventilating feelings.

The other Home which found it difficult to name a goal during research visits was in the process of being split into two by its authority. Staff were preoccupied with this prospective change, the details of which were not yet known. They used the research visits as opportunities to explore what this might mean for them, and to discuss rumours and their uncertain future. This was not named or acknowledged explicitly as a goal by the staff group as a whole in the meetings, though individuals referred to it. One could think of 'get ready for a major transition' to constitute an implicit goal. This staff also used research visits to discuss the weight of their current work.

In those Homes where goals were specified, some of those set initially were worked on in a reasonably systematic manner. The staff which wanted to work out a reward system did so. This was done in collaboration with the young people: it was agreed that a range of 'special treats' would be identified, from which young people could choose when they earned enough weekly points for good behaviour. It was the young people who determined what these special treats should be, and how their behaviour would be assessed by senior staff. This system was put into place and reviewed from time to time in residents' meetings.

The goal of getting more staff training proved to require ongoing attention. One could not say that the goal was achieved once and for all (impossible, given the nature of this goal).

One of the initial goals was to get locks put on bedroom doors. This had been put forward by the young people and accepted by staff. Staff did the necessary work of putting a request forward through regular departmental channels. Further action was then out of their hands. Over the succeeding months, this goal was regularly referred to and staff tried to find out where, in the Departmental decision-making system, the request now lay. A year later, this goal had still not been achieved. It was now third in the Department's priority list for small works, but money had run out, and action was deferred until such time as more money would become available.

In some instances goals were dropped. The circumstances in which this occurred were instructive.

One staff group had set as a goal trying to understand better what accounted for so many of its young people being school non-attenders, and planned to interview them. By the time of the next research visit, all the young people were back in school. This occurred partly in consequence of staff efforts and partly by chance. (Some of the school-attenders were new admissions.) The issue of school attendance no longer seemed so urgent. Staff expressed the intention to go ahead with interviewing the young people on the grounds that they would be better informed and therefore better prepared for similar problems in the future. Such efforts were, however, interrupted by crises demanding immediate attention. Interviewing the young people was not mentioned again and dropped out of this staff group's agenda. This and other comparable experiences showed that when a Home is heavily involved in what staff members call 'crisis management', previously identified goals tend to be set aside when the crisis is past.

Work also stopped on the goal of completing work on a brochure describing the Home, meant to be used as a 'welcome' for new young people. In the interval between setting (or resurrecting) this goal and the next visit, the staff had received a draft brochure which had been prepared by management. All Homes in the authority were meant to use it— there was room to insert the name and address of the Home and the list of staff names, but the brochure would otherwise be the same for every Home. This brochure was very different from the one that staff and young people had been working on. The latter had a cover designed by one of the young people. It referred to staff members by their first names and gave little character sketches. It included direct quotes from some of the young people as to how they experienced living in the Home. The management-produced brochure was not so personalised. It emphasised complaints procedures and other matters which management clearly felt were important to put before young people and parents. The status of the two brochures—both now in preparation—was not clear. Staff tried to figure out whether management's brochure would serve the same purpose as their own, or not, and whether the two brochures could be used in conjunction with one another or not. The general reaction was that their creativity and that of the young people had been blocked. Staff members said: 'What's the use?' The appearance of the Departmental brochure took the heart out of the staff's efforts, and although they discussed carrying on with devising a brochure of their own, and using both, work towards this goal slipped away and it was, in effect, abandoned. The Departmental brochure was produced, in due course, for this and other Homes in the authority. This event revealed how staff and managers can work at cross purposes without intending to do so. It transpired that, earlier, managers had asked all staff groups to prepare brochures for their own Homes but none had been produced. (Delays were almost certainly related to the need to respond to successive crises.) Management then went ahead to work out an all-purpose brochure, apparently without realising that a certain amount of work had been done at the local level.

Another staff group, in a different local authority, had also set as an initial goal designing a brochure for the Home. In fact they wanted to do two: one for parents and children and one for other professionals who might wish to place young people. This goal arose because the Social Services Department had asked all its Homes to design their own statement of purpose and function, and had allocated time to one of its managers to assist with this process. This manager's task was to bring together what staff wanted to include and what management felt had to be included. This Home designed a brochure which incorporated information for parents and children as well as information for professionals who might wish to place young people. They did this cooperatively with management, which required considerable time and a number of meetings. After much work the brochure was ready for publication. Publication, however, was delayed because money was not available. Nevertheless, when reflecting on what had come of their actions, staff members felt pleased with the product itself, and with having had their views listened to.

The staff group which was facing a split began to identify concrete goals and work towards them late on in the series of Study 2 visits, when the uncertainties of their situation became clarified. The staff which was preoccupied with an intractable problem continued to be so preoccupied throughout the course of Study 2. Not all goal-related work was at a standstill for either of these staff groups, but thinking about goals and plans was always against the background of certain ongoing preoccupations.

Two Uses of the Action Research Model

The Action Research Model as a Structure to Guide Goal-setting, Planning, and Taking Action

The action research model was introduced by the researchers because of its power to function as a guide to, and a way of thinking about, purposeful work. We knew from previous experience that it could constitute a structure for planning—not, of course, in the sense of an instruction manual, but in the sense of naming what needed to be thought about and taken into consideration, in a series of logically sequenced steps. Although we anticipated that staff groups might well already be operating in line with such a model, we thought that the model had the advantage of being explicit. It was meant to support good practice. By explicitly building in a 'reflecting on consequences' stage, it would facilitate learning from experience.

When we saw what actually happened when it was introduced, and how staff groups sometimes could and sometimes could not operate in line with the model, we realised that the model could also be used as a template whereby the goal-setting, planning, and other steps which actually took place could be understood. Used in this way, it could assist in understanding what gets in the way of pursuing goals, why and how goals might have to be changed, circumstances in which goal-setting and related action are compressed into very short periods of time, and circumstances and events which freed staff to identify and work towards goals.

The Action Research Model as a Template for Understanding the Realities of Practice

Understanding the use of the action research model as a template requires taking a closer look at how successive steps in the model work out in practice.

1. Taking a Reading of the Current Situation

Staff were in ongoing touch with the current situation in and around their Homes. 'Taking a reading of the situation' was something they did as a matter of course. This might be done informally, such that part of the 'reading' was explicitly stated while other parts might remain implicit. However, any staff group, when invited, or when it chose to, could name the salient events at any given time which required their time and attention. During Study 2 visits, staff members sifted through their recent experiences and commented on what was important to them. One staff group did this systematically: they designated a member of staff to keep a running list of significant events to report in the course of research visits.

Through listening to staff discussions, the researchers became aware of events which influenced the current situation and made it different from what it had been before. Often, the significant event was some change in the composition of the young people: someone had left, and someone else had come. Sometimes it was a crisis in the life of some young person: he or she had been in court, or father had visited unexpectedly. Sometimes a crisis occurred in the group of young people if, for example, a number of them had gone on a rampage or been picked up by the police. Sometimes the event stemmed from management: there was to be an internal inspection, or a member of staff heard that she was to be seconded onto a two-year full-time qualifying course.

Significant events could suggest new goals, or interrupt work on pre-viously identified ones.

2. Identifying a Specific Concrete Goal
The following are some examples of named goals:

'Richard has just joined this previously all-female staff group—we want him to integrate with us all and learn our ways.'

'We want to encourage Jay's Mum to visit her.'

'We want to persuade his [field] social worker that fostering is not what Paul wants, and to make a plan for him to stay here.'

'We want to stop the police thinking we have waking night staff, and ringing us up at all hours.'

'We want to improve relationships with angry neighbours.'

'We are trying to persuade management that we should not take an 11-year-old into a unit designated for older adolescent boys.'

'We are all trying to calm down after last weekend.'

Goals could be classified according to *their target* (e.g. whether they were directed to a particular young person, or someone in a young per-son's network; a member of staff; a field social worker; others in the Home's network; etc.); *their single or multiple character; their formal or infor-mal character* (e.g. whether written down in a care plan, or expressed in the minutes of staff meetings; or simply known and mutually understood to be present and 'in the air'); and/or *the time-span over which work would most likely need to be done* (e.g. long-term goals, such as 'prepare May for fostering'; shorter-term goals, such as 'prepare Eric for a return to school after a time-limited exclusion'; or immediate goals cast up by some unex-pected event, such as 'get Jane, who has just cut herself, to Accident and Emergency as soon as possible').

3. Devising an Action Plan which seems Likely to Move a Situation Towards Achieving the Identified Goal
Devising an action plan requires thinking-time—time and space for delib-eration between setting a goal and taking action. Reserving thinking-time is sometimes, but by no means always, possible in day-to-day life in a Children's Home. Sometimes it is possible but not done.

For example, suppose there is a long-term goal to attempt to reconcile a 14-year-old boy with his mother. An action plan might be arrived at quickly, which involves trial weekends at home. However, the action plan might have been agreed too quickly, without adequate consideration, for example, of the mood of the boy, the state of the mother, difficulties which could be anticipated, and the kinds of support which both boy and mother might need. Spending more time in deliberation might well lead to elaborating or refining a plan, or breaking it down into stages. It might point to the need for an overall strategy within which there are subsidiary goals which require their own action plans, and to the need constantly to monitor, so that actions can be modified in the light of events and goals adjusted when necessary.

With regard to many shorter-term or crisis-related goals there is simply no time to think out a plan in explicit terms. Staff members act and react, and if there is leisure afterwards, may give thought to why they took the action they took and how the action was connected to an implicit grasp of what they were trying to achieve at the time.

The realities are further complicated by the fact that staff cannot ask the world to stand still while they get on with making plans related to just one aspect of their work. As shown in Chapter 3, staff groups are faced with a multitude of situations, all of which imply goals and require action. Events move so rapidly, and new situations spring up so unexpectedly, that many staff feel to be in a state of crisis virtually all the time. This, of course, has profound consequences for whether and how 'purposeful work' can be undertaken in volatile circumstances.

It became very clear that *all* members of staff need to know what is hoped for and how work is meant to proceed, so that each staff member can contribute to achieving the goal as opportunities arise in everyday work and so that staff do not undo each other's efforts. There needs to be a 'good-enough' shared understanding of what is being aimed for so that effective work can take place.

Developing a 'good-enough' shared understanding does not preclude different members of staff taking on special responsibilities. The obvious example is the designation of a key-worker or link worker for particular young people. Other examples abound: for instance, the staff group which was working on a formal statement of the purpose and function of the Home agreed that one member of staff would draft a summary of a staff discussion on his computer, and bring it back to a future meeting; another staff group, faced with having to respond to new quality control measures being introduced by higher managers, designated one of their number to hold a discussion with their external line-manager on this matter.

4. Carrying out the Plan during an Agreed Implementation Period
Some goals, and some plans, lend themselves to being carried out during an agreed implementation period. Others do not. Time-scales are often set by the dates of review meetings. These are useful in that they help to

prevent drift. However, the best guess as to an appropriate implementation period may have to be modified in the light of unforeseen events occurring during the implementation period, or by the consequences of having put some sub-plan into operation.

With respect to some goals and associated plans, it becomes ludicrous to think in terms of a definite implementation period. If the goal is to 'help John to manage his pocket money', or to 'calm this chaotic 10-year-old', who is to say how long this will take, or even if it can be achieved?

Sometimes the implementation of a plan depends on the actions of people outside the staff group itself. For example, it might be a field social worker rather than members of a residential staff who is responsible for working with a child's mother; a return to school depends on the attitudes and actions of a headteacher. This raises the issue of who has the power to do what, and is one of the general issues around goal-setting and planning which will be returned to towards the end of this chapter.

5. Judging Consequences (with respect to whether the goal was achieved or not, or partially achieved) and Reflecting on the Usefulness and Appropriateness of the Plan and on any Unanticipated Processes or Outcomes
This step is essential if staff members are to provide feedback to themselves as a guide to future action. Plans do not always work out as intended; the goals initially set may prove to have been unrealistic or 'pie-in-the-sky'; working towards one goal may create unanticipated problems which themselves require some other goal to be set and some other plan to be made. If something has gone wrong, reflection is needed to understand why this has happened and whether it could have been prevented or something similar forestalled in the future.

It can be hard for staff to set time aside for reflecting on the consequences of having put some plan into action, yet it is a key way of learning from experience. This important step may be skipped over or given sparse attention, especially if a plan has been apparently successful and a goal achieved. In the face of everyday pressures of work, it can feel to be a luxury to dwell on past successes, even though much can be learned from doing so.

6. Initiating another Action Research Cycle (which may or may not be related to the original goal)
This step implies that one action research cycle has been completed and that a staff group is now ready to initiate another. Sometimes things work out in just this way. Examples are the story of Rosie, told towards the beginning of Chapter 5, and of Christine, the first practice instance provided in Chapter 11. In these cases, as in others, the work proceeded at a rather stretched-out pace, such that one could see (again using the

action research model as a template) that the sequence of action research cycles was orderly: the consequences of putting a plan, related to a named goal, into action, could be named and examined and was used as a basis for what was to be thought about or done next.

Sometimes a single action research cycle, with a beginning, middle and end and a satisfactory conclusion, could occur within the space of a single afternoon or a single day. When this was the case, staff could consider the chapter closed and direct their attention to something else. This was the case, for example, for the unit manager and staff who had a talk with a man living in the neighbourhood who became concerned at the possibility of abuse having occurred within the Home (ninth practice instance in Chapter 11), and for the staff who worked with the whole group of young people to try to resolve their rumbling complaints about the 'meanness' (stinginess) of the unit manager (eleventh practice instance in Chapter 11).

Often, situations are not straightforward. The model depicts successive discrete steps in purposeful work which follow neatly one from the other. Real life is not always this neat.

WHAT HAPPENS IN REAL LIFE WITH RESPECT TO SUCCESSIVE STEPS IN PURPOSEFUL WORK

When a goal was very generally stated in the first instance, it often had to be broken down into manageable steps. Sometimes this could not be done until actions were underway. In the middle of some action process, staff might reformulate their original thinking in terms of more specific and shorter term goals. The original, more generally stated goal was not abandoned, but staff came to see the shorter term and more concrete goals which it contained. 'Stepping-stone' goals could be identified which needed to be pursued in order to achieve the overall goal.

Sometimes explicitness came retrospectively. At the reflection stage, staff could see that they had been, in fact, working towards a particular goal even though it had not been stated explicitly at the time.

Serendipitous opportunities for benefiting young people sometimes arose in the context of day-to-day events. Making use of such opportunities were not part of a plan because no one knew the opportunity would arise. The following is an example:

Jim, a boy of 15, told the staff that he could do a more efficient job of doing the weekly food shopping than they did. They gave him responsibility for this task. He took it on and did it well. Staff showed their appreciation of his competence and help. (Researcher's notes.)

This amounted to 'on-the-spot' action which made use of an unexpected opportunity to further the general aim of assisting young people, including of course Jim, to exercise practical skills and enhance self-esteem.

Sometimes, in tracking a staff's work, one mainly sees the action, and both the goal and the plan remain implicit. They can be deduced from the action, but have not been stated explicitly. This tends to happen when an emergency situation demands immediate action, and whoever is on duty hardly has time to think, let alone formulate a goal and a plan:

A fairly new member of staff was usually and typically friendly and jokey with the group of young people. One day two of the girls began to fight one another physically. Without thinking or planning it in any way, he moved swiftly, speaking more loudly than he normally would, and firmly and decisively separated the girls. He had departed from his usual style, and afterwards realised that this was just what had been needed. (Researcher's notes.)

One could not say that a goal had been formulated, or that the member of staff had thought out an action plan which departed from his usual way of responding. He described how aware he was that girls were involved and that he was a male. He was familiar with Departmental guidelines on acceptable forms of physical constraint, and knew that if he were not careful he could be open to allegations that he had in some way abused the girls. All this went through his mind in a flash. In retrospect he could see that a spontaneous response was underpinned by reflection, logic, thought, and previous knowledge and skills, even though there was no time really to think, at the point when action was needed.

Sometimes a goal and a plan were collapsed into one statement, and not clearly differentiated. For example, when a staff member said 'the plan is to settle him down and return him home', the word 'plan' was used, but she was actually referring not to a plan but to a goal. The plan at that stage was unexplicated.

The connection between a staff group's efforts and the outcome may be apparent rather than real. For example, as reported earlier, when staff members wanted to get young people back to school, the goal was 'achieved' but it had nothing to do with staff efforts and everything to do with a turnover in the young people living in the Home.

GOAL-SETTING AND PLANNING PARTLY FORMULATED OUTSIDE THE RESIDENTIAL STAFF GROUP

In some of the examples already presented, the whole sequence of setting a goal, developing a suitable plan, taking action, noting consequences, and then engaging in further planning was done entirely by and within the staff group. In other instances, it was evident that others from within the Social Services Department became involved, or that actions on the part of others outside the Home had a bearing on whether and how a plan could be implemented, or was interrupted or transformed.

When making use of the action research model as a template, it is often necessary to apply it to a wider decision-making system—members of residential staff plus field social workers or managers within the wider organisation, or people in a child's or the Home's network. What happens with regard to goal-setting and successive stages cannot be understood unless the participation of these others is taken into account. Consider the following two examples.

Kevin, a 'Little Frozen Boy'

Kevin, now 12, first came to the unit when he was 6. He had, up to then, been living with his mother, a single parent with no other children, who had mental health problems. He had reportedly never experienced a hot bath or a meal sitting at a table. The unit manager who told his story said that he needed a lot of one-to-one work during the 14 months of his first placement in the Home, while fostering was being arranged. In the opinion of the unit manager and staff, Kevin needed both 'male and female role models', but he was placed by his field social worker with a single-parent divorced mother who had a son of her own the same age as Kevin, and who also fostered a 2-year-old. At this time Kevin was a remote child who kept his distance from adults. The unit manager felt that her opinions had been disregarded.

This placement broke down. Four other foster placements followed, each of which broke down after shorter or longer periods of time. Thus from the age of 8 to the age of 10, Kevin was in a series of foster placements. When 10, he returned to the Children's Home, and was still there, although foster care was again being planned. The unit manager described him as 'our little frozen boy'. Kevin remained remote despite consistent staff efforts to be friendly and show interest. Just recently, an episode had occurred which the unit manager described as a 'break-through'. Only a few days before, Kevin and the unit manager were talking about how difficult he found it to cuddle anyone, and he promised the unit manager that 'one day' he would do it spontaneously. The unit manager said that would be 'lovely', and suggested he might start the next day. He told her that his mother had never cuddled him. The next morning, while the unit manager was cooking breakfast, Kevin 'came hurtling through the dining room with his arms out and he said, "Oh it's good to see you", and he put his arms round me and he cuddled me. And I was absolutely delighted'. Kevin recognised, as did the unit manager, that he had achieved something he had never previously been able to do.

She suggested to him that having done it once he would now know how to do it again.

During this period another foster placement had been found for Kevin by the placement officer. He was due to leave the Home in another fortnight. The unit manager wanted to protest the current move, considering it ill-timed, but felt that the planning had gone so far that it was unlikely that Kevin would remain in the Home. Kevin himself knew about and accepted the plan. The new foster family included a father and a mother and two children older than Kevin. The unit manager knew nothing about them but had seen a photo of the family sent to Kevin. She felt strongly that Kevin needed a demonstrative couple to parent him—'people who will touch him and take an undivided interest in him'.

The unit manager hoped to be involved in Kevin's forthcoming transition to foster care. She had asked Kevin's field social worker if she might accompany Kevin to his first visit to the prospective foster parents (he had said that he would not go without her). The field social worker, whom the unit manager said was excellent, was considering this request. (Researcher's summary.)

What had happened was that six years after first entering care a crucial experience occurred for Kevin with the potential of making a real difference to his future. The kernel of this was Kevin 'hurtling through the dining room with his arms out and (saying), "Oh it's good to see you" ', and putting his arms round the unit manager. This was a new piece of behaviour on the part of a boy who up to this time had kept himself distant from adults, both physically and emotionally. It could be described as a 'crucial emotional experience', as discussed in Chapter 5. Such experiences are indeed crucial but they can only have a positive effect in the longer run if they are repeated, consolidated, and followed through. Long, patient work on the part of the unit manager had led up to this event. Furthermore, when she told Kevin 'now you will know how to do it again' she was paving the way for the necessary follow-up experiences if proper advantage was to be taken of the break-through. So far, it should be noted, Kevin had been unable to 'cuddle' anyone other than the unit manager.

It was just at this point that Kevin was to move to another foster home. The researcher's view coincided with the unit manager's. However good an idea this might be in the longer run, it was ill-timed. Kevin needed more time with the unit manager to consolidate this gain and begin to practise being 'able to do it again'. If the move was to occur, there was important transition work to be done, and the unit manager was in the best position to do it. What would be done next, however, was in the hands of the fostering officer and the field social worker. They would either see the point of involving the unit manager or it would not happen. It was not evident whether the field social worker knew about the break-through experience. The unit manager may or may not have told her about it as she had previous experience of 'not being listened to'.

In this case, in addition to the unit manager and staff, others involved in making decisions and plans concerning Kevin were a fostering officer, his field social worker, the foster parents who were prepared to accept him, and Kevin himself, who had accepted the plan.

Making use of the action research model as a template, and applying it to this situation, one can see first of all that it was not clear just who was involved in taking a reading of the current situation. It appeared that the fostering officer, the field social worker, and the unit manager had each done a 'reading' on his or her own, but had not shared or talked out their respective understandings of Kevin's situation. Neither the fostering officer nor the field social worker appeared to know about Kevin's breakthrough. There was a communication gap in that important information held by the unit manager had not reached others centrally involved in goal-setting and decision-making. In the face of this gap, there was no reason to reconsider the goal of placing Kevin with foster parents at just this time. An associated goal—that of assisting Kevin with the transition—had not as yet led to an action plan.

It was not known to the researchers (since it was not known to the unit manager, or at least not mentioned) what the thinking was which led to fostering again being tried for Kevin, nor who had set this goal. It seemed to the researchers that one of the things illustrated by this run of events is how difficult it can be to abort or modify a plan once action based on it is underway, even if changed circumstances suggest that a re-think would be appropriate.

Rosemary, a 14-Year-Old Girl whose Behaviour could not be Controlled

The unit manager said:

'A 14-year-old came into care in June. If there had been a foster place available she might not have come into [residential] care at all. She joined a very disruptive group and became very violent and hard to manage. We managed the situation as best we could, but a series of events led up to Rosemary being removed from the unit. She had got this boyfriend, and kept running off from here to live with this boyfriend, and we kept going and picking her up and collecting her and bringing her back. In between times, the field social workers said, "We're looking for a specialist placement" with foster parents that specialise with young people that have offended, and who get an enhanced payment. We realised that Rosemary needed something of her own, something

different, needed the individual attention—we couldn't give it 24 hours a day, seven days a week—there were the other residents. In between times she would run off. The police were going to the boyfriend's again, to see if she was there. We were going and seeing if she was there. The boyfriend's family were saying she was not there. But she was there, and the [field] social workers knew it. We weren't aware of what was happening'. The residential staff was in agreement that Rosemary should be moved into foster care. 'We would have liked to have been involved with this, and given some outreach work to talk to the foster carers and to Rosemary herself. Although she was a very difficult girl and displayed some very difficult problems, there was a link with a link worker: they'd got a good relationship, really. I felt very sorry for the staff because they'd worked with Rosemary for over a year, and she'd displayed all this behaviour and they were just cast aside.'

It is not easy to untangle this story. One would like to know more about the disruptive group and its impact on Rosemary, and whether the running away to the boyfriend's home was something constructive she was doing on her own behalf, given her particular current circumstances. Was Rosemary likely to continue to run away to her boyfriend's after the foster placement commenced? It is evident that there was conflict between the residential staff and the field social worker and that the residential staff, justifiably or not, mistrusted the field social worker. If Rosemary had indeed built up a good relationship with her link worker (and there was no reason to doubt this), then there was an opportunity for the link worker to play a part in the transition, but this was not part of the plan.

Those involved in goal-setting and planning with respect to Rosemary were field social workers, the unit manager, and residential staff. Rosemary showed clearly by her behaviour what she preferred—being with her boyfriend and his family—but she was not, apparently, a participant in working out goals. Indeed, in action research terms, her behaviour was part of set of events which were 'read' by all concerned as pointing to the appropriateness of foster care as a goal. The 'reading' which was taken was in fact based on incomplete information (no one knew what the boyfriend or the boyfriend's family meant to Rosemary); and on information not taken into account and possibly unknown by the field social worker (that Rosemary had a good relationship with her link worker). As with Kevin, the goal of assisting Rosemary with the transition into foster care was not in place. It is possible that the field social worker assumed that this was her province. Residential staff wanted to be involved in outreach work and transition work, but this was evidently not being considered—perhaps the social worker did not know that they wanted to be involved, or why.

Some Important Questions

In both these examples one can see that there were gaps in communication between residential staff and the field social workers concerned. In the first case, important therapeutic work was actually interrupted and in both cases the person in the best position to ease the young person's transition into another form of care was being excluded or in danger of being excluded.

This gives rise to three questions:

- In undertaking units of work, who does the goal-setting, who does the planning, and who carries out the actions?
- How do the efforts of residential staff fit in with the efforts and intentions of others?
- What marks the boundaries of a residential staff group's sphere of autonomous activity?

The answer to each of these questions is: it is not always clear. Sometimes, residential workers and field social workers, or residential workers and those responsible for placements, work at cross purposes with one another. What needs to be communicated, especially from residential workers to field staff, does not always get communicated. If communicated, residential workers feel that their views and opinions are not taken seriously. We conclude that there can be a mismatch or an imbalance between those who hold crucial information and those who hold decision-making powers, and that this can operate to the disadvantage of the young people concerned. We also conclude that it is very hard to reconsider or reverse plans once they have been set in motion.

Members of residential staff operate within certain spheres of autonomous activity which no one interferes with or interrupts. The unit manager's efforts with Kevin, for example, could proceed without interference as long as Kevin was resident in the Home. There was an overriding plan, however, which was to find foster parents for him. Because a foster family had been found, the plan rolled along, and there seemed to be no mechanism for reviewing the plan, or deciding to make more time for the unit manager to continue with the good work she was doing with him.

In looking at units of purposeful work *which take place altogether within the residential facility*, consensus was usually established with respect to goals and plans. When the unit of work extended beyond the boundaries of the residential Home, and others (especially field social workers and those responsible for placements) became actively involved, the situation changed. Although there remained consensus about the overall goal to benefit the child, consensus about sub-goals and about plans was not always achieved. Sometimes one part of the system undermined the efforts of another part.

What can be achieved through action research methods?

It will be clear that work gets done on issues important to a group. The group will be doing this kind of work already, especially through care plans worked out for individual young people. Action research encourages thinking in terms of a whole range of goals, some of which have to do with what goes on inside the Home, and some of which have to do with outside matters.

Besides work getting done towards important goals, the experience of moving through a series of action research cycles often leads to new information and new insights into the nature of the task, and into what helps and what hinders those concerned in working in the ways they most want to, and achieving what they hope to achieve. Often, the implicit becomes more explicit, and therefore more readily understood and communicated. In other words, action research assists in learning from experience.

HANDOUT ON ACTION RESEARCH

Action research is a way of thinking about and doing work which encourages people in Children's Homes to identify goals which everyone thinks are important to pursue, make plans which fit those goals, put the plans into action, and carefully examine the consequences.

Action research as a series of cycles

Action research works in a series of cycles, each one having to do with a particular goal. It is best if any one cycle does not go on for too long—three to five or six weeks is best. This in turn means that goals have to be specific and concrete, not too general. A very large goal can usually be broken down into a number of smaller ones.

The four steps in a single cycle of action research

An action research cycle always starts with identifying a goal (step 1); proceeds to making a plan (step 2); and then to carrying it out (step 3). A cycle finishes with a careful evaluation of outcomes and consequences (step 4).

A goal which is considered important enough to work on may have to do with the routines and rules in the Home, with an individual young person, with the young people as a group, with improving or modifying the physical facility, with some issue concerning the schools or the police, etc., with neighbours, or with an issue arising within the staff group or between those working or living in the Home and others in the unit's larger organisation.

The plan is, of course, thought out to fit the goal. The group as a whole then decides who should be involved in putting a plan into action. This may be everyone or some part of the group, or different people may have different parts to play.

Step 4—the evaluation—deserves time and thought: Did the plan achieve what it set out to? If yes, what helped it to succeed? If not, what accounted for this? For example, was the goal unrealistic in the first place? Did other more urgent matters take precedence over work on it? Did the plan run into obstacles which were not anticipated? Which were outside the control of those trying to make it work? Were there additional consequences beyond the hoped-for outcomes?

If a particular goal is achieved, then the group goes on to identify another goal, and proceeds through a further action research cycle. If a particular goal is not achieved, the group may decide to work out a different plan directed to the same goal, or it may decide to change the goal if they come to see the original goal as unrealistic. Or, the way things worked out may suggest a different goal which needs working on before going back to the original goal.

11

BUILDING A PICTURE OF GOOD PRACTICE

A picture of what residential child care practice is, and what differentiates good and poor practice, can be derived from the many accounts of situations faced by residential staff which required a response from them.

'Practice' is what staff members do in direct interaction with individual young people and groups of young people, and what they do on behalf of young people when interacting and negotiating with others. Practice also has to do with what staff members refrain from doing in the various spheres of their work. In other words, practice is behaviour. 'Behaviour' should be taken to include tone and volume of voice, body posture, eye contact, and forms of physical contact.

Behaviour, however, is connected to the thinking and feeling which goes on inside the practitioner. While practice consists of behaviour (which is visible and can be observed), what is said and done by staff is related to the values and attitudes held by them, to the meanings they place on events as those events unfold, and to personal emotional reactions to events.

This chapter and the one which follows need to be taken together, for Chapter 11 is the basis for what is said in Chapter 12. This chapter shows how features of good practice and of poor practice can be derived from examining concrete and unique instances of practice. Chapter 12 brings together conclusions about characteristics of good practice.

The approach being taken is to arrive at an understanding of good practice by demonstration and illustration. This avoids two extremes which we judge would be less helpful. One extreme would be to formulate generalised exhortations to virtuous practice in abstract terms, such as 'improve children's self-confidence', or 'promote a sense of identity'. The other extreme would be to offer detailed prescriptions, such as 'accompany to school any child who is reluctant to attend', or 'urge parents to attend review meetings'. The first extreme offers no guidance about actual behaviours. The second offers specificity but does not acknowledge that circumstances may require exceptions to usually useful guidelines. Our intention, instead, is to draw attention to a repertoire of courses of action involved in good practice. To make constructive use of this repertoire, practitioners and managers will need to choose actions in the light of each specific case.

The premise from which we begin this chapter is that good practice is that which contributes positively to the welfare and personal develop-ment of children and young people who cannot live with their own families and who may have been damaged by past experiences. 'Welfare and personal development' includes protecting young people from harm; taking advantage of all current opportunities to assist them to develop emotionally, interpersonally, educationally, and physically; repairing, to the extent that this is possible, the consequences of past trauma; helping a young person to function in line with societal norms such that he or she does not get into personally disadvantageous positions with the law or with others; and assisting each young person to become able to lead a satisfactory life without causing unusual distress or harm to others or being the recipient of harm from self or others.

This statement is consistent with the Children Act 1989, an important piece of legislation in England and Wales which brings together and updates earlier legislation, and emphasises the relationship between chil-dren and young people, their carers, and state responsibilities. The Act states that it is 'the general duty of every local authority to safeguard and promote the welfare of children within the area who are in need' (Part III, 17). The phrase 'to safeguard and promote the welfare of children' is used repeatedly both in the Act and in Volume 4 of the Guidance and Regula-tions accompanying the Act, which pertains to residential care. Volume 4 of the Guidance and Regulations further states that:

> Residential care is a positive and desirable way of providing stability and care for some children which they themselves often prefer to other kinds of place-ment. Homes should set out to treat each child as an individual person and to promote and safeguard his welfare in every way. . . . Homes . . . must ex-ercise the concern that a good parent would by providing a safe environment which promotes the child's development and protects him from exposure to harm in his contacts with other people or experiences in the community.
>
> (The Children Act 1989 Guidance and Regulations
> Volume 4, Residential Care, Section 1.1)

INSTANCES OF PRACTICE AVAILABLE THROUGH THE RESEARCH

A large number of instances of practice were available from the data. From Study 1 there were accounts of discrete episodes. In Study 2, related instances of practice sometimes took place over months and went through numerous phases. Practice sometimes occurred in 'passing moments' and could last only seconds. All formed a basis for understanding good practice and of lapses from good practice.

Our procedure was to examine concrete instances of practice against the general statement of what good practice comprises, which begins this chapter. With respect to each concrete instance, a judgement needed to be made as to which behaviours—and associated thoughts and feelings—on the part of members of staff were good practice and which were departures from good practice.

The next section shows how this was done. Description and commentary are kept separate, to avoid interpretation creeping into description. Description had to be 'straight' description, including actual events and any expressions of opinion or interpretation of events on the part of staff members, or references to personal feelings. What care workers thought and felt were a part of the episode itself. Researchers' opinions and interpretations are a separate matter. In every case a description of an instance of practice is presented first. This is followed by the researchers' views about features of practice—good or poor—demonstrated by the episode.

EXAMPLES OF INSTANCES OF PRACTICE, WITH COMMENTARIES BY THE RESEARCHERS

1. *Seeking to re-establish a girl of 15 in school after she had been excluded for fighting*

Christine, 15, was excluded from school because of fighting with another girl. She herself was unhappy about this, especially as exams were coming up. Christine was on a part-time work placement at the time, and the staff arranged for her to continue with this, even though she was not attending school. At the same time, and in the course of several visits to the school, the staff tried to persuade the Headteacher to have Christine back. The headteacher, however, consistently said that she would not re-admit Christine. The staff then approached several other schools in the hope that they would accept Christine, but all refused. Eventually a school was found which was willing to consider accepting her. While the head of this potential new school was still pondering this, the staff sought and assembled character references for Christine from teachers who liked her in the first school. They established that the other girl who had been in the fight was equally responsible for it. Christine was offered a place in the new school. The school was inconvenient because of its geographical distance (six miles away) and Christine had lost her friends. The transition was difficult for Christine, and staff tried to help her by making visits to the school with her before she began to attend. After a two-week period of feeling unsettled in the new school, she managed the transition successfully.

The researchers judged, from this example, that it is good practice to work at the 'frontier of a young person's needs'. At the beginning of this episode, what Christine needed, and also wanted, was to get back into school in time to take her exams. This was Christine's most important and immediate need at the time, and it defined the goal that the staff was working towards. It is also good practice to perceive opportunities arising in a young person's environment for benefiting him or her. In this case, Christine happened to be on a work placement. If the staff could arrange for this to continue, then Christine would benefit from some structured activity in her weekly timetable and not be totally at loose ends. She would not be cut off totally from familiar routines. This was achieved. Good practice includes *not* persevering with an effort when experience shows it is not working. In this case, when it became evident that the headteacher would definitely not have Christine back, the staff shifted their tactics, though not their goal. They began to approach other schools. It is good practice to try to increase the likelihood of a good outcome from one's efforts in every way possible. In this case, when a school was found which was willing to consider accepting Christine, the staff tried to increase her chances of being accepted by assembling evidence in her favour, to put before the new headteacher. It is a part of good practice to shift one's goal on behalf of a young person in response to changed circumstances. Once Christine was accepted at the new school, the 'frontier of her needs' shifted. What she most needed now was help in making a difficult transition. The staff accordingly shifted its goal and devised a new plan to fit the new goal. This involved taking action to assist Christine to settle in to her new school.

It can be difficult to judge altogether accurately whether pressing on with one course of action will eventually pay off, or whether further effort will be futile and therefore some other tactic should be tried. With reference to outcomes: the outcome for Christine was good in that she got back into school in time for her exams. This can be regarded as a medium-term outcome for Christine. How it fits with, or contributes to, longer-term hoped-for outcomes for her is not known, either by the researchers or by the staff concerned. One can, however, say with confidence that it constituted a positive medium-term outcome.

2. *A spontaneous, brief response to a very indirect expression of a personal worry on the part of a 14-year-old girl*

Three young people and two staff were sitting in the lounge of the Home, chatting. (A researcher was also present.) A girl who had recently reached the age of 16 was discussing her plans to find a flat of her own. Jane, a 14-year-old, said, 'I'll be 16 in two years.' Ann, a member of staff, said, 'You have plenty of time. Besides, we don't just chuck people out.'

This example shows that sensitivity to a young person's feelings under-lies good practice. Ann caught Jane's anxiety even though it was very indirectly expressed. Jane's feelings were shown more by tone of voice than by what she said. Ann's comment was quick and intuitive and shows how a spontaneous, unplanned response can be an instance of good practice. In a split second, with no real time to think it out, Ann offered reassurance. Further, good practice includes building up a picture of a young person and increasing understanding of him or her through close observation in the course of everyday events. In this case, Ann registered Jane's anxiety and, we can assume, added it to her understand-ing of Jane.

There was no indication from Jane as to whether she registered this reassuring response, so we do not know what the short-term outcome was (i.e. did Jane feel reassured, or did the offer of reassurance pass her by?). We can be more confident of another kind of outcome—the worker's increased understanding of Jane—which can be expected to become a more developed basis for good practice as further opportunities arise.

3. *Dealing with a disturbance in a mini-bus*

A group of young people had enjoyed an outing and were being driven back to the Home in a mini-bus by a member of staff. They were excited, and began to create a disturbance—shouting, laughing, and throwing things. The staff member pulled over at the first opportunity and stopped the mini-bus. He told the young people that he could not proceed until they calmed down, because their behaviour was distracting him, and they were at risk of an accident. He made no further comment, but waited until the group calmed down, and then proceeded.

In this example the staff member remained calm in the face of a disturbance among the young people. There are several reasons why it is good practice to remain calm in the face of excitement, uproar, or the unexpected. One is that to respond to excitement with more excitement tends to escalate a situation which, in this case, was already showing signs of getting out of control. Another reason has to do with the fact that young people often expect reproof or punishment, and they expect violence to be met with further violence. This is a familiar scenario to them, to which they know how to respond. It confirms their world view in which adults are enemies. In this case the member of staff did not reprove the young people or do anything to escalate the situation, nor did he confirm any expectation the young people might have held that the response to violence is more vio-lence. Another feature of good practice shown by this example is that it demonstrated to the young people that certain consequences follow log-ically from their behaviour. In this case it was logical for the staff member to stop the mini-bus and wait for order to be re-established. It would have been bad practice had he responded with some punitive action which was arbitrarily related to the young people's behaviour.

Was the member of staff being 'soft' on the young people by this response? The researchers thought not, for the episode was an opportunity to demonstrate to them that unruly behaviour has logical consequences. A 'harder' or more punitive or retaliatory approach would have failed to have made use of this opportunity, and also would have demonstrated to the young people that adults are prepared to use their power against them—an assumption all too likely to be a part of their world view already.

4. *Preventing a 13-year-old girl, known to have tried to harm herself, from running out of the house at night*

Philippa, a girl of 13, had been to bed but came down at midnight, clearly intending to go out of the house. When Mary, the member of staff on duty, tried to intervene, Philippa spat at her. As Mary said afterward, she was 'covered with it'. Mary persuaded Philippa to come into the lounge, and said she knew she was upset, and, 'I talked it over with her, and she appeared quite calm. She had had a phone call which upset her. She came down in her nightie. I said, "Come on, love, you're upset". She said, "Get away from me, you fucking bitch", but then she came into the lounge, sat down, had a drink, and apologised.' Later, Philippa said that she was surprised that anyone would care enough about her to stop her.

As the previous example also shows, it is good practice to keep one's wits about one in the face of the unexpected—in this case, behaviour on the part of a young person likely to put her at risk, and a verbal and physical attack on the worker. However Mary may have felt inside, she avoided behaving in an angry or reproachful or punitive way—any of which could have escalated the situation and none of which would have provided the help that Philippa needed. In this situation, there was no real time, at first, to think, yet the staff member did the right thing: first stopping Philippa from running off, then seeking to calm her down, then talking it over. This again shows that good practice can be immediate, spontaneous, and 'intuitive'. It can also be good practice to offer support and/or nurturance in some concrete form which is at the same time a symbolic expression of a staff member's feelings of interest, concern, and wish to help. Offering a hot drink may seem mundane, but in this example it was a way of offering nurturance in a concrete form. Mary offered a sympathetic, listening ear—another feature of good practice. Finally, this example shows that good practice can combine control and care. Control, when it is needed, is an aspect of care.

5. *Staff and young people having an enjoyable outing together*

Three members of staff took six young people on an outing to a theme park. There were exciting (and frightening) rides, and games of skill. They all enjoyed themselves. Several young people prided themselves on their courage and pointed out that they were more courageous than one of the members of staff, who was frightened and declined to go on one of the rides. One boy, in particular, kept repeating that he had got the highest score of anyone in a game which required a good deal of manual dexterity. Staff members said afterward that all the young people had behaved well—they did not steal food, or swear.

A part of good practice includes providing opportunities for young people to demonstrate and increase physical skills, demonstrate personal courage, stretch themselves, feel good about themselves. Good practice includes showing young people that enjoyable times can be had with adults. This can be particularly important if their previous experiences with adults have mostly been very negative. Good practice also includes making opportunities for young people to have a sense of being a part of a social group, and for behaving acceptably in public.

6. *Negotiating with the Social Services Department for a new way of ordering clothing*

A unit manager had noticed that it took a long time for an agreement for clothing to be purchased for young people to come through from the Department. He tracked an order for socks through a long chain of people who had to approve and process the order, and noted the time from placing the order to being able to go out and buy the socks. He presented this information to his line-manager, calling attention to how much the socks must have cost when the time of all those concerned had been taken into account. He suggested that a new system be tried: that the Home be given a clothing allowance. The line-manager took the matter further, and eventually, the new arrangement was agreed. Under the new system the young people were able to make their own choices, and get the needed item sooner.

This account shows that good practice includes noticing whether some established procedure works against the best interests of the young people. It further shows that it is good practice to devise a plan which is likely to work if turned into action. In this case, the plan included assembling information and evidence, avoiding a complaining or resentful stance (which tends to stir up opposition), and presenting the case for a change in policy through accepted channels within the organisation.

This episode did not involve face-to-face work with any of the young people and it was not undertaken with the welfare of any specific young person in mind. The young people might not even have known that the unit manager was making these efforts. This is an instance of work with others on behalf of the young people in general. The outcome was positive in that the new procedure gave the young people more choice, and avoided delays in getting what was needed.

7. Responding to a situation in which one young person stole bus tokens meant to be used by all

All the bus tokens had been stolen and the young people were told there could be no more trips out because there was no money for the bus fares. Soon after, one of the girls returned the tokens. She was praised for doing so. A member of staff said, 'Everybody makes mistakes.'

The researchers judged that it is good practice to acknowledge a young person's courage in owning up to having done wrong, and to express appreciation of it. This episode, like several previous ones, made use of a situation known to all the young people to remind them that 'behaviour has consequences'. In this case the message was: no bus tokens, no trips out.

The short-term outcome in this instance was satisfactory in that the bus tokens were returned, the group was not deprived of further outings, and 'lessons' were offered that people can make mistakes and retrieve them, and that consequences which may be unwanted can follow from behaviour. How, or whether, this might feed into longer-term positive outcomes for any of the young people is not known.

8. Responding to a young person's pain, and offering support, not once, but many times

Trevor, a boy of 13, was still in an extremely distressed state following the death of his mother, which had occurred nearly a year ago. He had made a number of suicide attempts during that period and was still considered to be at risk of committing suicide. His father felt that he could not cope with him and asked for him to be taken into care. When Trevor arrived at the Home, his desperately painful grief was evident. Staff sat with him, listening to his powerful expressions of grief and rage, sometimes for long periods of time. In describing their interactions with this boy, a member of staff said: 'You listen, you offer support, you try to be honest.' He added, 'It's been difficult for all of us.' Another member of staff said, 'The animal sounds alone tear you to bits.' Staff members working with Trevor reported having to go out of the room for brief periods just to recover. 'We help each other. I couldn't escape from it. John (member of staff) came in, made a drink, and brought us both one.' 'It went on until 3 or 4 o'clock. Three of us had to talk it out afterward.' Shortly afterward, Trevor was moved to another Children's Home, nearer to his own home. This was in line with Departmental policy—a place nearer to home had not previously been available. The work which the staff had been doing with Trevor of course stopped. When talking about their experience with Trevor afterwards, not all staff felt that they had done good work with him. One member of staff thought that the work had fallen short, and wondered whether they had 'just been holding his hand'. Another member of staff argued that the boy had trusted the staff enough to show himself, and that what they had done had been a good, appropriate course of action.

This episode points to a feature of good practice—working at the frontier of a young person's needs. In this case it was important for Trevor to work through his grief. Members of staff functioned as 'mourner's helpers' by listening, by staying with him, and by tolerating his pain. It is good practice to continue to work with a young person at the frontier of his or her needs despite the personal pain a staff member is, in consequence, experiencing. In this case, staff members were much pained by the rawness of Trevor's feelings, but with help from one another they managed to tolerate this and to stay with Trevor. By inference, it is poor practice if staff members protect themselves from experiencing pain generated by a young person's circumstances or state by, for example, withdrawal or avoidance or offering false reassurance. In this case it would have been poor practice if the staff had avoided Trevor or left him to it when he clearly needed the comfort of someone's presence. It would have been poor practice to try to reassure him when he was for the moment unreassurable, or, worse yet, to try to cheer him up. It is poor practice to interrupt good practice. In this case the good work which the staff was doing with Trevor was interrupted by his being moved. Turning to another aspect of this episode—Trevor's transfer—the researchers judged that it is poor practice to follow Departmental guidelines slavishly when it is evident that, in a particular circumstance, this is against a young person's best interests. In this case, it was Departmental policy to place young people in facilities nearer to their own homes, but Trevor was transferred at a time close to the anniversary of his mother's death—the worst possible time for him—and at a point when the staff was doing constructive 'mourner's helper' work with Trevor. This was either poor practice on the part of the placement officer, or there may have been a gap in communication between what the staff knew and what management needed to know to make a good decision. Such a communication gap is another form of poor practice—this time, located in the care system.

In their work with Trevor, staff were deprived of the extended time which would certainly be required to take Trevor further towards recovery from his bereavement. Within the time available, which was too short for Trevor's needs, the practice was excellent. It can also be noted that not all the staff felt satisfied with the work they were doing (the researchers thought it was excellent). The difference of opinion was connected with what different members of staff hoped and expected to achieve. It is also possible that an understanding of the role of the 'mourner's helper' was not a part of the staff's knowledge base, and/or that the staff was un-easily aware that their efforts had been interrupted and had not gone far enough. The longer-term outcome for Trevor can only be revealed by events.

9. Dealing with a man living in the neighbourhood who had been told by a young person that he had been mistreated by a member of staff

Colin, 12, went missing from school, turned up at a friend's house, and com-plained to the friend's father about having been mistreated in the Children's Home. The situation was described by the unit manager: 'We had a phone call in the afternoon saying that he had gone missing. We had people looking around and reported it to the police as required. In the course of the evening we had a phone call from the father of a friend of Colin's. Our boy had gone from school to his friend's home, and while there told the parent that he was frightened to come back to the Children's Home, and, basically, that he was not being treated fairly. This obviously needed dealing with. A colleague and I went to his parent's home to talk to him. My view of why Colin was saying this was that he was having problems in school, but this was a surmise and difficult to get across to a member of the public. We talked at length with this parent (the boys were upstairs) about why Colin was complaining, whether it was justified or not, and we also advised him as to the courses of action which he could take as well. He could, for example, go to the police. We offered our explanation but also said that he did not have to believe it.' Colin was asked to come down and talk about the incident. He said that he had had a fight with somebody at school, and also had problems with his work. He had got angry, and ran off. He then became frightened to go back to the Children's Home, expecting to be told off. The unit manager commented later, 'He got into this big hole and he couldn't get out of it', and went on to say, 'The story that the boy told the parent had a grain of truth in it. There had been a situation in which he had been out of control and was wrecking his bedroom. He was held by two members of staff. One had got their arms round him from the back and was holding his arms. The boy was sitting on this person's knee at the time. He was being prevented from damaging his room, and also himself, since he was in a real rage. Colin used this example as a means of trying to convince the parent that he was being mistreated.' The unit manager went on to say, 'We were fairly happy with the way this discussion went and so was the parent. We told the parent that we would like him to come back to the Home with us, and said that if he still had feelings about how Colin was being treated he could report it to the police or take other action. The parent came back with us, and was satisfied. The incident was reported to the Social Services, who investigated and were satisfied that there were no grounds for complaints against the Home.'

The researchers judged that it is a feature of good practice to confront a potentially fraught situation without delay. In this case, it was good practice to try to prevent any form of threat to the Home from escalating, on the grounds that, if the Home came under attack and became non-viable, work with and on behalf of young people could not go forward. It is good practice to avoid getting into an adversarial relationship with a member of the public, and to be open and honest rather than defensive and evasive. It is good practice, too, to follow Departmental procedures, by reporting incidents to the Department through established procedures. It is good practice to cooperate in the investigation of incidents.

This example points to certain personal qualities which underpin good practice: in this case, courage and forthrightness. This unit manager was prepared to take the risk involved in pointing out to a member of the public that it was his right to lodge a complaint against the Home if he considered it appropriate to do so.

10. Working with a 14-year-old girl who was bossy and demanding with other young people and with the staff

Sarah was frequently bossy towards other young people, insisting that they do things for her, or do things her way. She was also very demanding of staff, following them about and talking when they were busy with something else. Staff members felt that it was important to try to help Sarah to modify her behaviour, since she was alienating the other young people and becoming more and more disliked, and was taking up proportionately more staff time than they thought appropriate. They thought of her as attention-seeking. The staff tried to reason with Sarah, pointing out how her behaviour was affecting others. They decided to ignore her when she was especially demanding. Neither of these efforts had any effect on Sarah's behaviour. Thinking further, staff members came to a different opinion as to the meaning of Sarah's behaviour. They came to see her as having very low self-esteem and believing that no one liked or valued her. They saw her 'attention-seeking' behaviour as desperate efforts to get a response from others. On the basis of this revised understanding, staff members felt more sympathetic towards Sarah than before, and changed their approach. They began to spend time with her when she had not asked for it, and found opportunities to credit and praise her for her good qualities. After a time Sarah became at least somewhat less bossy and demanding. As this occurred, the young people began to feel and act more positively towards Sarah, and staff members' positive feelings were maintained.

With respect to Sarah, a key aspect of the work was the re-thinking which staff members did when their first efforts to assist her to change her behaviour had no effect. It is likely that their initial efforts, meant to be helpful, succeeded only in communicating to Sarah that she was being unreasonable and that her behaviour was unacceptable. If so, this would only increase her bad feelings about herself. The second set of responses was more effective because it took into account possible underlying feelings. Further, the staff now liked her better, which was bound to be conveyed and have an effect. The goal which pertained to Sarah's behaviour remained the same. However, another goal was added, which had to do with her feelings about herself. The approaches taken to working with Sarah, under the two different sets of assumptions about the meaning of her behaviour, were quite different. The second approach initiated an upward spiral.

11. *Dealing with young people's complaints in a series of meetings*

The young people in a Home had been complaining about James, the new unit manager, saying he was tight with money. They demanded a residents' meeting. Staff responded with the suggestion that they first meet as a whole group, so that the staff could hear the complaints, that the young people then choose a spokesperson who would attend an especially-called staff meeting, and that there then be a further meeting of the whole group of staff and young people. This was done, all in the space of a single day. In the first meeting, 'the kids pulled the staff to bits'. Paul was chosen as spokesperson for the young people and did well. In the last meeting of the day, 'No one was offended'; 'We all applauded Paul' (the spokesperson). The unit manager acknowledged being tight with money and gave some of the reasons (e.g. Christmas expenses), saying also that it was part of his job. The young people accepted this and things calmed down.

The researchers considered that it was good practice to respond quickly to an indication of unrest or dissatisfaction within the group of young people, to seek to forestall a blow-up on the part of the young people when a problem situation is still in its early stages, and to take young people's complaints seriously. It is also good practice to do any necessary talking-through within a structure which allows for the frank expression of feelings and opinions while at the same time keeping it within definite boundaries of time and space. It is good practice for a staff to listen to young people's complaints without reproaching them and without displaying a defensive attitude in response to being criticised. It is also good practice for staff to share their feelings and their points of view with young people when they and the young people are in conflict or potential conflict, providing this can be done (as said above) without reproach or defensiveness. Thinking a little more broadly, it is good practice to have a structure already in place—in this case, regular residents meetings—which can be activated when needed, at the initiative of either the staff or the young people. Still another feature of good practice demonstrated by this episode is the use of a group situation for the benefit of some particular young person, for example by giving him or her a special role to play, or by taking the opportunity to credit him or her for doing something well. In this case, Paul's self-confidence was boosted by being chosen as spokesperson, doing well, and being praised for it. Finally, it is good practice to make use of a group situation to demonstrate to all the young people concerned that conflict or potential conflict can be resolved through talking matters out rather than resorting to the exercise of strength (to determine who wins out), or trickery, or concealing feelings.

This piece of practice was contained within a single working day. It is a good example of preventing a potentially explosive situation, and also demonstrates how staff worked effectively together. A single staff member expressing defensiveness or reproach could have spoiled the good work that was being done.

EXAMINING THE PRACTICE INSTANCES DESCRIBED IN EARLIER CHAPTERS

Many of the illustrations provided in earlier chapters could be examined in a manner comparable to the 11 instances of practice described and discussed here.

For example, an account was provided in Chapter 5 of work with Rosie, a 17-year-old who was soon to leave the Home. This account demonstrated how a staff group was alert to changes in Rosie's circumstances and to her reactions to them, and adapted their work with her accordingly.

In Chapter 6, on the mix of young people in the Home, a situation was described which demonstrated that it is good practice, when engaging in one-to-one work with one young person, to be alert to possible negative consequences for others, and to take steps to avert such consequences. Conversely, it is poor practice to fail to notice such 'knock-on' undesirable consequences.

In Chapter 10 an account was given of work with Kevin, an emotionally frozen boy of 12. With reference to the direct practice involved, it was possible to say that it is good practice to be in touch with that child's state and needs, to make use opportunities to benefit the child arising in the course of everyday living, and to be sensitive to what the child can tolerate at any one time and to assist him forward without pressurising him and risking triggering some counter-reaction or retreat. It is good practice to 'pave the way' for change and to give the child space and time to move forward at his own pace.

HOW MANY EXAMPLES DOES ONE NEED TO BUILD A PICTURE OF GOOD PRACTICE?

Many more instances of practice were available to the researchers than those described in this and other chapters. When considering the implications of a series of instances of practice one gets to a point where further examples do not generate understandings different in their essentials from those already examined, even though each new example is unique.

'Grounded Theory' (Strauss & Corbin, 1990) makes the point that it is justifiable to stop examining more instances of some phenomenon when further examples cannot be expected to yield further insights into the issue under investigation. This is a judgement made by the researcher. It is always possible that the 200th instance will yield something altogether new when the preceding 50 have not, but it is unlikely.

A FURTHER STEP . . .

What has been said in this chapter about features of good or of poor practice has been tied to the examples which gave rise to them. There remains a further step—that of detaching the inferences from the examples in which they were embedded, and grouping and ordering them into a coherent statement of what constitutes good practice, and lapses from good practice. This is done in the next chapter.

12

CHARACTERISTICS OF GOOD PRACTICE

The analysis of a number of specific concrete instances of practice, as reported and referred to in the previous chapter, generated a number of statements of characteristics of good or of poor practice. The next step was to extract these from the contexts in which they occurred, and sort and categorise them. This further step allows characteristics of good practice to be named in terms which transcend the specifics of the situations in which the practice occurred. It is a form of content analysis. The difference between it and earlier ways of using content analysis is that, earlier, content analysis was based on raw data while here, it is based on processed data.

We proceeded by sorting statements about practice according to the focus of the work. This is in line with what has been done earlier, in Chapter 3, when identifying five task arenas within which staff groups work, and in Chapters 5 to 9, where each task arena was examined more closely. In this chapter we add a sixth focus, which has to do with the structures, procedures, and customs established within the Home. We also examine, separately, working with the network around the child and the network around the Home.

Most of the points made below refer to characteristics of good practice. Poor practice can be taken to be the converse of the points made.

ARENAS OF PRACTICE

Establishing Structures, Procedures and Customs inside the Home

Good practice includes:

- providing orderly (but not overly rigid) structures and routines for day to day living;
- being prepared, sometimes, to relax rules if enforcing them rigidly means losing an opportunity to do some good work with a child or the group, or if rigid enforcement conveys an uncaring attitude;

- creating situations in which a young person can demonstrate existing skills or develop new ones;
- holding regular residents' meetings, in which matters of concern to all can be discussed and decisions can be made;
- being ready to call special residents' or house meetings if something occurs which needs everyone's immediate attention;
- arranging treats to be enjoyed inside and outside the Home;
- making certain that any sanctions which are in place are reasonable and are known to all the young people, preferably through their having played a part in devising them; and
- establishing customs or having in mind special activities which can be introduced to turn a situation around when a problem situation appears to be building up.

Working Directly with Individual Young People

Here, we use as sub-categories the three 'fronts' at which working with individual young people occurs, as identified and discussed in Chapter 5: containing and controlling; working at the 'frontier of young people's needs'; and seeking to provide reparative experiences.

Good practice related to containing and controlling a young person includes:

- being sensitive to early signs that an upset is on its way, and intervening to prevent it;
- avoiding exciting further an already excited young person;
- trying to 'talk a young person down' from a state of excitement or from destructive (verbal or physical) behaviour which is already underway; and
- using acceptable forms of physical restraint when necessary, but also trying to reduce the frequency of the need for physical restraint.

Good practice with an impulsive or frequently out-of-control young person includes taking advantage of periods of relative calm to talk to, soothe, seek to understand, and show interest in the young person.

Good practice relating to working at the frontier of a young person's needs includes:

- giving thought to what lies at the 'frontier of a young person's needs' (which will be different from person to person and for the same person at different times);

- defining goals which pertain to that frontier and making plans which, if followed, are likely to move towards the goals (conversely, it is poor practice to define goals which are irrelevant to the young person's frontier, or so far beyond it that a failure experience is bound to occur; it is also poor practice to define goals in so abstract or ambitious a way that one cannot devise an operational plan which fits them);
- consulting with a young person about goals which might be pursued, while keeping in mind that a responsible adult might see goals differently from an impulsive or rebellious adolescent (for example, concerning drugs or alcohol);
- perceiving and taking advantage of opportunities arising in a young person's environment to benefit him or her, whether or not these relate to a currently emphasised goal;
- avoiding persevering with a plan when experience shows it is not working: the goal may remain the same, but a different approach or plan is needed;
- trying to increase the likelihood of a good outcome in every way possible—when a goal has been defined, this means thinking out different possible routes towards achieving it, including indirect ones which might support the main effort;
- continuing to work with a young person at the frontier of his or her needs despite the personal pain a staff member may, in consequence, be experiencing (also, by inference, one can say that it is poor practice if staff members protect themselves from experiencing pain generated by a young person's circumstances or emotional state by, for example, withdrawal or avoidance or offering false reassurance); and
- shifting one's goal on behalf of young people in response to changed circumstances—if the original goal has been achieved or is shown to have been unrealistic.

For many young people, attention needs to be directed towards providing 'reparative' experiences which make up for, and gradually heal, the consequences of earlier trauma. This involves:

- developing an understanding of what needs repairing in individual instances;
- finding ways to disconfirm a young person's fixed beliefs and expectations—for example, that all adults are untrustworthy, or hostile, or to be feared; and
- finding opportunities to provide such experiences in one-to-one contact *and* in the context of day-to-day living; appreciating that if what

happens in one-to-one contact is not supported by what happens in ordinary-day-to day interactions, it will be nullified.

With reference to all three of these fronts, good practice includes:

- being ready to listen, both to the evidently momentous and the apparently mundane;
- being sensitive to a young person's readiness, or not, to talk and to share feelings or experiences;
- combining non-verbal or symbolic forms of caring with verbal, explicit ones;
- noticing good or admirable behaviour and crediting a young person for it; and
- marking special occasions in a young person's life with a celebration.

Good practice is based on as full and as accurate an understanding of each young person as possible. This requires paying close attention to day-by-day behaviour, listening with care to what a young person says and how he or she says it, and avoiding jumping to conclusions: in particular, avoiding *immediately* believing that surface behaviour is a direct expression of underlying feelings.

Good practice is as much a matter of non-verbal behaviour and tone of voice as what is actually said. Non-verbal behaviour and tone of voice sometimes reach a young person when words do not.

Good practice will rarely if ever be based on accepting as 'explanations' such superficial catch-phrases as 'he is manipulative'; 'she is attention-seeking'; 'he only wants to get his own way'; 'she is uncooperative'. Such phrases mix up, in one unthought-out bundle, observed behaviours, assumptions about the young person's motivations, and personal emotional response to the young person's behaviour. Phrases such as these stop practitioners from thinking further, and are not a satisfactory basis for good practice.

In addition to planned work towards goals, a quick, intuitive response to a young person, occurring in a matter of seconds, can be an instance of good practice. In this research we were struck by how often some brief and spontaneous comment or piece of behaviour was just right for the circumstances. A staff member caught a child's mood and responded to it, or lightened a tense situation through humour, or responded in a sensitive way to some unexpected event when there was no time to think things out. Such apt, intuitive responses are likely to be based on an accumulated understanding of the young person, held somewhere in the mind at all times, and on the ability to perceive a special opportunity arising in the context of immediate, often fleeting, circumstances.

Working with Groups of Young People

Working with groups of young people is not only necessary in residential care but also offers crucial opportunities for personal gain. Good practice includes:

- providing opportunities for young people to work together, with one another and with the adults;
- using interactions occurring in the group as a whole or between pairs and small groups of young people to assist individuals to develop more satisfactory ways of handling disagreements, and to learn to express their feelings and wants explicitly without alienating others;
- noting and making use of opportunities arising in the course of everyday interaction and conversation for young people to learn from one another's experiences;
- showing young people that enjoyable times can be had with adults;
- steering young people towards forms of conflict resolution which emphasise seeking consensus and compromise by peaceful means rather than through the exercise of power, such that only one person or subgroup can 'win';
- assisting individual young people to establish a respected place for themselves in the Home;
- creating opportunities for individual young people to make positive contributions to the Home and the household;
- creating opportunities, during everyday life, for young people to demonstrate and increase their physical skills, demonstrate personal courage, stretch themselves, feel good about themselves;
- crediting the group as a whole for their real accomplishments, for example, in helping a new young person to feel at home, or in handling some tense situation among themselves; and
- reviewing group and interpersonal events with the young people for what can be learned about how each presents himself or herself to others, how own behaviour can sometimes elicit unwanted responses, and how own behaviour impacts on others.

In addition to the constructive work which can be done for the benefit of individuals within a group context, observing group interactions assists hugely in developing a fuller understanding of each young person by noting how he or she operates with others: the emotional stance taken towards others, responses to the positive approaches of others, responses to the anger of others, expressions of envy, and the 'favourite' interpersonal positions into which a young person manoeuvres himself or herself. It is good practice to improve one's understanding of each young person by all the means available, including noticing his or her behaviour in group situations.

Situations sometimes blow up in residential settings which involve most, if not all, of a group of young people. This can take the form of mass absconding, or committing offences together, or taking drugs together, or engaging in destructive behaviour inside or outside the Home—damaging property or one another or outsiders. If a blow-up of some kind is anticipated, good practice consists of:

- trying to notice early warning signs and intervene early, before a situation gets altogether out of control—useful tactics include separating potential combatants ahead of time, or distracting the whole group into another activity, or providing some energy-consuming activity for all or some of the young people; and
- airing problems early on, and taking advantage of structures and customs already in place to do so (usually, residents' meetings).

If a blow-up could not be prevented and is already occurring, good practice includes:

- remaining calm and trying to keep one's wits in the face of excitement, uproar, or the unexpected (to do otherwise can make a difficult situation worse—unexpected events, especially challenging ones, stir up feelings in a worker which it may not be appropriate to act upon; in particular, responding to anger or to attacks in kind is likely to escalate an already difficult situation);
- (in some circumstances) simply a period of *waiting* if the group is excited or even rowdy, but no real harm is being done, in order to give the group the opportunity to calm down on its own. This requires careful attention to whether the situation is escalating or not, for if it is escalating, waiting will make things worse;
- (in some circumstances) intervening immediately because harm is being done or is threatened, and trying to calm a situation down before addressing it in any other way;
- 'talking it out' after the group has calmed down; and
- calling on outside help when it is needed: colleagues or, when necessary, the police.

Harm can come to individual young people through interactions in the group as a whole or a sub-group, through interactions between pairs. Good practice includes:

- remaining alert to such damaging interactions as scapegoating, bullying, ostracism, etc., and then
- appreciating that each of the young people involved needs to be understood—both the apparent victim and the apparent perpetrator—

and that each may need help in handling the situation better and perceiving how his or her own behaviour might be contributing to a difficult situation (for example, a young person might be manoeuvring himself or herself into being someone else's victim).

If staff feel that sanctions are needed, or that a reward or incentive system would be helpful, good practice includes:

- making this a matter for discussion with young people, while holding final power, in case the young people support harsher sanctions than staff think appropriate; explaining one's reasons if young people's preferences are overruled. (It is poor practice to transfer power fully to young people, since staff could fall into going along with some decision which they think is unwise, or else getting into an adversarial relationship with young people.)

Also in connection with seeking to maintain orderly behaviour in the group as a whole, and working towards the development of self-control, good practice includes:

- demonstrating to young people that behaviour leads to consequences that are evidently and plausibly related to the behaviour itself: that good behaviour brings rewards, and unacceptable behaviour is connected with unwanted consequences. This means avoiding imposing arbitrary punishments or sanctions which pain young people but have nothing to do with their behaviour, *and* seeking to connect rewards to actual behaviour ('rewards' include expressing appreciation and praising young people for their accomplishments);
- using sanctions which follow logically from the offence, and, conversely, avoiding sanctions which are arbitrarily related to the offence.

A final point: good practice includes:

- providing positive models through one's own behaviour—for example, by showing that mistakes can be acknowledged without loss of face; that feelings can be expressed without hurting oneself or others.

Working with Members of Each Young Person's own Network

The Children Act 1989 recommends working in partnership with young people's parents. Good practice involves:

- seeking every opportunity to work together with parents and, where possible, to improve a young person's capacity to relate to a parent and a parent's capacity to relate to the young person;
- supporting contact between a young person and his or her parent(s), for example, by making space in the house in which young people can meet with members of their family without interruption;
- recognising practical and psychological limitations to partnership work, especially where abuse has occurred or a parent has serious mental health problems, or has irrevocably rejected the son or daughter; and
- being guided in individual instances by as careful a reading of the realities of the situation as possible, rather than by wishful thinking or essentially romantic notions about the value of family life.

With respect to other network members, good practice includes:

- perceiving opportunities for establishing or strengthening emotional ties between a young person and other family members—including, for example, siblings and grandparents, but at the same time appreciating limitations on what may be possible;
- judging when it will be in the child's best interests to make special contact with teachers and headteachers, in order to develop a shared view of the child's needs, and anticipate and try to forestall problems;
- appreciating that when a young person comes into residential care his or her personal network expands to include the staff and the other young people in the Home; good practice also includes being alert to indications that potentially constructive personal relationships are beginning to be formed, and nurturing these; and
- being alert to interpersonal relationships which are damaging or could be damaging, and trying to limit and curtail negative consequences, and arm young people against being drawn into unacceptable behaviour or being harmed by other young people inside or outside the Home.

Working with the Network around the Home

This point relates to the fact that, around the Home, there exists a network of people and organisations which is relatively stable and independent of the young people who happen to be living in the Home at any one time. Good practice includes:

- appreciating that the network around the Home needs to be nurtured and kept in a 'healthy' and constructive state—which, in practice, means creating opportunities to maintain good relationships with neighbours, schools and teachers, the local Education Welfare Officers, the local police, GPs, and anyone else with a regular relationship with the Home; and

- making this a regular part of the work whether or not particular network members are currently involved with young people.

Attending to the Needs of Staff Members and Maintaining the Viability of the Staff Group

Good practice includes:

- integrating new staff into the team while maintaining consistency in practice;
- making time to discuss and review units of work, examining plans which worked out as intended and those which did not, and interventions and activities which were effective and those which were not, with the intention of learning from experience;
- paying attention to staff morale and trying to control and manage stress levels so that time and energy is not diverted away from the young people;
- finding ways to acknowledge and air differences of opinion without generating internal conflict and divisiveness;
- acknowledging and seeking to deal with persistent internal conflict which interferes with the quality or consistency of the work; and
- appreciating when outside help may be needed to achieve any of the above.

Working within the Larger Organisation to Benefit the Home and its Residents

Good practice includes:

- being scrupulous in conforming to the organisation's requirements about record-keeping, reporting incidents to the Child Protection Team, and cooperating in internal inspections and investigations;
- noticing whether some established organisational procedure works against the best interests of the young people, thinking out what would put the matter right if turned into action, and approaching external managers in ways that do not stir up resistance—this includes assembling evidence and making use of proper channels within the organisation;

- negotiating with external managers, field social workers, and/or those responsible for placements about the admission of new young people, with the intention of maintaining as favourable a mix as possible (*NB:* it is true that the power to place and move young people tends to lie outside the power of the staff; however, successful negotiations do take place, and it can be poor practice to stop working towards this goal too soon); and
- making own opinions known and marshalling evidence if external managers and/or field social workers embark on a course of action which residential staff consider is likely to be against the best interests of young people, or will interrupt good but still uncompleted work with young people.

GOOD PRACTICE: GENERAL POINTS

Good practice includes:

- noticing when a changing situation requires a shift in goals, in the focus of the work, and in the kind of work undertaken;
- being in touch with what is needed and likely to work for *this* young person, in *this* set of circumstances or for *this* group of young people— i.e. appreciating the uniqueness of every person and every situation;
- being aware of one's internal feelings, and exercising control over how one expresses them—taking care that one's own behaviour does not escalate a difficult situation, and that, whatever the provocation, one's behaviour is a response to the young person's needs rather than one's own; and
- being realistically aware of limits on own autonomy, and the influence of others on the quality of practice. (Practice often involves others within the organisation or within the Home's or young person's network. Whether good practice can occur or not, or is interrupted, is sometimes outside staff control. When this is the case it is good practice to explore matters with relevant others, and to argue the case with those who in staff opinion are blocking good practice.)

Poor practice involves the reverse of these: persisting in a course of action when events show that it is not effective or no longer appropriate to changed circumstances; working to formulae or to universal rules which are not always applicable to the current situation; allowing personal feelings to be expressed in action, without reflection or thought as to likely consequences; giving up too soon in seeking to influence others in the care system.

Good practice can never be the province of one care worker alone. All care staff, plus others involved in day-to-day care, need to be in touch with a young person's state and needs and be familiar with Departmental procedures, so that whatever is done, by whichever staff on duty, has some consistency to it, and staff members do not work at cross purposes. 'Consistency' should not be taken to mean that all behave in precisely the same way, but that what is done is rooted in shared understandings and mutually agreed goals.

LAPSES FROM GOOD PRACTICE; ERRORS AND THEIR RETRIEVAL

Residential work with children and young people is so demanding and exacting that lapses from good practice are bound to occur from time to time, even in the most skilful of staff members. Some of these matter a great deal and some matter less.

Among the not-so-serious lapses are occasional failures to notice something which could contribute to understanding a young person more fully, or occasional failures to take advantage of some opportunity for benefiting a young person that occurs among daily happenings. A member of staff might behave in some less than tactful manner with someone in the world outside the Home. A staff member might fail to follow up on something as quickly as might be desired—not necessarily through error but through the pressure of circumstances. No one can be alert to everything all of the time, or tactful all the time, and no one can be in more than one place at the same time. If lapses of these kind occur it is likely that another opportunity will arise, or that threads which had to be dropped can be picked up later.

More serious errors include basing actions on one's own pain or stress or anger, such that harshness, revenge, or defensiveness creep into behaviour. It is a serious error to fail persistently to note a young person's feelings or concerns, or to misunderstand his or her motives. It is a serious error to behave in down-putting ways towards young people. In short, it is a serious error if a member of staff behaves in some way which makes things worse for a young person, or persistently fails to perceive and use situations arising which could benefit the young person.

Some errors are hard to retrieve. It takes a long time to make up for them. For example, if a member of staff has done something to alienate a parent, it might take some very hard work over a period of time to mend relationships.

Some errors can be retrieved relatively quickly, and if so the overall effect can be positive. For example, suppose that a unit manager made a rule and afterwards realised that it could not be enforced. This is an error, for if such a rule is left to stand, it is a virtual invitation to the young people to break it. If the unit manager realised this, he or she could simply tell the young people that the rule was not a good one but the behaviour it was seeking to influence nevertheless has to be kept in check. He or she might ask their help in working out something better. As another example, suppose that a member of staff has applied an inappropriate sanction perhaps impulsively cancelling a visit to the cinema after an episode of unruliness in the house. As has been argued earlier, such a sanction is inappropriate because (a) it is arbitrarily rather than logically related to the behaviour which led to it, and (b) it demonstrates to the young people that the member of staff is prepared to use his or her superior power against them. To put this right, the staff member might name his or her behaviour as an error and say why, and put in place some alternative response such as talking the episode over and trying to get to the bottom of it, or asking the young people how *they* think the problem could be addressed. As already mentioned, acknowledging a mistake is good practice, in that it is one of the ways in which staff can provide a positive model for young people.

We found, in this research, that lapses from good practice were very often not so much bad practice as unfocused or unthought-out practice. When setting goals, for example, staff members might not clearly distinguish between a goal and a plan, or they might be imprecise in naming or defining a goal, or they might jump into a plan without considering which goal it actually bears on, or even if it bears on a goal at all. Or staff might fail to revise a goal or a plan in the light of changed circumstances. A member of staff might fail to catch a young person's mood or feeling, especially if it has been expressed indirectly or in subtle ways.

It is desirable to avoid errors as much as possible, to maintain good practice for as much of the time as possible, to avoid interrupting good practice, and to avoid placing obstacles in the way of good practice. This is not exclusively the responsibility of a residential staff, for many factors other than staff knowledge, values, attitudes and skills enter into the maintenance, or not, of good practice. The multiplicity of factors which support good practice, or hinder it, are discussed in the next chapter, and a framework is introduced which assists in seeing what can be done to influence a situation towards better practice, more of the time.

13

FACTORS WHICH SUPPORT OR HINDER GOOD PRACTICE

In earlier chapters it became clear from time to time that certain factors were in place which either supported or hindered good practice on the part of staff. For example, members of staff described mature young people who helped them to maintain order in the Home. They also described particular young people who so occupied their time that others were relatively neglected. At times, they referred to rumours about the future of the Home which unsettled both themselves and the young people. They sometimes complained that they were not informed by managers about prospective changes early enough to prepare for them properly. And so on.

In this chapter we draw together what was learned about factors which support or hinder good practice. They thus become more visible than when embedded in discussions of other matters, as in previous chapters.

The first step was to identify factors which helped, or hindered, staff in carrying out good practice. The second step was to decide which factors belonged together, to place them in clusters, and to give each cluster a title. The clusters which emerged were:

(a) Relationships between managers and the staff of Homes
(b) Relationships between residential staff and field social workers
(c) Admission and transfer policies and procedures
(d) Planning and monitoring procedures in place in the SSD, for individual young people
(e) The operation of ground rules and guidelines originating in the larger organisation
(f) Structures and procedures within a Home; interactions within staff groups, and between staff and young people
(g) The mix of young people
(h) The courts
(i) The wider networks

(j)   Staff appointment policies and procedures
(k)   Training.

There were from 2 to 29 items in the various clusters. Items often occur in pairs, since a positive force, which supports good practice, might be related to a negative force which hinders good practice. The number of items in a cluster is not an indication of the importance, or otherwise, of the cluster.

There is a practical reason for wishing to call attention to supportive and hindering factors. To improve and sustain good practice, it is well for practitioners and managers to know which factors support good practice so that these can be nurtured and strengthened. It is also well to know which factors interfere with good practice, so that actions can be taken which remove them or reduce their power. Kurt Lewin's schema, force-field analysis, exactly suits the task of displaying factors which help or hinder moving towards a defined goal, and seeing which actions might be taken to move nearer to a preferred goal.

Force-field Diagrams

Force-field schemas are devices for showing, in graphic form, factors which bear on achieving (or not achieving) nameable goals. They help to grasp, almost at a glance, a complex situation in which many factors may be operating.

Kurt Lewin developed force-field analysis and made use of it in many action research projects. His idea was that a 'field of forces' can be identified, and that the analysis of a social situation in force-field terms can then be put to practical use for effecting change. Force-field analysis and force-field diagrams have been used widely by others. It is relevant to all manner of situations in which a goal can be defined and there is a gap between the current situation and the preferred state represented by the goal. To see Lewin's original presentation of a force-field diagram, see Lewin, (1951, p. 226) and Newcomb and Hartley (1947, pp. 330–344). Our adaptation of this disgram is shown in Figure 3 and in Figures 4a to 4k in this chapter and Figures 5a to 5f in Chapter 14.

The Force-field Schema Shown and Described in General Terms

A generalised force-field diagram—that is, one which does not as yet pertain to any real situation and is in a sense 'empty'—is shown in Figure 3.

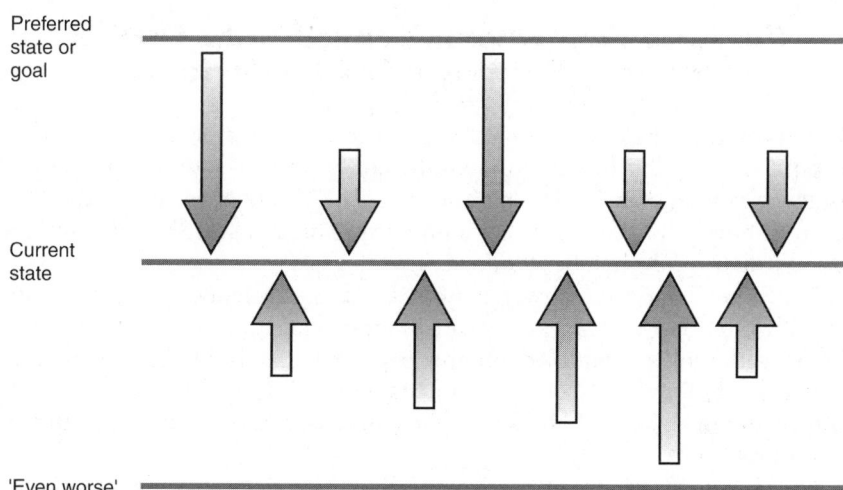

Preferred
state or
goal

Current
state

'Even worse'

Figure 3 A Generalised force-field diagram

In this diagram:

- The top horizontal line represents a preferred state or goal.
- The middle horizontal line represents the current state.
- The bottom horizontal line (which is not always needed) is a reminder that any given situation could be worse than it is now.
- Upward pointing arrows represent forces which press towards achieving the goal. They are *facilitating* or *supportive* or *helping* factors (in Lewin's terms, 'driving' forces).
- Downward pointing arrows represent forces which prevent movement towards the goal. They are *hindering* forces (in Lewin's terms, 'restraining' forces).
- The length or thickness of an arrow indicates its strength.
- The middle line, representing the current state, is never exactly 'still'— it moves up and down in response to fluctuations in the forces in the field—but not very much. The forces which are in place tend to be in some kind of balance even though small changes occur. Lewin pointed out that any current state is in 'quasi-stationary equilibrium'.
- The diagram as a whole is referred to as a 'force field'.

Movement towards the goal occurs if:

- supportive forces can be strengthened or new ones introduced;
- hindering forces can be weakened or removed;
- any new supportive force which is introduced does not trigger a countervailing hindering force.

The Force-field Schema applied to the Goal of Improving Practice in Children's Homes

When the force-field structure is applied to practice as it occurs in Children's Homes, the upper horizontal line, or goal, is defined as 'better practice', the middle horizontal line as 'current state of practice', and the bottom horizontal line as 'poorer practice'. Forces which help or hinder good practice can then be fitted into the diagram.

The nine diagrams shown in Figures 4a–4k are exactly the same in structure as the 'empty' force-field diagram just presented, apart from being differently orientated on the page. Each pertains to one of the clusters listed earlier. Each diagram has inserted into it forces relevant to the cluster which, as this research has shown, either support or hinder good practice.

In reading these diagrams one needs to keep in mind that the three terms 'current practice', 'better practice' and 'poorer practice' are not headings but denote positions within the force field. Arrows pointing towards the right press towards the goal of better practice. They are *facilitating* or *supportive* or *helping* factors. Arrows pointing towards the left work against movement towards the goal of better practice. They are *hindering* factors. Taken together, all of these factors keep practice in its current state. There has been no attempt to make some arrows longer or thicker than others. Anyone applying it to his or her own situation will have to decide which factors do or do not apply, and which are the stronger or the weaker ones. In order to effect change in any given situation, the factors need to be examined with care to judge which can be influenced and which not. A situation will move nearer to the goal of better practice if hindering factors can be weakened or removed, and/or if facilitating factors can be strengthened or new facilitating factors introduced.

Relationships between Managers and the Staff of Homes

Relationships between external managers and the staff of Homes proved to be an important influence on practice (see Figure 4a). Whether relationships helped or hindered good practice often depended on the nature and timing of communication. Decisions affecting staff were typically made unilaterally by middle or top managers. Communication was from the top, down. There were channels for managers to communicate their decisions and guidelines to staff, but, often, effective channels for residential workers to communicate their needs or to share their experiences with external managers were not in place. Residential workers were aware of the negative consequences of this, but managers often were not, since

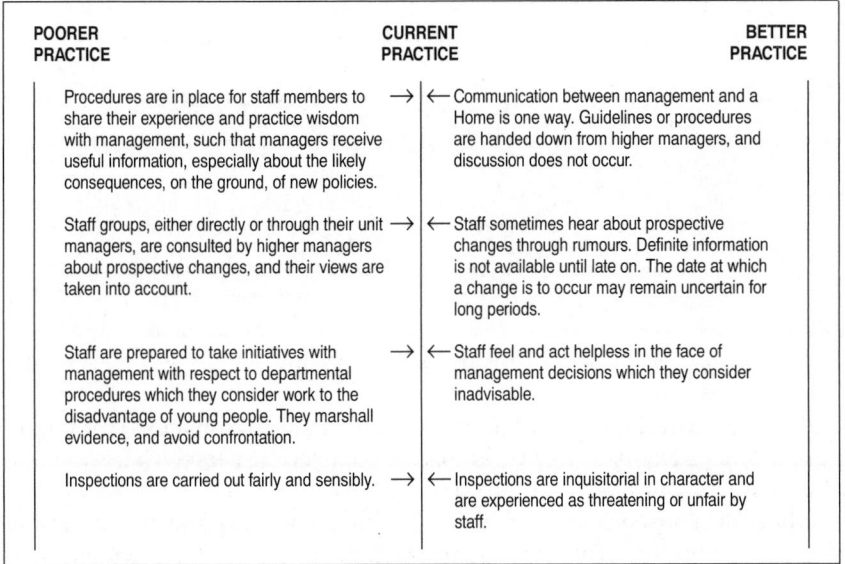

POORER PRACTICE	CURRENT PRACTICE	BETTER PRACTICE
Procedures are in place for staff members to share their experience and practice wisdom with management, such that managers receive useful information, especially about the likely consequences, on the ground, of new policies. →	← Communication between management and a Home is one way. Guidelines or procedures are handed down from higher managers, and discussion does not occur.	
Staff groups, either directly or through their unit managers, are consulted by higher managers about prospective changes, and their views are taken into account. →	← Staff sometimes hear about prospective changes through rumours. Definite information is not available until late on. The date at which a change is to occur may remain uncertain for long periods.	
Staff are prepared to take initiatives with management with respect to departmental procedures which they consider work to the disadvantage of young people. They marshall evidence, and avoid confrontation. →	← Staff feel and act helpless in the face of management decisions which they consider inadvisable.	
Inspections are carried out fairly and sensibly. →	← Inspections are inquisitorial in character and are experienced as threatening or unfair by staff.	

Figure 4a   Relationships between managers and the staff of Homes

they did not know that they were being deprived of useful information concerning likely consequences of new policies they had in mind. The morale of staff members suffered when information about their future came to them through rumour, or the press, rather than directly from their own external managers. Low morale affects practice by reducing energy levels or distracting staff from their primary tasks.

Relationship between Residential Staff and Field Social Workers

Relationships between residential staff and field social workers (Figure 4b) influenced the quality of practice adversely when lines of responsibility and spheres of autonomy were not clearly drawn. Disagreements about preferable courses of action occurred. Residential workers, because of their lower status in the organisation, usually had less say. When there was open and frequent discussion between residential staff and field social workers, clarity as to jurisdiction, and a sense of partnership and of working together, good practice was supported.

Admission and Transfer Policies and Procedures

Admission and transfer policies and procedures (Figure 4c) have an adverse effect on practice if they meet Departmental or administrative needs

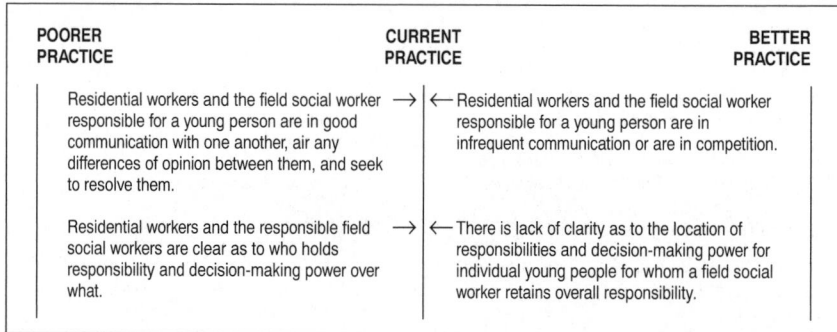

POORER PRACTICE	CURRENT PRACTICE	BETTER PRACTICE
Residential workers and the field social worker responsible for a young person are in good communication with one another, air any differences of opinion between them, and seek to resolve them. $\rightarrow$	$\leftarrow$ Residential workers and the field social worker responsible for a young person are in infrequent communication or are in competition.	
Residential workers and the responsible field social workers are clear as to who holds responsibility and decision-making power over what. $\rightarrow$	$\leftarrow$ There is lack of clarity as to the location of responsibilities and decision-making power for individual young people for whom a field social worker retains overall responsibility.	

Figure 4b   Relationships between residential staff and field social workers

and do not include ways of taking the individual circumstances of young people into account. Practice is also influenced adversely if residential staff, who are familiar with the mix of young people in the Home and can predict the consequences of an admission, have no say in admission decisions. Similarly, practice is influenced adversely if residential staff

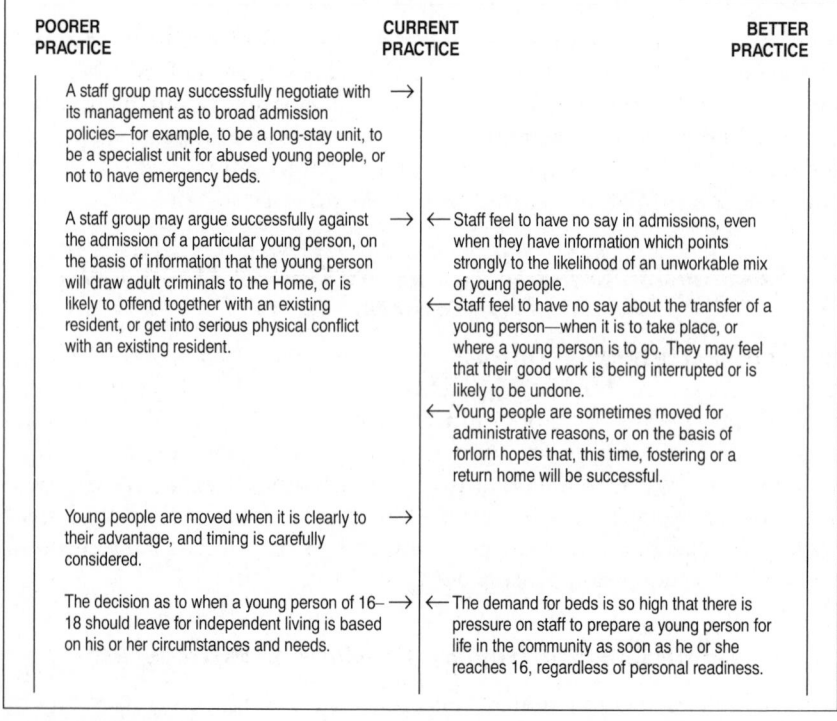

POORER PRACTICE	CURRENT PRACTICE	BETTER PRACTICE
A staff group may successfully negotiate with its management as to broad admission policies—for example, to be a long-stay unit, to be a specialist unit for abused young people, or not to have emergency beds. $\rightarrow$		
A staff group may argue successfully against the admission of a particular young person, on the basis of information that the young person will draw adult criminals to the Home, or is likely to offend together with an existing resident, or get into serious physical conflict with an existing resident. $\rightarrow$	$\leftarrow$ Staff feel to have no say in admissions, even when they have information which points strongly to the likelihood of an unworkable mix of young people. $\leftarrow$ Staff feel to have no say about the transfer of a young person—when it is to take place, or where a young person is to go. They may feel that their good work is being interrupted or is likely to be undone. $\leftarrow$ Young people are sometimes moved for administrative reasons, or on the basis of forlorn hopes that, this time, fostering or a return home will be successful.	
Young people are moved when it is clearly to their advantage, and timing is carefully considered. $\rightarrow$		
The decision as to when a young person of 16–18 should leave for independent living is based on his or her circumstances and needs. $\rightarrow$	$\leftarrow$ The demand for beds is so high that there is pressure on staff to prepare a young person for life in the community as soon as he or she reaches 16, regardless of personal readiness.	

Figure 4c   Admission and transfer policies and procedures

have no say in transfers and the timing of transfers, since they are in close touch with work currently being done with a young person, and will know if a transfer is, or is not, in the young person's best interests.

Planning and Monitoring Procedures in Place in the SSD for Individual Young People

Planning and monitoring procedures, with respect to individual young people living in Children's Homes, importantly affects the quality of practice (Figure 4d). Typical structures are care plans and review meetings—the latter attended by field social workers, residential workers, others concerned with a young person, and, often, a parent and the young person himself or herself. The effectiveness of these structures depends on whether they are actually used, and how they work out in practice. Much depends on such matters as whether all those with an interest in a young person have a chance to express their opinions, whether conflict and tension levels within group meetings can be managed, and the like.

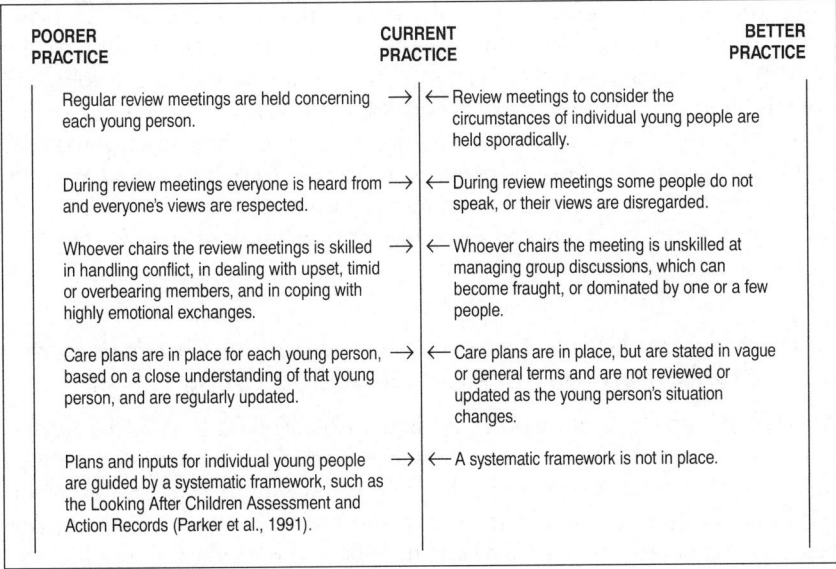

POORER PRACTICE	CURRENT PRACTICE	BETTER PRACTICE
Regular review meetings are held concerning each young person. →	← Review meetings to consider the circumstances of individual young people are held sporadically.	
During review meetings everyone is heard from and everyone's views are respected. →	← During review meetings some people do not speak, or their views are disregarded.	
Whoever chairs the review meetings is skilled in handling conflict, in dealing with upset, timid or overbearing members, and in coping with highly emotional exchanges. →	← Whoever chairs the meeting is unskilled at managing group discussions, which can become fraught, or dominated by one or a few people.	
Care plans are in place for each young person, based on a close understanding of that young person, and are regularly updated. →	← Care plans are in place, but are stated in vague or general terms and are not reviewed or updated as the young person's situation changes.	
Plans and inputs for individual young people are guided by a systematic framework, such as the Looking After Children Assessment and Action Records (Parker et al., 1991). →	← A systematic framework is not in place.	

Figure 4d Planning and monitoring procedures in place in the SSD for individual young people

The Operation of Ground Rules and Guidelines Originating in the Larger Organisations

In England and Wales, Social Services Departments have sought to make operational, in their own organisations, provisions of the Children Act

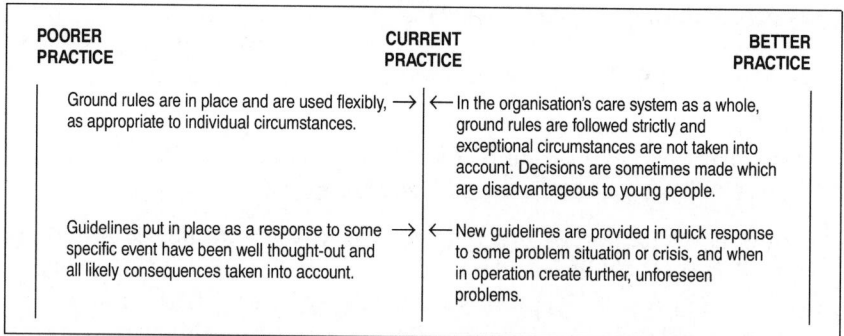

POORER PRACTICE	CURRENT PRACTICE	BETTER PRACTICE
Ground rules are in place and are used flexibly, → as appropriate to individual circumstances.	← In the organisation's care system as a whole, ground rules are followed strictly and exceptional circumstances are not taken into account. Decisions are sometimes made which are disadvantageous to young people.	
Guidelines put in place as a response to some → specific event have been well thought-out and all likely consequences taken into account.	← New guidelines are provided in quick response to some problem situation or crisis, and when in operation create further, unforeseen problems.	

Figure 4e   The operation of ground rules and guidelines originating in the larger organisation

1989. Typically, they do this by devising ground rules and guidelines to be followed by staff groups in Children's Homes and those responsible for placing children and young people (Figure 4e). These support good practice in the majority of instances, but exceptions occur. Sometimes, close knowledge of a child and his or her circumstances indicates that adherence to the rule is not in the child's best interests. It follows that good practice is supported if ground rules and guidelines are followed flexibly. Some guidelines apply to all the Children's Homes for which a Social Services Department is responsible. Some apply to particular Homes and have been put in place as a solution to some particular problem or crisis. The latter can work against good practice if the full consequences, some of them negative, have not been considered—in other words, if solving one problem causes another.

Structures and Procedures within a Home; Interactions with Staff Groups and between Staff and Young People

All staff groups operate to certain structures, procedures, and routines which are internal to the Home or meant to be followed when on outings (Figure 4f). Some of these are prescribed by external managers higher up in the Departmental hierarchy, and were discussed under the previous heading. Some are devised by staff members themselves. Some are formally stated while others evolve informally. Many structures and procedures support good practice, for example, by providing young people with a sense of security, orderliness, and regularity, by showing respect for young people and helping them to develop competences, or by ensuring planning time and opportunities for members of staff to communicate with one another. Very rigid adherence to procedures and routines meant to maintain order can lead to poor practice. Practice is better

POORER PRACTICE	CURRENT PRACTICE	BETTER PRACTICE
The unit manager works with his or her staff, is steady and reliable, and is prepared to be the person of last resort. →	← The unit manager is anxious, overbearing or judgemental.	
Staff have time to discuss general issues bearing on their work and do not concentrate only on housekeeping decisions; there are opportunities to learn from own experience. →	← Staff are continuouosly pressed for time, and manage only to discuss that which has to do with the day-to-day running of the Home.	
There is a full or nearly full complement of staff, and the staff group is relatively stable. →	← Staff shortages are such that there is much reliance on relief staff or overtime, with consequent poor continuity of care, or fatigue.	
In addition to dealing with whatever emergencies or crises a shift brings, staff have time to plan ahead, for example, for review meetings, holidays, birthday celebrations. →	Staff lack time: one or more young people who are excluded from school and are in the home all day make extra demands on staff, and ← deprive staff of time for discussion or paperwork. Staff members are faced with particularly difficult or stress-inducing situations, and are drained of energy. Some members of staff may be on sick leave because of stress.	
Structures and procedures are in place within a Home which provide opportunities for staff to talk together to develop and update their understanding of individual young people and of relationships and behaviours among groups of young people. →		
Staff have adequate time during a working shift to complete paper-work. →	← In order to conform to a Department's requirements for record-keeping, members of staff sometimes have to work far into the night.	
When working out rotas, care is taken to place new, inexperienced staff with more experienced staff. →	← The rota is such that two inexperienced staff members may be on duty together.	
Staff have structures in place for meeting with the young people: to plan, share views, hear and deal with complaints before they build up. →	← Some young people are wise to the power they have over members of staff through making, or threatening to make, allegations.	
	← Staff and young people are in an adversarial relationship with one another. Young people attack staff and are outside staff control.	
Staff have procedures in place for informing those starting a shift of significant events which have occurred in their absence. →	← Communication from one shift to the next is haphazard.	
A key worker or link worker system is in place, and in addition everyone understands what a young person needs and what goals are being worked towards, so anyone who is at hand can interact appropriately with a young person. →	← Members of staff work at cross purposes, in consequence of poor communications or unresolved differences of opinion.	

Figure 4f Structures and procedures within a Home; interactions within staff groups, and between staff and young people (*continues overleaf*)

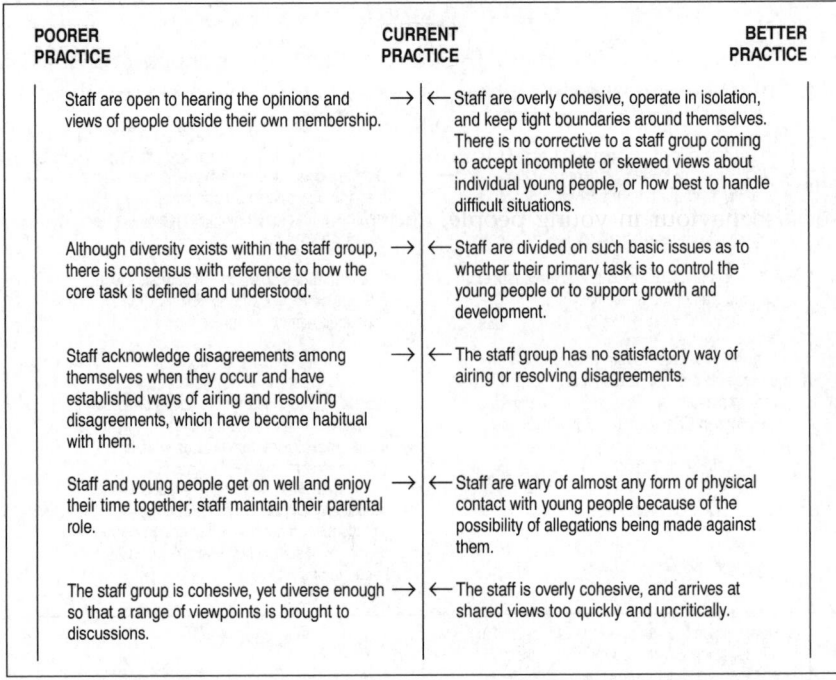

POORER PRACTICE	CURRENT PRACTICE	BETTER PRACTICE
Staff are open to hearing the opinions and views of people outside their own membership. →	← Staff are overly cohesive, operate in isolation, and keep tight boundaries around themselves. There is no corrective to a staff group coming to accept incomplete or skewed views about individual young people, or how best to handle difficult situations.	
Although diversity exists within the staff group, there is consensus with reference to how the core task is defined and understood. →	← Staff are divided on such basic issues as to whether their primary task is to control the young people or to support growth and development.	
Staff acknowledge disagreements among themselves when they occur and have established ways of airing and resolving disagreements, which have become habitual with them. →	← The staff group has no satisfactory way of airing or resolving disagreements.	
Staff and young people get on well and enjoy their time together; staff maintain their parental role. →	← Staff are wary of almost any form of physical contact with young people because of the possibility of allegations being made against them.	
The staff group is cohesive, yet diverse enough so that a range of viewpoints is brought to discussions. →	← The staff is overly cohesive, and arrives at shared views too quickly and uncritically.	

Figure 4f   *(continued)*

if the circumstances which suggest that routines or rules should be relaxed are taken into account. Sometimes a structure which ought to be in place is not—for example, regular staff meetings in which views on basic care issues can be discussed. Sometimes a structure is in place but is not used, usually because staff are overpressed or overstressed.

If staff members do not have sufficient time to communicate, about both immediate and broader issues, practice will suffer. Unresolvable conflict within a staff group impairs the quality of practice. Good practice is supported if staff groups have established means for airing and resolving disagreements.

Good practice is supported by amicable relationships between staff and young people, and if staff maintain their parental role without being overbearing.

The Mix of Young People

Some mixes of young people are a recipe for explosive situations (Figure 4g). Chaotic conditions inside and around the Home interfere with staff efforts to create security and orderliness. Good practice is supported if new admissions do not occur in rapid succession within a short space of time.

The Courts

Sometimes decisions are made by courts which from the point of view of staff interfere with good practice (Figure 4h). This is particularly the case if there are long delays in a court making a decision, or if a young person is 'let off' and returned to the Home, where he or she boasts of having 'got away with it'. This undermines staff efforts to encourage satisfactory social behaviour in young people, and may influence young people towards further offending.

The Wider Networks

Good practice is facilitated if a staff group can rely on the accessibility, cooperation, and understanding of the police, schools, the Health Service, and other outside people and organisations with whom they must interact on behalf of young people (Figure 4i). A school's power to exclude young people means that staff may not be able to meet their responsibility

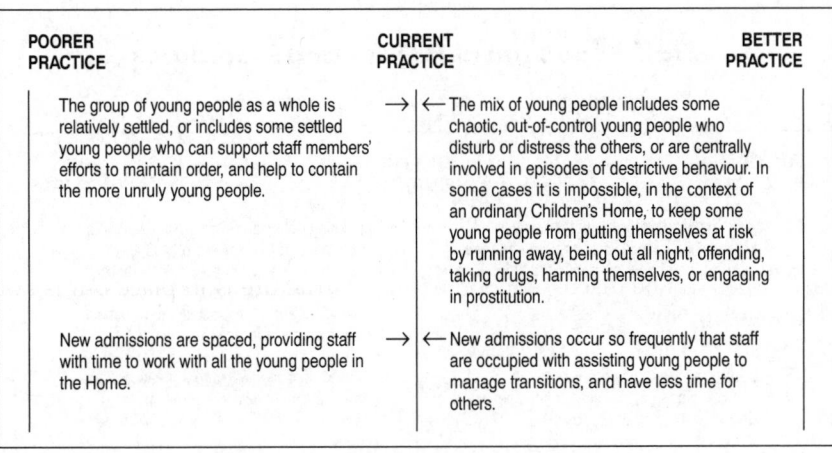

POORER PRACTICE	CURRENT PRACTICE	BETTER PRACTICE
The group of young people as a whole is relatively settled, or includes some settled young people who can support staff members' efforts to maintain order, and help to contain the more unruly young people. →	← The mix of young people includes some chaotic, out-of-control young people who disturb or distress the others, or are centrally involved in episodes of destructive behaviour. In some cases it is impossible, in the context of an ordinary Children's Home, to keep some young people from putting themselves at risk by running away, being out all night, offending, taking drugs, harming themselves, or engaging in prostitution.	
New admissions are spaced, providing staff with time to work with all the young people in the Home. →	← New admissions occur so frequently that staff are occupied with assisting young people to manage transitions, and have less time for others.	

Figure 4g   The mix of young people

POORER PRACTICE	CURRENT PRACTICE	BETTER PRACTICE
Decisions made by courts sometimes lead to a → young person being moved elsewhere. If the young person has been particularly disruptive, staff members feel that this is appropriate and benefits all concerned.	← Decisions made by courts sometimes lead young people to feel that they have got away with something: in consequence they become less responsive to staff members' efforts to lead them away from offending.	

Figure 4h   The courts

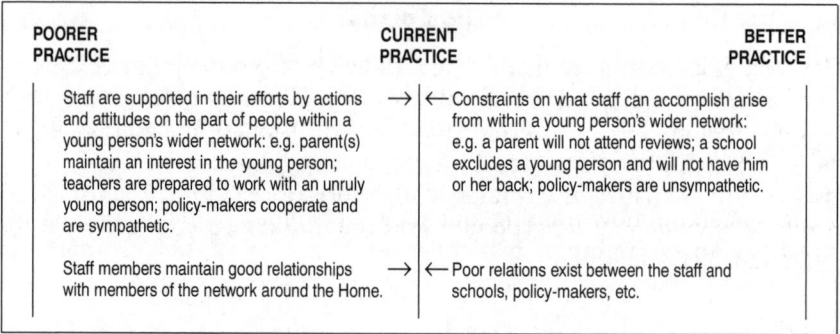

Figure 4i   The wider network

to support young people's education and continuity of education, and also means that time must be spent during the day with excluded young people, at the expense of doing other forms of work. Problems arising within a young person's family and personal network can interfere with staff efforts.

Staff Appointment Policies and Procedures

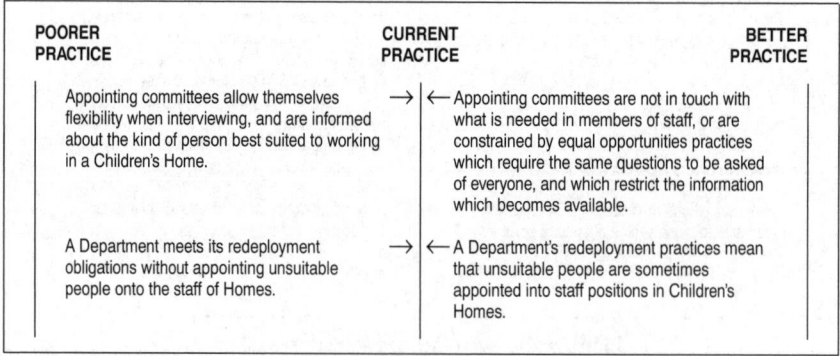

Figure 4j   Staff appointment policies and procedures

Good practice is assisted if appointing committees operate to well thought-out procedures based on a good understanding of what makes for a good or promising staff member (Figure 4j). Conversely, a committee may not fully appreciate the demands made on residential care workers and the kind of person therefore best suited to provide care for young people. An appointing committee may be required by management to follow strict interviewing procedures which deprive it of relevant information. Redeployment policies may lead to the appointment of an unsuitable person into a care post. Any such deficiencies might lead to poor appointments being made. Practice then suffers.

Training and Supervision

Figure 4k shows how training and supervision may help or hinder good practice. An organisation may release a member of staff to attend a qualifying course, whether full time or part time, and pay his or her fees.

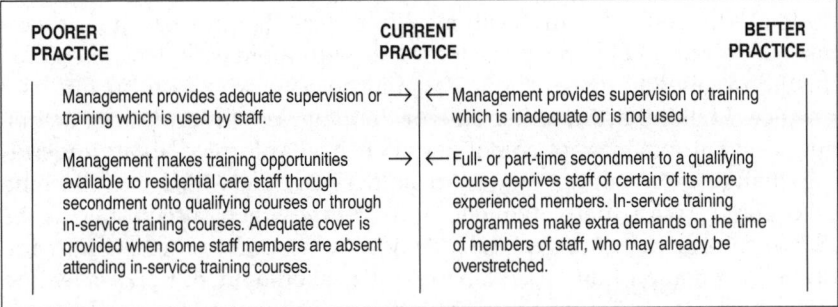

Figure 4k   Training and supervision

Seconding one member of staff onto a qualifying course of two years' duration may support good practice in the long run but can cause problems in the short run if the Home becomes short-staffed in consequence, or must make do with relief staff or inexperienced staff. In-service training opportunities may facilitate good practice but tend to increase workloads. Opportunities for supervision and consultation support good practice but will be less effective if provided infrequently, or only with respect to emergency situations, after the fact.

THE MULTIPLICITY OF FACTORS WHICH SUPPORT OR HINDER GOOD PRACTICE

These nine force-field diagrams need to be looked at together. It is evident that an array of factors support or hinder good practice. Some are located within a staff group, but some are not. Not all of them are under the control of staff. It follows from this that responsibility for bringing about good practice lies within a staff group, in the larger organisation, and in wider networks. This point is fundamental to seeing which changes might be made in order to improve practice, and by whom.

INTERVENING IN A FORCE FIELD IN ORDER TO MOVE NEARER TO A GOAL

In moving nearer to a goal—in this case, improved practice or the maintenance of satisfactory practice the strategy is to strengthen factors which support good practice or introduce new ones; and/or to weaken or eliminate factors which hinder or interfere with good practice.

For example, looking at supportive factors calls attention to the advantages of a young person's key or link worker being in good touch and communication with his or her field social worker. If this is not already the case, or if practice is haphazard in this respect, it would be helpful to try to assure better communication. When working out rotas, it is advantageous to place new, inexperienced staff with more experienced staff. If this is not already being done, it would be helpful to introduce it as a practice. Looking at the other side of the diagram, to hindering factors, one sees that if managers do not keep staff well informed about impending changes, but allow rumour to hold sway, then staff may become preoccupied with their own fate and at times their attention may be diverted from the young people. Action is indicated which would improve information flow. If a Department's redeployment policies lead to the appointment of inappropriate staff into Children's Homes, then it is clear that the policy needs to be re-examined and modified.

Every force in Figures 4a to 4k can be examined to see if it applies to particular circumstances and if it can be influenced.

It is possible that a force meant to assist in achieving the goal generates a counter-force which nullifies the effort. For example, an internal inspection system is almost always in place and is intended to detect bad practice and support good practice. If well conducted, it is a helping force. But if inspectors are experienced by staff as inquisitorial or an indication of management's distrust of them, countervailing hindering forces might well be triggered. Staff members who feel that they are under threat may close ranks and share *less* of their experiences with management. Good intentions attached to the system are undone because insufficient attention has been given to the possibility of unanticipated counter-forces appearing in the force field, which hinder good practice. It is for this reason that Lewin warned that it is well to be cautious about introducing new helping forces without trying to anticipate their full consequences.

It becomes clear that many different people can potentially take actions likely to improve child care practice. Each will have the power to influence some forces and not others. It is likely that some forces can be influenced quite easily and within a short period of time, while others may take longer, involving many sub-steps.

It is possible to take any force appearing as a helping or a hindering factor and create a new force-field diagram. What appeared as a force in the first diagram is inserted in a new diagram as the current situation which needs to shift towards some more preferred situation. Both the current situation and the goal relating to it can be specified. For example, suppose that someone wants to weaken the helping force, 'there is lack of clarity about the location of responsibility and decision-making between residential staff and field social workers'. This could be put in a new force-field diagram as the middle line, naming a current state. The preferred state would be something like 'increase clarity with respect to responsibility and decision-making power'. One would then insert into the force-field diagram all supportive and hindering forces believed to be in place. These would then be examined to see which could be influenced so as to shift towards the goal.

A force-field diagram can contain a huge number of factors. Decisions have to be made as to which should be made the special focus of a new force field. Usually, one does not need to move through more than three or four successive force-field formulations before reaching a fuller understanding of a situation which previously may have seemed mysterious or intractable.

How does one know which forces to insert into a force-field diagram? The researchers identified supportive and hindering forces through a form of research which paid close attention to what staff said about their work and to the examples of practice they provided. Tapping into experience is the essential part. This could be done by a consultant as well as by researchers.

If a start is made *somewhere* within a force field, if some action is undertaken and the consequences noted, and if further thinking is done about forces which seem particularly important, then change is not impossible. One should not, however, make it sound too easy. Sometimes actions are undertaken which are suggested by a force-field analysis, which then reveal further factors which are virtually impossible to influence. This is not necessarily a setback. It is helpful to differentiate the truly intractable from the apparently intractable because this prevents the repetition of efforts which are bound to be futile. Sometimes work on one aspect of a force field reveals that a hindering factor is in place which no one was aware of. This, too, can feel like a setback but it need not be, since it contributes to a fuller understanding of the situation, and can suggest actions not considered before.

MAKING PRACTICAL USE OF A FORCE-FIELD ANALYSIS

The practical uses to which a force-field diagram can be put will already be evident. In a Dissemination Day for those organisations who participated in Study 2, people were invited who were concerned with child care and functioned in different parts and levels of the organisation—residential workers, field social workers, external line-managers, higher managers, training officers, and councillors. The force-field diagram was presented and opportunities to discuss it were provided. Those who attended were invited to identify those factors which they judged to be present and operative in their own organisations, and then to discuss changes which might be made.

It needs to be emphasised that *all* that was shown by the research to help or hinder good practice was put into the force-field diagrams. The diagrams thus were a conglomerated depiction of forces. Particular forces might, but might not, be present in any specific situation, and some might be more salient and powerful than others. Those actually working for an organisation are best placed to know which are operative and important in their own Homes and their own organisation and it is they who need to examine the diagrams with their own experience in mind. In applying force-field diagrams to their own situation, we do not recommend that they be used utterly systematically. This would take too long and be too laborious. When a force field is scanned with a specific Home or a specific situation in mind, certain forces are bound to stand out as more significant than others. That points to the place to start.

A REMAINING QUESTION

The point of there being good practice is to increase the likelihood of good outcomes for young people. The point of this chapter has been to identify factors which support or get in the way of good practice, so that actions can be taken to improve and maintain good practice. There remains a crucial question: *If all supportive factors were in place and practice was consistently good, would outcomes for individual young people also be good?* This issue is addressed in the next chapter.

14

FACTORS WHICH INFLUENCE OUTCOMES FOR INDIVIDUAL YOUNG PEOPLE

All concerned with the out-of-home care of children and young people hope that they will enjoy the best possible life while they are being looked after in residential or foster care. All concerned hope for the best possible outcomes for them. Good practice is regarded as important because it contributes to a good quality of life in current circumstances, as well as to good longer-term outcomes. This chapter examines the connections between good practice and good outcomes, and asks: What further factors influence outcomes?

HOW STAFF MEMBERS THINK ABOUT OUTCOMES

As staff members get to know the young people living in the Home, they develop views as to what would constitute a good outcome for each of them. What staff think would be a good outcome for Terry will be different from what they consider to be a good outcome for Kelly, and this will be different again from their ideas about a good outcome for Samantha. Thinking about what would constitute a good outcome *while the work is going on* is much the same as defining goals. The outcome has not yet occurred but it can be imagined: it is a hoped-for future state.

Hoped-for outcomes are conceptualised differently for different young people because each young person is in a different state when he or she enters the Home. The issues that need to be worked on or towards are therefore also different. For a young person who has been out of school for many months, a hoped-for outcome might well be regular school attendance and progress at school. If a girl enters the Home in an acute state of distress over having been abandoned recently by her mother, the longer-term hoped-for outcome might be to restore the family unit, or if this proves impossible, to help her to come to terms with her new situation and find ways forward. A shorter-term hoped-for outcome would be to help the young person to deal with current distress. If a young boy, on point of entry, shows poor control over rage and anger and frequently attacks others, a good outcome in his case would be better control over his behaviour and more amiable relationships with peers.

There always comes a time when staff take stock and judge whether a hoped-for outcome has been achieved or not. One such time is the point at which young people leave the Home or are about to leave the Home. It is then that 'point-of-departure' outcomes are evaluated. Staff members also form judgements at different points during a young person's stay, in connection with goals they have set, or their hopes and aspirations. We have called the latter 'way-station' outcomes.

What staff hope and look for in 'way-station' outcomes include such achievements as 'getting back into school'; 'getting back on an even keel after a suicide attempt'; 'spending a weekend at home without violence occurring'; 'thinking through what to do after learning that she is pregnant'. Outcomes such as these are marked by easily observable events: a young person is back at school, or not, or has spent a weekend at home with or without getting into another violent encounter with a parent.

Some shorter-term 'way-station' outcomes are less easy to specify and less easy to observe. More judgement enters in. Sometimes something does not happen, which staff expected to happen on the basis of past experience with a particular young person. For example, staff noted, after the fact, that a young person 'has resisted being drawn into truanting by two new admissions who scorn school and do not attend'. This is a positive outcome even though it consisted of something which has not happened. The staff knew that the young person was at a knife-edge with respect to school attendance and vulnerable to being influenced into truanting.

Sometimes staff judgements of an outcome are based on registering a number of small indications of the state of a young person's feelings or attitudes rather than noting some particular, easily observable event. For example, staff might judge that a young person is 'happy about a prospective move into fostering, having previously dreaded it', or 'is more settled and less agitated'. Sometimes staff cannot be absolutely certain that something positive has occurred—for example, they might say that a young person 'has apparently recovered from the disappointment occasioned by mother cancelling a visit'.

Young people leave the Home either for independent living or transfer to another placement or to return to their own homes. At the time of a young person leaving, staff tend not only to compare the young person's current state with some earlier state, but also develop a point of view as to whether any gains were consolidated or not. We have described outcomes judged at such times 'point of transfer or departure outcomes'.

With respect to some young people who were moving into independent or semi-independent living, staff felt that substantial gains had been achieved, and they felt confident that the young person had 'turned the corner' or was 'on the right road'. They judged that gains had been consolidated, and that, unless something untoward happened, the young person was in a good position to continue to make gains. With respect to other young people, staff remained uncertain ('he still could go either way') or else were convinced that the move to independent living was premature.

When a younger child or young person left, either to return home or to go to another placement, staff members could often name gains and feel confident that the young person was ready for the move and that everything possible had been done to prepare him or her for it. They considered that gains achieved while in their care had been consolidated and would accompany the young person into his or her next life context. At other times, staff members were convinced that the move was premature and the timing wrong, and that while some gains had been achieved more could have been done had they had more time. Sometimes staff mourned the departure of a child. Someone would comment sadly, 'We could have worked with him'; or, 'It was the worst possible time to move her'. If the move was back to the child's own home, staff might feel happy because a reconciliation had been effected and pleased with the part they had played in it. If a young person had left home in an adolescent tiff and had requested being taken into care, staff members might have felt that placement in residential care (or any kind of care) had been inappropriate in the first place, and were glad to see the young person return home to parents who had not wanted him or her to leave. With respect to other young people, staff members might feel that a young person's own home was the worst place for him or her to be. This was because of the danger of further abuse, or because the family situation was such that further offending or further disorderly behaviour in the community was likely to occur. There were also occasions when young people left a Children's Home because the residential staff group and others felt that the Home could not help or contain them. In such situations staff members often felt and said that no real gain had been achieved. They might feel that a good outcome was unlikely, unless the new setting could provide special help.

From what we have heard and seen, we know that staff members are cautious about forming opinions about longer-term outcomes. Staff often did not know and did not find out if the predictions they made at the point of young person's departure from the Home were borne out by subsequent events, or not. Occasionally, information came their way. In one case, a unit manager reported meeting a young man in the street who had been in their care some years previously. He was with his wife and young child, and told the unit manager, 'You did well by me'. The unit manager had not been at all sure that this young person, at the point when he had left them, had been sufficiently helped for her to be confident about his future. As things turned out, he had either been sufficiently helped, or lucky, or both. Now and then several, or particular members, of the staff were still in touch with a young person and were pleased with how things were going ('She has got a job'; 'He is in the navy'), or else very concerned indeed. In one case, where a boy was serving a custodial sentence, the unit manager was much concerned because the boy was being persecuted by his current companions (he had committed a sexual offence against younger children) and, in her opinion, was deteriorating. In this case, the boy wrote to the unit manager almost daily, and she was his only life-line.

No one can predict the future, and no outcome is 'final'. Staff members know this. They are happy if a young person shows gains which appear to be well established, and seems to be on a good track and able to continue along it. The following illustrate the kinds of outcomes which satisfy staff:

- A young person whose relationship with his parents had broken down is now on good terms with them and is looking forward to returning home.
- A young person who was approaching care-leaving age and was fearful of leaving care, was helped with her anxieties and is now living comfortably with an older sibling.
- A young person who was fearful of going to school and had little confidence in his ability to do well, now attends regularly and takes pleasure in his accomplishments.
- A young person, now 16, who was on drugs four years ago and entered care on that account, is off drugs and is looking forward to living on her own with the support of her mother and sister, who have retained interest in her. She is confident of the future, and staff feel that she is likely to maintain her gains.
- A young person who had committed a number of offences and was a school refuser, has not committed any offence for the past eight months and regularly attends school.

In summary: when residential staff think about outcomes, they think in terms of particular young people, and outcomes are judged in terms of that young person's previous state. Outcomes are likely to be judged at particular points in the course of ongoing work with a young person ('way-station' outcomes) and also at the point when the young person leaves the Home ('point of transfer or departure' outcomes). Staff are cautious about predicting longer-term outcomes, but do feel more confident or less confident as to whether gains have been consolidated and are likely to persist.

Definitions of Good, Poor, and Uncertain Outcomes for Individual Children

- An outcome can be said to be good if a young person has moved beyond his or her previous state in a desirable or positive direction, if he or she appears to have stabilised in the new state, and (if applicable) if he or she is ready for an impending move out of the Home.
- An outcome can be said to be poor if a young person has shown no progress or improvement compared with his or her previous state, or is worse off than before, and/or is not ready for an impending transition.
- An outcome can be said to be uncertain, even if some progress has been made, if those who know the child judge that gains have not been consolidated and if the young person is considered still to be in a vulnerable state.

These definitions can contain outcomes related to such different areas as health, schooling, relationships with parents, offending, and so on, since any of these could appear as aspects of the previous unsatisfactory state, and of the current state.

FACTORS WHICH SUPPORT OR HINDER YOUNG PEOPLE MOVING TOWARDS GOOD OUTCOMES

Having provided a definition of a good outcome, it becomes possible to return to the question posed at the beginning of this chapter: What is the connection between good practice and good outcomes, and what further factors influence outcomes?

Again, information contained in accounts of situations encountered in practice and derived from observations will be drawn upon. The 40 or so more general comments made by unit managers when interviewed for Study 1 are also relevant. As in the previous chapter, the many factors so identified fell into clusters. These are:

(a) The state of a young person's family and personal network
(b) A young person's personal characteristics
(c) The state of a young person's peer group and the young person's position in it

(d) A young person's current lifestyle
(e) A young person's care career: past, recent past, and current
(f) The state of the Home and a young person's relationship with staff
(g) The quality of practice.

In presenting what was learned about factors influencing good or poor outcomes, we will again make use of a series of force-field diagrams (Figures 5a to 5g), one for each of the seven clusters.

The State of a Young Person's Family and Personal Network

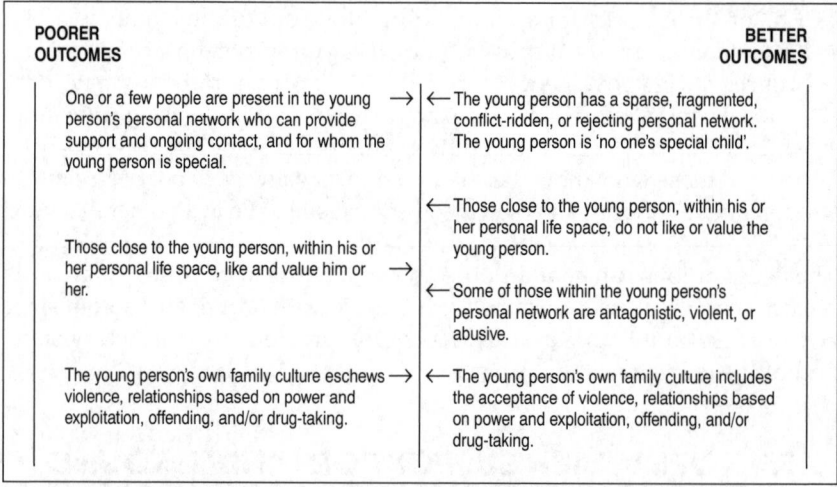

POORER OUTCOMES	BETTER OUTCOMES
One or a few people are present in the young person's personal network who can provide support and ongoing contact, and for whom the young person is special. →	←The young person has a sparse, fragmented, conflict-ridden, or rejecting personal network. The young person is 'no one's special child'.
	←Those close to the young person, within his or her personal life space, do not like or value the young person.
Those close to the young person, within his or her personal life space, like and value him or her. →	←Some of those within the young person's personal network are antagonistic, violent, or abusive.
The young person's own family culture eschews → violence, relationships based on power and exploitation, offending, and/or drug-taking.	←The young person's own family culture includes the acceptance of violence, relationships based on power and exploitation, offending, and/or drug-taking.

Figure 5a The state of a young person's family and personal network

The force-field shown in Figure 5a emphasises that good outcomes depend in part on the nature of support available to the young person in his or her family and personal network, and the 'healthiness' or 'noxiousness' of that personal network. If there are strengths within the family or the personal network, they will support a staff group's efforts on behalf of the young person, and there will be real possibilities for partnership work with parents and others. Further, when a young person leaves the Children's Home to return home or for independent living, the network will be in place to support him or her through the transition.

A Young Person's Personal Characteristics

Personal characteristics (Figure 5b) may be such as to support staff's helping efforts or to undermine them. 'Personal characteristics' are not

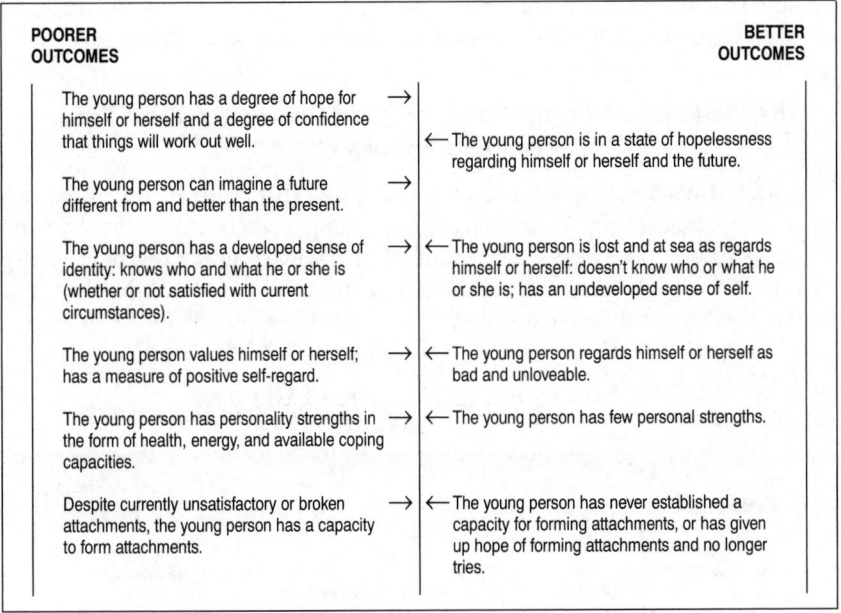

Figure 5b A young person's personal characteristics

quite the same as a young person's developmental stage at the point of entering the Home. The example was provided earlier of an 8-year-old who 'behaved like an 18-month-old'. That child was developmentally halted due to extremely disadvantageous previous life circumstances, but

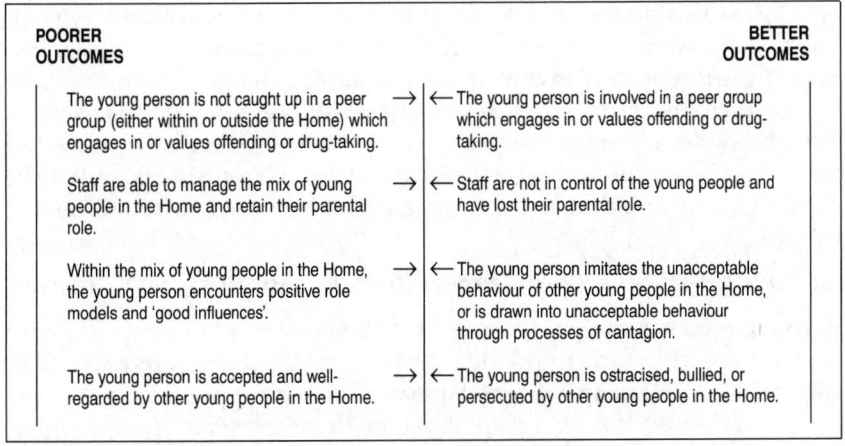

Figure 5c The state of the young person's peer group, and the young person's position in it

he nevertheless had the personal capacity to respond to staff efforts, and relatively quickly achieved life skills more in keeping with his age.

The State of a Young Person's Peer Group, and the Young Person's Position in it

That the state of the peer group has a powerful bearing on outcomes needs no elaboration. A noxious peer group which exists outside the Home is likely to be outside the control of the staff, while the peer group inside the Home is something the staff group works with all the time and is in a position to influence.

A Young Person's Current Lifestyle

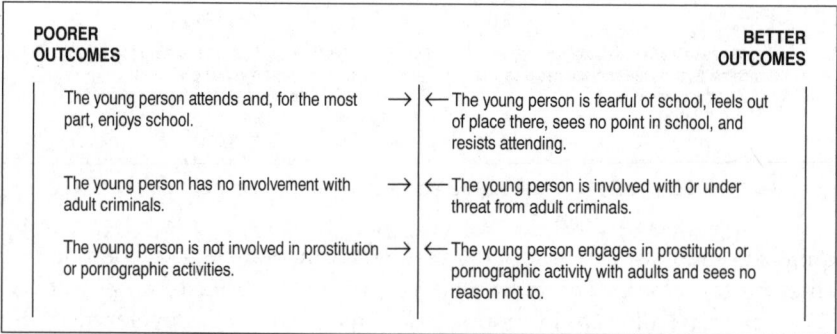

POORER OUTCOMES		BETTER OUTCOMES
The young person attends and, for the most part, enjoys school.	→ ←	The young person is fearful of school, feels out of place there, sees no point in school, and resists attending.
The young person has no involvement with adult criminals.	→ ←	The young person is involved with or under threat from adult criminals.
The young person is not involved in prostitution or pornographic activities.	→ ←	The young person engages in prostitution or pornographic activity with adults and sees no reason not to.

Figure 5d   A young person's current lifestyle

An already established disadvantageous lifestyle much reduces the likelihood of a good outcome (Figure 5d). Some young people are fixed into a life of prostitution or of involvement with adult criminals which pre-dates admission to the Home. Attachment to such lifestyles can be very hard to influence if, for example, the young person clearly prefers it to any alternative, or if powerful forces—outside the Home and outside the influence of the staff—are holding the young person in his or her current lifestyle.

A Young Person's Care Career: Past, Recent Past, and Current

A young person's care career may place him or her in a poor position to respond to staff efforts to provide care or help. Frequent moves while in substitute care work against good outcomes. A young person may protect himself or herself from the pain of yet another separation from carers or yet another experience of personal failure by maintaining a distance from those who could potentially help them. One sometimes sees a

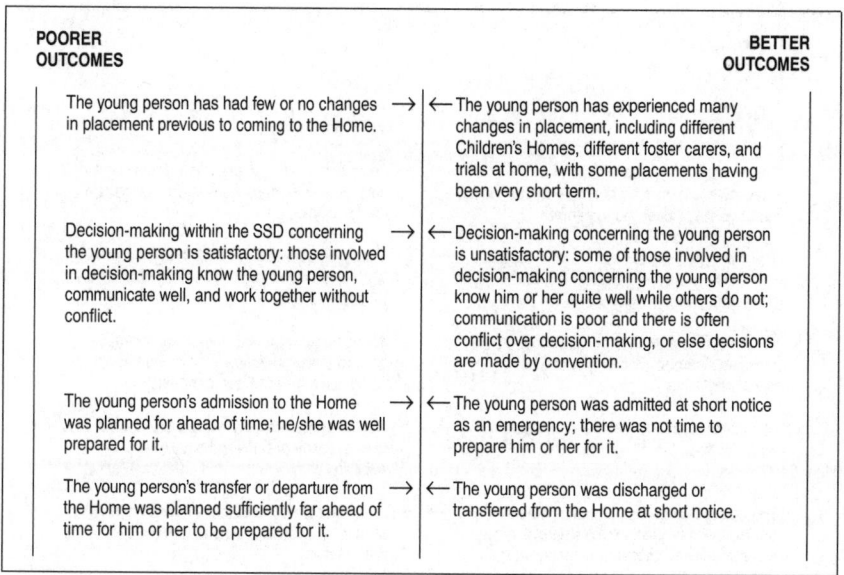

POORER OUTCOMES	BETTER OUTCOMES
The young person has had few or no changes in placement previous to coming to the Home. →	← The young person has experienced many changes in placement, including different Children's Homes, different foster carers, and trials at home, with some placements having been very short term.
Decision-making within the SSD concerning the young person is satisfactory: those involved in decision-making know the young person, communicate well, and work together without conflict. →	← Decision-making concerning the young person is unsatisfactory: some of those involved in decision-making concerning the young person know him or her quite well while others do not; communication is poor and there is often conflict over decision-making, or else decisions are made by convention.
The young person's admission to the Home was planned for ahead of time; he/she was well prepared for it. →	← The young person was admitted at short notice as an emergency; there was not time to prepare him or her for it.
The young person's transfer or departure from the Home was planned sufficiently far ahead of time for him or her to be prepared for it. →	← The young person was discharged or transferred from the Home at short notice.

Figure 5e A young person's care career: past, recent past, and current

disadvantageous care career continuing right up to the present, if yet more changes in placement occur, without adequate reason or preparation.

The State of the Home and a Young Person's Relationship with Staff

The state of the Home has an impact on outcomes for young people generally. If the atmosphere is tense or chaotic, it can be hard for any individual young person to settle down or escape being drawn into unacceptable behaviour. Young people who enter the Home and stay for very short periods before moving on are sometimes the centre for disturbances. They may draw others into imitative behaviour, or, at the least, distract staff from the work they have been doing with the young people already resident. Children and young people admitted for short periods of 'respite care' can have the same effect. Different young people may form quite different relationships with staff or particular members of staff. When mutual regard and respect are present, positive experiences and good outcomes are more likely. Good outcomes are also supported if staff and the young person are working towards the same goals on behalf of the young person. Poorer outcomes are associated with conflict between a young person and staff over goals.

POORER OUTCOMES		BETTER OUTCOMES
The Home is relatively calm and orderly.	→ ←	The Home is in a chaotic, disorderly state much of the time.
The mix of young people in the Home is favourable and on the whole has a constructive impact on individual young people.	→ ←	The mix of young people in the Home has an unfavourable or destructive impact on certain young people.
The mix of young people does not include extremes of some long-stay and some very short-stay young people.	→ ←	Some young people have been in the Home for 3–4 years while others come and go, and stay for only short periods.
The resources of the Home allow abusers and previously abused young people to be separated at night.	→ ←	Young people who have been abused may have to share bedrooms with young people who have abused others in the past.
The Home is relatively stable in its staff composition.	→ ←	Staff changes are frequent or there are just a few established staff with heavy reliance on relief staff.
The young person likes and feels able to rely on one or more staff in the residential setting: he or she has been able to form emotional attachments with current carers.	→ ←	The young person distances himself or herself from staff, or mistrusts them, or makes them his or her enemy.
Members of staff are sensitive to young people's needs and notice their moods	→ ←	Members of staff are preoccupied, busy, distracted, or insensitive.
The young person and the staff are able to work together towards understood and agreed goals.	→ ←	The young person is in conflict with the staff over goals; or the staff and/or others make decisions concerning the young person which he or she does not understand and/or is not consulted about.

Figure 5f   The state of the Home and a young person's relationship with staff

The Quality of Practice

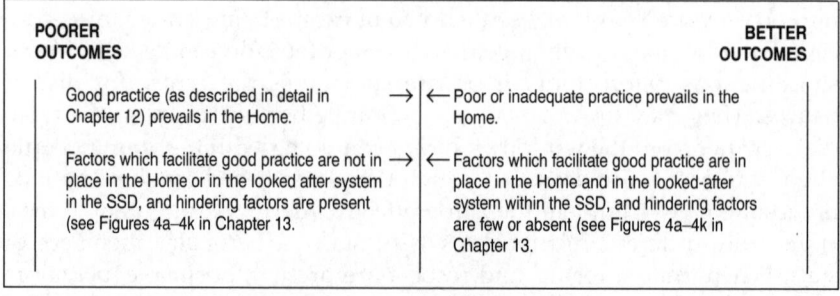

POORER OUTCOMES		BETTER OUTCOMES
Good practice (as described in detail in Chapter 12) prevails in the Home.	→ ←	Poor or inadequate practice prevails in the Home.
Factors which facilitate good practice are not in place in the Home or in the looked after system in the SSD, and hindering factors are present (see Figures 4a–4k in Chapter 13.	→ ←	Factors which facilitate good practice are in place in the Home and in the looked-after system within the SSD, and hindering factors are few or absent (see Figures 4a–4k in Chapter 13.

Figure 5g   The quality of practice

For a full spelling out of the quality of practice in the Home and the presence or absence of factors which support good practice, see Chapter

12, which described good practice, and Chapter 13, which presented force-field diagrams (Figures 4a–4k) of factors which facilitate or hinder good practice.

Of all the clusters of factors related to good outcomes, it is only the final one which has to do directly with the quality of practice. Within other clusters, good practice sometimes plays a part, but it is often the case that a facilitating factor or a hindering factor is independent of what a staff does or does not do, and is outside staff control. The conclusion one must come to is that good outcomes are influenced by a number of facilitating factors, of which good practice is one. The happiest situation is one in which good practice occurs together with a range of other facilitating factors. This point needs to be emphasised because it is sometimes assumed that outcomes would improve if only practice were better. The fact is that there is an inexact relationship between good practice and good outcomes. It all depends on the totality of supporting or hindering factors which are in place.

It also follows that it would be an error to accept the quality of an outcome as a direct indicator of good or of bad practice.

IMPLICATIONS FOR ACTIONS WHICH COULD IMPROVE THE LIKELIHOOD OF MOVING TOWARDS GOOD OUTCOMES FOR INDIVIDUAL YOUNG PEOPLE

Force-field diagrams can assist in suggesting actions which could increase the likelihood of moving towards good outcomes for individual young people. If any of the supporting factors could be strengthened, or if any of the hindering factors could be removed or weakened, the likelihood of good outcomes would increase. Some factors will be more open to influence than others. Some factors can be influenced in the short term; some only in the long term. Some are virtually impossible to influence because they are held in place by forces outside staff members' (or management's) capacity to influence.

In thinking out a strategy for increasing the likelihood of good outcomes for young people *in general*, it makes sense to concentrate on those forces which can be influenced. The force field suggests that certain hindering factors could be weakened and certain facilitating factors strengthened.

- Further unnecessary changes in placement could be avoided.
- Some unplanned admissions, at least, could be avoided.
- Placements could take into account the mix of young people already living in the Home.

- Promising parts of a young person's family and personal network could be identified and worked with on his or her behalf.
- Discharging a young person at short notice without taking into account the work staff are doing at the time and the state of readiness of the young person at the time, could be avoided.
- The decision-making structure and procedures in the larger organisation could be examined and improved, so that those who need information of various kinds actually get it.
- The practice skills of a staff group could be improved by a variety of means.

OUTCOMES: CURRENT THINKING IN THE FIELD

In an extensive discussion of how 'outcomes' might best be considered, Parker and colleagues point to the importance of perspective, and distinguish between public outcomes, service outcomes, professional outcomes, family outcomes, and child outcomes. They also point out that a distinction can be made between general outcomes and specific outcomes, and call attention to the crucial issue of the *point* or *points* at which outcomes can and should be assessed, and the sequential nature of outcomes (Parker, Ward, Jackson, Aldgate, & Wedge, 1991).

Biehal and her colleagues, taking into account the work of Knapp (1989) and Parker *et al.* (1991) distinguish between final outcomes ('changes in child welfare defined along the dimensions spanned by society's objectives for child care or child development generally, which are measures of the quality of life'); and intermediate outcomes ('measures of the quality of care, desirable in themselves and for the impact they have on final outcomes') (Biehal, Clayden, Stein, & Wade, 1995, pp. 249–250.)

There is general agreement that outcomes for individual young people need to take individual circumstances into account. Parker *et al.* (1991, p. 34) state:

> Partial success in this or that area for one child may be no outstanding achievement for another, depending upon their relative starting positions, their different handicaps or inherent capabilities.

Biehal and her colleagues, in identifying factors influencing outcomes, includes 'personal starting point (individual circumstances)'. (Biehal *et al.*, 1995, p. 251).

When discussing 'service outcomes', Parker *et al.* (1991, p. 21) point out that service providers—i.e. those 'concerned with the overall

performance of an organisation'—are likely to express outcomes in aggre-
gate or statistical terms, and that ' "statistical outcomes" are not what
interest the parents of children with whom the services are engaged'.

Most staff groups who participated in our research had a developed
sense of what constituted constructive inputs, or good practice, on their
part. They sometimes could point to things which they had done, with or
on behalf of a young person, which led to some desirable outcome.
However, they appreciated that many factors other than their own practice influenced outcomes—especially a young person's family circumstances, and how entrenched he or she might already be in some
particular lifestyle. In this, they are consistent with Parker *et al*, (1991,
p. 28) who say that '. . . even the simplest outcome is shaped by some
forces that are either unconnected with the service or that lie largely
outside its power to control', and with Biehal *et al*, (1995, p. 251) who
(when looking at outcomes for young people leaving care at care-leaving
age) list, as factors influencing outcomes, not only 'professional support',
but also 'local housing and labour markets, preparation, support from
non-professional sources, qualifications, personal development after leaving care, and personal starting point'. Those concerned with the quality of
outcomes for young people emphasise the importance of the quality of
practice, but acknowledge the impact of other factors.

In this chapter, and the three preceding ones, we have examined the
issues of the quality of practice, factors influencing the quality of practice,
and the quality of outcomes for individual young people. In the next
chapter we turn to the issues of the quality of Homes and the performance of staff groups.

15

THE QUALITY OF HOMES AS CARE SETTINGS

This chapter, as the title indicates, focuses on the quality of Homes as care settings. It is thus the fifth in a series of chapters which have 'quality' as their theme. Chapters 11 and 12 have provided particulars of good practice and have pointed to lapses from good practice. Chapter 13 identified factors which support or hinder good practice, and Chapter 14 addressed the issue of quality of outcomes for individual young people, identifying factors which increase or decrease the likelihood of good outcomes occurring.

It is obvious enough that a good Home is one in which practice is excellent and outcomes for individual young people are as favourable as could be expected, given their overall circumstances. Such a statement calls attention to the importance of the staff group in shaping and maintaining a satisfactory Home. It does not assist in understanding how satisfactory Homes can best be described, and differentiated from those which give cause for concern.

To approach the issue of how Homes and staff groups can be described and differentiated, we will make use of features of *culture* and of *group dynamics* introduced in Chapter 1. From among what was said there, we have selected those features of culture and of group dynamics which, as shown by research findings, bear on staff functioning in Children's Homes. Our focus is on *what staff groups are like*, and our intention is to examine relatively abiding features of staff groups which transcend the inevitable ups and downs described earlier in Chapter 4 and the vicissitudes of everyday life and work.

UNDERSTANDING THE CULTURES AND INTERACTIVE DYNAMICS OF STAFF GROUPS

The features of culture and interactive dynamics to be emphasised are:

- unit managers' leadership styles;
- attitudinal sets in staff groups;

- interactive styles within staff groups and between staff and young people;
- levels of cohesiveness within the staff group;
- norms, structures, procedures, routines, and customs;
- the nature of staff group boundaries; and
- values, related goals, and goal systems.

Unit Managers' Leadership Styles

Unit managers differ substantially and each puts a personal stamp on the role. One sees differences in leadership style, in personal strength and the capacity to be the person of last resort, in how the task is conceptualised, and in assumptions about needed internal structures and rules.

With respect to leadership styles:

The participative unit manager works closely and side by side with the staff without neglecting the special responsibilities attached to the role. Such a manager gets to know individual staff members well—in particular, their strengths and vulnerabilities, their capacities to cope with different sorts of situations arising in the Home, and their preferred ways of handling stress. The participative unit manager is thus in a position to support individual members of staff, without being heavy-handed about it, and to utilise well the diverse strengths contained in the staff group as a whole. He or she respects staff and shows this in behaviour. One such unit manager declared: 'Everyone is senior here'—meaning that everyone is thoroughly well experienced and equipped for the task. Participative managers make a positive contribution to the Home's capacity to provide good care.

The distant unit manager may be physically present but leaves a good deal to his or her staff, especially with regard to direct work with young people. He or she tends to function at one remove from young people, concentrating on the administrative parts of the task. A distant manager may have a considerable impact on the structures and procedures within the Home, but is less likely to offer a model for interacting with young people, or be available to help and support staff when crises build up. Staff members can 'work around' such a manager, forming themselves into an effective team. One or several of their number may take on leadership functions not being provided by the unit manager. Nevertheless, staff lack an official leader. The Home may or may not be well placed to provide good care, depending on how staff members rally round to make up for the unit manager's psychological absence.

The anxious unit manager appears to be overfaced by the task. He or she may withdraw (literally or emotionally) when things get tough; or be invasive with the staff, frequently calling meetings in an effort to retain control and keep things 'right'. The behaviour of the anxious manager is directed more to alleviating his or her own anxiety than to working on the care task. Matters of routine may be handled satisfactorily, and the Home may function well enough when there are no special crises. When crises occur (and they are inevitable) the unit manager's anxiety intensifies, and may spread to the staff group. The Home is not well placed to provide good care *consistently*, and good practice is hard to sustain.

We were struck by how important it is that a unit manager be prepared to be 'the person of last resort' when a crisis occurs. By this is meant that the unit manager will be available to staff under fraught conditions, prepared to step in, prepared to take action, prepared to face whatever crops up. Such a stance strengthens a staff group and supports staff members in doing their best work. Participative unit managers are most likely to be able to be the person of last resort. The anxious manager cannot be a person of last resort for his or her staff, and the distant manager leaves it to others.

We did not see instances of *over-controlling management* as a leadership style on its own. When it occurred, it seemed to be a manifestation of a unit manager's anxiety. Over-control is dysfunctional, since attempts to oversee all aspects of staff members' work leave little room for personal discretion. In Children's Homes, staff members always have to exercise discretion because they are so frequently faced with situations requiring an immediate response, with no time to consult.

Another leadership style we did not observe is the *charismatic leader*, though we have heard and read of such. Charismatic leaders tend to cue staff members into being followers. This is a disadvantage in Children's Homes because staff initiative and flexibility of response is reduced. Diversity in point of view, valuable when seeking to understand and take action in the face of some puzzling situation, may be much reduced.

Unit managers have an impact on staff and the Home through their conception of the task with respect to young people, especially the relative emphasis put on care and control, and also with respect to relationships with the larger organisation. A unit manager who knows the ropes of the organisation and is prepared to work within Departmental structures and procedures for the benefit of the Home is in a better position than a unit manager who rails against management and feels helpless in the face of decisions taken by managers. Unit managers do not always agree with the decisions taken by those who occupy management positions above them. When this is the case, some unit managers tend to give in; others try to negotiate. Some managers are more skilled than others at such negotiations.

Attitudinal Sets in Staff Groups

Attitudinal sets can persist over fairly long periods of time, and may be directed to young people, management, or people and organisations in a Home's network.

For example, the members of a staff group may believe and assume that once a young person is excluded from school it will be very difficult to reinstate him or her, or that residential staff carry little weight in review meetings, or that their external managers are likely to blame them if things go wrong. Attitudinal sets differ in how reality-based they are. They are, of course, related to what really happens or has happened in the real world (they are not fantasies), but once established they sometimes persist in the face of contrary evidence. It is then that an attitudinal set becomes a problem. It is well understood in the field of group dynamics that 'consensus lends validity'—that is, anything which is accepted unanimously by a whole group comes to be seen as 'truth', or 'the way things are and need to be'.

Attitudinal sets get translated into behaviour, some facilitative of good work and good practice, and others not. For example, the assumption that external managers high up in the organisation will not be interested in staff views, or take them seriously, can stop staff from trying to convey their opinions up the organisational hierarchy. The assumption that a particular young person is 'manipulative' can put a stop to thinking harder about how that young person's behaviour can best be understood.

Staff groups establish characteristic attitudes towards young people as a whole which influence their prevailing interactive styles. Evidence for this tends to accumulate through occasional, sometimes off-hand comments about 'the way we operate' and through observing many diverse interactions in different contexts, over time. Members of one staff group said all of the following over a period of time, in the course of a number of Study 2 visits:

'It is important that residential workers are interested in doing the job.' 'You've got to like kids.' 'You have to be able to listen to the kids' (to which someone added:) 'and understand them.' 'You can't lie to the kids or mislead them.' 'You have to be honest.' 'You have to show your personality all the time. Kids can "suss" adults.' 'Kids know when you care.' 'Kids know when you are interested in them.' 'If you make mistakes they will know if it is done in their interest. They will make allowances for you.' 'It's important that each kid knows that when he walks in the front door, it's a fresh start.' 'You have to listen.' 'You try to be honest in your feelings.' (Drawn from a researcher's notes.)

These statements comprise a shared set of attitudes towards young people which emphasise interest, respect and honesty, and a readiness to listen and to try to understand. These attitudes found expression in a multitude of day-to-day, large and small, events and interactions, which added up to a characteristic way of interacting and working with the young people, to their benefit.

Interactive Styles within Staff Groups and between Staff and Young People

Differences in interactive style within a staff group, which have a bearing on the quality of care provided, have to do with ways of offering mutual support, preferred ways of dealing with internal disagreements, and uses of humour.

When staff members know they will get support and understanding from one another when crises arise or morale is low, they are in a better position to weather and deal with fraught situations. There is a sense of being on safe ground. Members of staff know they can count on one another to understand what they have been faced with on a particularly difficult shift, and to be helpful and responsive and responsible. They know that they can call upon staff members not on duty to come in if needed, and that members of staff will stay on after their shift ends, if necessary, to deal with a crisis. This obviously improves staff functioning, in the specific sense of being able to marshall resources when a crisis occurs, and in the more general sense of maintaining staff morale.

Staff groups differ in how they respond to internal conflict. Some staff groups allow disagreements to rumble on, and seem not to deal with them at all. Some staff groups seem to put a stop to discussion when they begin to perceive that disagreement is in the air, thus maintaining the appearance but not the reality of cohesiveness. Some staff groups are in the habit of talking things out, and manage to maintain cohesiveness while at the same time airing differences of opinion and point of view. The latter pattern is clearly preferable, for alternative views are taken into account when searching for a satisfactory understanding of a situation, or course of action.

Some staff groups make constructive use of humour. We have observed a rather wry or ironic form of humour which functions well as an elliptical means of sharing feelings and opinions, and a way of alleviating stress. As an example, all of the following was part of the same conversation:

A staff group whose admissions were almost always on an emergency basis was told to prepare for a planned placement. A staff member commented that a planned placement was one that they knew about a week in advance. The next two comments were, 'We're all gonna have a party!' 'Yeah, we're gonna have a party!' The staff member who had been told by an external manager to hold a bed for the planned placement had asked him what to do if the Home received an emergency referral that night—should they accept it? The manager had said, 'Yes'. Hearing this, another member of staff said, 'I think that's brilliant! Stack them up!' The staff reflected that they had had two planned placements in the last year and a half, out of more than 60 placements in all. Referring to one of these, a member of staff said 'What kind of a planned placement was that? Straight from C —— (a secure unit) to here. I mean that was some plan, wasn't it? That was sad for that lad, I mean that was awful. That lad could not cope.' Another staff member remarked that it had been for respite care, to which the reply was, 'Why can't I go to C —— for respite?' (Researcher's notes.)

Reading this without also hearing the tone of voice in which comments were made could lead one to believe that anger or resentment was being expressed. However, tone of voice showed that these staff members were enjoying a huge joke together.

Staff groups also differ with respect to their prevailing interactive styles with young people. Some appear to be heavier-handed than others. Play-fighting, especially with boys, was an interactive style seen in some Homes. Staff apparently assume that affection underlies the rough behaviour, but the researchers noted that play-fighting always involves the exercise of power on the part of staff over young people. On these grounds it can be regarded as a disadvantageous interactive style. Some staff groups managed to be egalitarian in their approach to young people while at the same time maintaining their adult responsibilities. Such staff groups were well placed to carry out good practice.

An interesting difference between staff groups is their use of humour with the young people. In some Homes good-hearted humour is part of a 'house style' which lightens a charged atmosphere, is a way of expressing affection for young people, and constitutes a palatable (to the young people) way of exercising control. For example:

A boy of 13 was soon to move to a specialised facility outside the Authority. He was asking members of staff for money in a half-joking way, 'And I'm going to get £5 from you, and £3 from you, and . . .', etc. A relatively new member of staff said, 'Why do I have to pay so much? I've only known you for three weeks.' Another member of staff said, as a joke, 'I don't believe in money. Money corrupts.' (Researcher's notes.)

Staff, of course, had no intention of giving this boy money and the boy undoubtedly knew it or he would not have expressed his request in a half-joking way. By using humour, staff avoided reproaching or getting into a confrontation with the boy. The episode passed off as a light-hearted exchange.

In some instances, humour can have a hostile edge, which turns it into something entirely different.

Interactive styles may emphasise cooperation and participative decision-making and planning, benevolent oversight, pleasurable sharing and an atmosphere of enjoyment. Staff groups marked by these styles are well placed to carry out good practice. In contrast, interactive styles may emphasise over-control, with power firmly lodged in the staff group. Or, staff may distance themselves from young people, perhaps because they are preoccupied with other matters. Or, there may be tensions between staff and young people, and an air of 'who is winning at the moment?'. Staff groups marked by these styles are not well placed to carry out good practice.

Levels of Cohesiveness within the Staff Group

Some staff groups are more unified or cohesive than others. A reasonably united, cohesive staff group tends to be mutually supportive, although, as was seen in Chapter 9 (on how staff seek to maintain viability), staff members place limitations on supportive behaviour, curtailing it if a colleague has behaved in some way which violates personal or group norms.

Knowing that support will be available from one another if needed greatly enhances staff members' ability to deal with difficult situations, and reduces stress. Situations sometimes arise inside the Home which place one staff member in a particularly vulnerable position—for example, a young person has alleged abuse, or has physically attacked a member of staff, or persistently 'targets' a member of staff in a way which amounts to ongoing persecution. The staff member concerned naturally experiences considerable personal distress. If other staff members rally around and offer support, the problem may not always be solved but the pain and stress are less. Staff members have said that they are thoroughly aware that they themselves could easily be placed in a similar vulnerable position. A member of staff may be under tension for reasons which have nothing to do with the Home—for example, illness, or illness in the family. Again, other staff members rally round, for example, by being prepared to ease the workload for the person concerned, or to cover a necessary absence.

Some staff groups lack unity and cohesiveness. They may be split into two or more sub-groups which hold incompatible views about how best to manage and work with young people. Or, the unit manager might be fighting the whole staff, by wishing to institute procedures which others find unacceptable or risky. The staff group is less well placed to provide good care.

It should be mentioned, although we did not observe it, that a staff group can become overly cohesive. Staff members may support one another in maintaining ways of thinking about young people, and preferred practices, which actually work against young people's welfare. They may be so unified and cohesive that there is nothing within the staff group to challenge universally shared assumptions and associated behaviours.

Norms, Structures, Procedures, Routines, and Customs

Certain structures, procedures, routines, and customs are widely seen and therefore are not a basis for differentiating between Homes. For instance, the staff groups we came to know were similar, by and large, in the kinds of norms they tried to establish in their Homes—in particular, they pressed towards establishing orderly daily routines, were considerate towards one another and tried to encourage considerate behaviour in young people. It would be unusual for birthdays not to be celebrated, or for special outings not to be planned, or for Christmas and other holidays not to be marked.

Some structures and procedures are widely seen but differ in their detail. For example, virtually all staff groups hold handover meetings when there is a change in shifts. Most often, these are attended by staff only, but in some cases young people also attend. Residents' or children's meetings are often in place, but differ in how they operate. One staff group sought to formalise its children's meetings by always meeting around a table, and always providing everyone present with a drink and a pad of paper and a pencil, for making notes. As another example, some staff groups make use of a reward or incentive system, based on the weekly earning of 'points' by the young people, while others do not. These variations mark differences between Homes which may or may not be related to differences in the quality of care.

Customs grow up, and are specific to Homes—for example, Sunday visits to the seaside, the cinema, or a theme park. Some Homes establish bedtime rituals, or particular kinds of treats to be enjoyed inside the Home during the evening. Staff groups find their own ways of creating enjoyable and learningful experiences for young people and a home-like, rewarding atmosphere.

Rules about such matters as bedtimes, or eating between meals, tend to be in place, but staff members (individually and collectively) differ in how strictly they are applied. Homes also differ in whether house rules are devised by staff, or taken from guidelines provided by management, or worked out in discussion with young people. In general, Homes are in a better position to provide good care if staff members work out rules in conjunction with the young people, and show some flexibility in their use.

Some of the customs and practices which staff establish stem from sensitivities to the importance of gender, race, and religious beliefs. Some staff referred explicitly to the advantages of gender balance within a staff group. This had to do with recognising that both male and female staff were needed to provide positive role models for boys and girls. It was appreciated that girls, especially, might feel free to talk about certain matters with a female rather than a male member of staff. Staff might become concerned about a prevailing house style—for example, a macho style—and come to the view that it might change if there were more female staff. It was generally the case that staff were aware of the import-ance of good relationships between the boys and girls in the Home. Race and ethnic background were explicitly named as an issue in some Homes and not in others, usually in relation to the current mix of young people. In one Home the fact that one young person was black was never referred to. In another, white staff were very distressed by racist taunts from the young people against the only black member of staff. In still another Home, white members of staff showed little sensitivity about race, and some disputed a black staff member's expressed feelings of isolation. Religious beliefs were not much mentioned, though a related issue—dietary requirements on the part of young people from different ethnic or religious backgrounds—was taken seriously.

Some norms, structures, procedures, routines, and customs make defi-nite contributions to the quality of care. Bedtime rituals, for example, support cosiness and a sense of belonging. Regular residents' meetings provide opportunities for young people to develop competence of many kinds—planning, decision-making, listening to the points of view of oth-ers, finding non-combatant ways to resolve disagreements, and so on.

The Nature of Staff Group Boundaries

Staff groups differ with respect to the firmness of the boundary they place around themselves. Some are welcoming to outsiders, ready to share, and open to outside influence. Other staff groups keep things to themselves and, especially when a crisis arises, prefer to deal with it internally.

Boundaries that are too tight, however, carry the risk of beliefs, atti-tudes, and practices being maintained which are dysfunctional and amount to poor practice. Isolation from others creates a breeding ground for the development and maintenance of shared beliefs which, when put into practice, work against the best interests of young people or staff.

A staff group may also be characterised by a boundary which is too open. Every detail of what goes on in the Home is shared with others outside the Home as soon as it occurs. Such staff groups may make more demands on outsiders than is necessary, and surrender decision-making to others.

Boundaries that are too tight or too permeable are signs that the staff group is in, or is in danger of entering, an unhealthy state which could have a bearing on the quality of care that staff can provide.

Values, Related Goals, and Goal Systems

It is useful to distinguish between *espoused values*, which are what a staff group says that it values, and *values-in-action*, which have to do with whether and how espoused values are translated into action. The two may correspond, or diverge.

Our data revealed no real difference between staff groups with respect to espoused values, insofar as they expressed a fundamental commitment to the welfare and personal development of the young people. We often heard staff members say that it was unacceptable to them to be merely 'warehouses' for young people, or 'babysitters'. They wanted to make a positive difference to the young people in their care.

Espoused values were so similar across the whole sample of Homes that, important as they are, they proved to be a poor basis for differentiating between Homes.

What of the consonance, or otherwise, between espoused values and values-in-action? In our data and on the whole, consonance prevailed, but there were also examples of dissonance. For example, staff who became over-controlling, or characteristically made use of hostile forms of humour, were behaving in ways inconsistent with their espoused values. Some dissonances were outside staff control. If turnover was very rapid, for instance, staff members literally did not have enough time to do more than 'warehouse' young people.

Within the field of group dynamics, distinctions are made between overall goals and instrumental goals, and between shared public goals and covertly held shared goals. Private, personally held goals are also a part of an overall goal system. All this can be observed in Children's Homes. The publicly espoused value of benefiting each young person is an overall goal. Within it, one sees in operation a whole set of sub-goals or instrumental goals which contribute to achieving the overall goal. Staff may hold further goals which are not directly related to the young people—for example, protecting the continued existence of the Home, keeping out of trouble with the neighbours, or avoiding being the subject of commentary in the local newspapers. Some of these may be held covertly. Individual members of staff may have their private goals—to gain promotion, or protect family members from realising how distressed they sometimes get in consequence of events at work.

Whether the multiple goals which make up a goal system facilitate good work or get in its way depends on whether and how they fit together. Problems arise if sub-goals do not mesh well with overall goals, or further goals unrelated to work with young people become dominant and distract staff from their care task, or private goals become so preoccupying that they get in the way of doing good work.

DEVELOPING A SENSE OF THE DISTINCTIVE CULTURAL TOTALITY OR *GESTALT* OF A STAFF GROUP

What has been said so far names and discusses a number of dimensions along which staff groups may be compared. We have not as yet described staff groups in terms of the essence of their prevailing culture. To do so requires reaching beyond dimensions or component parts and developing a point of view about the totality or *gestalt* of a culture.

Charles Case describes the totality of a culture in the following terms:

> Culture is the social heritage that is developed out of the biological responses and the life processes. It is the web of relationships holding people together in various viable groups. It is the structure of predictability in the behaviour of the members of society which tells each person who he is and who other people are. It provides the techniques for dealing with life problems, and for directing the shape of one's existence. Culture is a guiding system, a behavioral map, a grammar of behavior, constantly working to shape behavior in its outward form. In essence culture is communication.
>
> (Case, 1977, pp. 16–17)

Case is referring to a totality which is hard to put into words. He uses such phrases as 'the web of relationships'; 'the structure of predictability'; 'a grammar of behavior'. These are metaphors which are used to *convey* what a culture is and the functions it serves.

Arriving at a sense of the special quality—the essence—of different staff groups requires that attention be paid to all the dimensions discussed separately above. It requires one to notice iterations and regularities which are present over a period of time, stories which staff tell which reveal their stance towards the world or how they respond to particular kinds of situations, atmosphere and tensions (which may change from time to time, but tend to vary around a prevailing equilibrium), how staff members tend to feel in consequence of their belonging to the staff group (for example, pleased and fulfilled through their membership or, conversely, exploited, stressed, or overly constrained by it), how a staff group responds to outsiders, and whether some members of a culture gain at the expense of others, who lose out.

Different cultural totalities can be described briefly as follows:

- the competent and mutually supportive staff group which seeks to keep tight boundaries around itself and be self-sufficient;
- the secure and competent staff group which works appropriately both inside and across the boundaries of the Home;
- the relaxed, creative staff group, whose members maintain good relationships with the young people—most of whom are with them for long periods—and do good work with them;
- the insecure staff group;
- the distracted staff group, whose members are preoccupied with worries about their future or their struggles with their own management, and have reduced energy for the care task;
- the staff group which has become accustomed to working continually under crisis conditions, because of difficult mixes of young people or frequent admissions and transfers of young people;
- the staff group which is marked by a persistent and apparently unresolvable internal conflict;
- the staff group which emphasises individual work with each young person and has not yet understood how to work with and within groups to benefit individuals; and
- the fragmented staff, which cannot be said to have a culture at all.

It will be clear that some types of staff group are better placed than others to carry out good practice.

Worst-placed staff groups are those which are fragmented or marked by internal conflict. Staff groups marked by insecurity are able to do routine work but can fail when faced by extraordinary events or crises. Staff groups which are consistently at odds with their external managers, or preoccupied with worries about their future, are distracted from their primary task and hard-pressed to do their best work. They may struggle against the odds and carry out good practice much or some of the time, but are likely to pay a price in stress.

Best-placed staff groups are those whose practice is consistent with their values, who understand how to work with individual young people in the context of group living, and who manage and use well the diversity among themselves. They do not operate on yesterday's assumptions, but keep in touch with events as they unfold and change, and adjust their thinking and behaviour accordingly. Some such staff groups draw tight boundaries around themselves while others work easily with people across their own boundaries. The latter are rather better placed than the former.

Staff groups which work well with individuals but are insensitive to the dynamics of groups are in a 'middling' state. They fail to see and use all the opportunities to benefit young people which arise when the whole group, or sub-groups, are in interaction.

'GOOD' and 'BAD' HOMES AND THE SPECIAL CASE OF STAFF-PERPETRATED ABUSE

In recent years it has come to light that in several Children's Homes members of staff, or a unit manager, have physically or sexually abused young people living in the Home, or the whole staff group has engaged in questionable forms of practice. The fact that abuse of this kind can occur anywhere is, of course, a matter for concern. Concern is all the greater because, in some cases, abuse went on, undetected, for considerable periods of time.

This concern is sometimes expressed as a need to be able to differentiate between 'good' and 'bad' Homes. These terms are labels, and 'bad' is an epithet. They are short-cut ways of referring to complex issues. We have preferred to think of Homes and staff groups as differing in how well-placed they are to carry out good quality care. This allows an exploration of differences between Homes, some of which bear on the quality of the care that can be provided and some of which do not. It facilitates recognising that Homes are rarely all bad or all good, and it emphasises identifying features of staff functioning which make a difference to the quality of care, especially if they are repeated over time.

We are unable to offer evidence as to what goes wrong when actual abuse occurs, or suggestions about how to detect it. Nevertheless our research suggests certain lines of thought which could be useful. In particular, if the boundaries around a staff group and Home are very tight, any abusive tendencies within the staff group will be harder to detect. If a unit manager exercises a powerful, controlling leadership style, staff members may find it hard to resist being influenced. If staff members have only a fragile hold on espoused values, there is a greater likelihood that there will be divergence between espoused values and values-in-action. If staff members sense that something is going wrong but find it personally threatening to think the unthinkable, they may develop shared collusive defences of denial, distancing or rationalisation. If a strongly held shared belief develops that some questionable form of practice is in fact acceptable or even desirable, it will not easily be dislodged without outside intervention. These are suggestions as to dynamics which might be in place. They need testing by those investigating incidents or suspected incidents, or through research. The intention, of course, is to forestall further abuse by being alert to warning signs and by intervening early.

UNDERSTANDING THE QUALITY OF STAFF GROUPS AND THEIR PRACTICE

Some criteria which can be employed in evaluating staff groups are easy to note and to form judgements about—for example, the provision of good food, a clean environment, and basic care. Others are much more difficult—for example, a staff group's capacity to form a full and evidence-based understanding of a young person's unique situation, or a capacity to shift aspirations and plans in response to changing circumstances, or skills in making use of the mix of the young people for the benefit of individuals.

It is an error to concentrate on criteria for which evidence is readily available simply because it *is* available. Other criteria may be equally or more important even though it is harder to assemble evidence.

Outcomes for individual young people—whether favourable or unfavourable—should not be used as sole or major criteria for judging the quality of Homes or of practice. Looking to outcomes is important, and it is demonstrably the case that quality of practice influences outcomes. On the other hand, a poor outcome does not necessarily imply poor practice, for, as Chapter 14 shows, many factors over and beyond the quality of practice influence outcomes. The very best practice does not guarantee a good outcome.

Local circumstances need to be taken into account when judging the performance of a staff group. Particular staff groups operate within certain constraints, which need to be noted when assessing their performance. Time constraints, for example, influence what a staff group can achieve with individual young people. A spate of uproars within a Home, or mass offending by residents, or a sudden rise in school refusals, may have more to do with the mix of children in residence than the quality of staff.

It is advisable to base an evaluation on a series of 'readings' rather than just one. A single reading runs the risk of basing a judgement on a current bad patch. Earlier, in Chapter 4, it was shown that Homes go through ups and downs, good and bad patches. A Home which is in a good patch is likely to impress observers as being a Home which is in a satisfactory state. A Home which is in a bad patch may strike observers as being in an unsatisfactory state. A Home which has been in a good patch can slip into a bad patch if certain adverse circumstances arise, and a Home which has been in a bad patch can recover from it through staff efforts or if circumstances become more favourable.

Staff groups which are not well placed to do good work at a given time, and who might be judged to be performing poorly, are open to change. Fragmentation and internal conflict may be healed. Skills in working with groups of young people and the group of young people as a whole can be acquired. Countervailing forces which interfere with good work may change or be open to influence.

16

GENERAL COMMENTS ON THE CHALLENGES AND COMPLEXITIES WHICH STAFF GROUPS FACE IN CHILDREN'S HOMES

What, of what has been learned through this research, is applicable to the residential care of children anywhere? and What are the limitations to generalising? The answers to these questions depend on what can plausibly be assumed to be the case wherever children and young people are looked after in groups in residential settings, and on the level at which generalisations are made.

With respect to some issues, broader relevance can be assumed and plausibly defended. For example, it is known from this and other research and from clinical observations that contagion can occur in groups of children and young people—in such diverse settings as Children's Homes, summer camps, and schools. It is reasonable to assume that contagion *could* occur in Children's Homes anywhere, and that an understanding of this phenomenon will have general relevance. As another example: what this research showed about conditions under which positive change can occur for children and young people fits what is known about the dynamics of therapeutic change. An understanding of change processes also assists in understanding factors that limit change, which may be located in the child or in the child's personal network. It is reasonable to assume that similar dynamics are to be found elsewhere.

Some of the particularities of the Children's Homes in this study and their organisational contexts will not be found elsewhere. This means that one has to be careful about generalising but does not rule out all forms of generalisation. For example, the organisations in which our Children's

Homes were located were large and hierarchical. This will not be the case everywhere. We found that certain chains of communication were characteristic of this kind of organisational structure. Different kinds of information were located in particular parts of the organisation, and often not communicated, or not communicated in effective ways. One obviously cannot assume that all organisations are so structured, and that all of the consequences observed in this research will occur. Generalisation at that level is not appropriate. Yet, most Children's Homes will be located within some sort of larger organisation. There might, for example, be a board of governors, or a loose federation of Homes with a steering group or advisory group. Whatever the differences in organisational structure and context, certain intra-organisational issues will be important—for example, communication patterns, the location of decision-making power with respect to admissions and transfers, and how responsibilities are distributed or shared between those providing direct care and others in the organisation. At this level, generalisation is justified—the research calls attention to important features of organisation and the likelihood that they will have an impact on how Homes operate and on their effectiveness in looking after children. A child's personal network—its character and how it changes—will always be important. There will always be a larger network around a Home, with accompanying needs for staff to work with other organisations such as police, education, and health services.

With respect to some issues, relevance to other Homes and other contexts cannot be assumed but can be tested. For example, at the time this research was carried out, the possibility that children and young people might make allegations of physical or sexual abuse against members of staff was very much in the air. Abuse was known to have occurred in the past, and the Children Act 1989 took this into account in its emphasis on children's rights, including the right to register complaints. This had effects on life and work in Children's Homes. The possibility of allegations of abuse being made by young people or their relatives became an ongoing worry for many members of staff. Allegations, when actually made to the larger organisation, were always investigated, and sometimes upheld, but often not. Practice was affected in that staff members became wary. Young people knew that they had the power to make allegations and sometimes threatened staff ('I'll *get* you under the Act!') None of this might be the case elsewhere. Yet, going back to the issue of the level at which one generalises, the issue of how children are to be protected from the *possibility* of abuse is important anywhere. So also is the still broader issue of who holds what kind of power over whom.

As another example, the current trend in England and Wales is to seek early fostering for younger children, and, indeed, this also tends to be the aim for older children. Fostering is often harder to achieve for adolescents, or is rejected by them. All this has had an impact on the composition of Children's Homes in that most (though not all) of the young people now living in them are adolescents. One cannot assume that this trend is the case elsewhere. However, it is clear that the age range (and the life stage or mix of life stages) of those living in a Home has a bearing on interpersonal interactions among the children and young people, and on the situations which members of staff find themselves facing. For example, the presence of highly sexualised adolescent girls led to situations within Homes which staff groups had to find ways to cope with.

Certain limitations on generalisations come to mind. This research was mainly undertaken on relatively small Homes. If a Children's Home is a great deal larger and has more than seven or eight young people, it might be the case that further dynamics related to the mix of children might prove to be important.

GENERAL ASSERTIONS

With all the above in mind, the assertions made in the following sections are likely to be relevant anywhere, or important to bear in mind when examining specific circumstances wherever they occur.

The task of working with children in residential settings is complex, diverse, and demanding

All the tasks we heard about, or observed to be facing staff, fitted into at least one of the following categories: working with and being managed by their larger organisation; working with people and organisations in their wider networks (including the networks of each child); and surviving as a staff team which meets the needs of children. We suggest that these apply to any unit providing residential care, but would expect differences as to what is prominent within each of these, depending on particular circumstances.

This research showed that one of the realities of working life is that staff members face the unexpected every time they come into work and are faced with multiple tasks most of the time—most of them important and many of them urgent. Some staff are in a reactive position much of the time and have little time to reflect or to plan. Whether this proves to be the case elsewhere is likely to depend on how disturbed and how demanding the young people are, and on the turnover of young people. This is an important point because it is related to a staff group's capacity to think and to plan, and to learn from experience.

The issue of staff autonomy—spheres in which it occurs and limitations on it—is bound to be important for all staff groups

The quality of practice is bound to suffer if the boundaries on staff's freedom of operation are such that they cannot make decisions based on their particular and close knowledge of groups or individual children. To put this another way, the quality of practice is bound to suffer if key decisions affecting a child or the Home are made by people who do not have full information about the current situation, or who are working towards aims different from those of the staff group.

Tensions between members of staff and their own managers, or between members of staff and significant members of their wider network (such as teachers, the police) arise when a staff group is responsible for something (such as a child attending school) but does not have the power to insist that a school take a child back who has been excluded from school. In this research, it was often the case that people inside the organisation but outside the Home had power over placements and transfers. Conflict arose when staff had information which suggested that a wrong decision was being made, but had no real power to influence it. We do not assume that such conflicts are inevitable, but believe it is an issue which needs to be monitored, given the frequency of hierarchical organisational structures and processes, where power tends to be located at or near the top and some forms of relevant information tend to be located at the bottom, with direct carers.

Staff autonomy is also limited by the powers of other organisations with which staff must work. One organisation may have power over resources needed by a staff group for one of its young people—for example, a school or Education Department can decide whether to accept a young person or not, leaving a staff group relatively helpless in meeting its responsibility to assure that each young person is being educated. Inter-organisational conflict could occur anywhere, and like intra-organisational tensions, needs to be monitored.

Certain positive potentials are present in group living

The presence of a number of carers, rather than one or two, is an advantage to some children. A young person who cannot tolerate the closeness and intensity of family living, or who, with good reason, finds it threatening, can be well looked after in a Children's Home and at the same time not be exclusively reliant on just one or few adult carers. The availability of a number of adult carers allows a young person to gravitate to one or to another—to a comfortable and nurturing middle-aged woman, or a younger, athletic male, or a 'big sister'. Some young people, especially adolescents, cannot tolerate parental figures and it is useful for them to have available some responsible adults who are older, but not much older, than themselves. In this respect younger staff members function well as role models for the young people. A number of adult carers are able to share the load of looking after a difficult child, or managing a difficult and fraught situation.

Within the peer group inside a Home, young people may form supportive friendships with one another. Opportunities are present to learn to get on together within a group, to work together, to tolerate potential rivals, to learn to look out for those younger or more vulnerable than themselves, and to develop practical skills and skills of living.

Group care offers the special potential of young people getting in touch with and taking into account the impact of their behaviour on others.

We suggest that these potential advantages are to be found in residential child care generally.

Certain negative potentials are present in group living. Particularly important are the potential for emotional and behavioral contagion and for various forms of destructive interaction

One child may be persecuted or otherwise placed in a disadvantageous position by another, or others. The whole group may sometimes get caught up in some episode of emotional and behavioral contagion, and get out of control. One or several children may be drawn into behaving unacceptably, in ways not previously characteristic of them, through processes of imitation. A newly admitted young person who is particularly disturbed or demanding may intimidate others, or disrupt some good piece of practice that has been going on, or simply unsettle the Home, making it a less safe and less secure base for the child.

The job of being a care worker in a Children's Home carries with it potentials for high reward and high stress

We think that this must be the case universally. Children and young people who come into residential care have had their lives disrupted by the very fact of entry, and many have experienced severe trauma previously. Many are disturbed and/or operate outside usual social norms. Some such children are hard to 'turn around'. Staff members experience substantial reward if they are able to help such young people to move forward. In day-to-day work, staff members take pleasure in seeing the young people enjoying themselves, or making small personal gains which add up over time. Some activities undertaken with the young people are pleasurable for all concerned. Some rewards come from working together in a close, supportive staff team, or from a sense that the staff group is understood and appreciated by the larger organisation and others in the network. A very personal form of reward comes from feeling able to cope with whatever comes along: a sense of self-esteem, self-worth, and effectance (i.e. that what one does makes a difference).

At the same time there are stresses: staff members become fatigued and may feel emotionally drained. There can be a sense of helplessness if the staff group has to work with very difficult mixes of young people and has no control over this through having no control over admissions. At times staff members may be at the receiving end of discourtesy, verbal abuse, or physical attacks from the young people. There can be worries about what *might* happen, worries about young people who have run away, worries about certain of the young people who seem to be on an inexorable downward course; worries about the physical safety of some of the young people or of the staff; worries related to rumours about the future of the Home. Staff members may be stretched to breaking point if the Home is in a period of crisis, or under-resourced.

One can argue that underlying the specifics of rewards and stresses are certain common human needs which are either satisfied or not by experiences on the job. They may be satisfied at some times and not at others. Such common needs include being able to achieve the goals one sets for oneself; feeling to be on top of the job rather than helpless; feeling to be effective rather than feeling to have no positive effect, whatever one tries.

Ups and downs, or 'good patches' and 'bad patches', are features of Children's Homes

All the unit managers and all the staff groups with whom we were in contact through this research said that Children's Homes go through good patches and bad patches, and could give vivid examples of each. They had ideas about what triggers bad patches and what helps to sustain good patches. When we reported this to others, outside the research, with comparable experience, they too immediately recognised the phenomenon of fluctuations between good and bad patches. We thus have reason to believe that good and bad patches, and the dynamics associated with them, are general phenomena.

The mix of children or young people in the Home makes a crucial difference to what occurs and can occur, and to what staff groups can accomplish on behalf of the children

We found, on the basis of the data available to us, that 'the mix' needs to have a kind of reservoir of personal strengths, such that any violent and disruptive tendencies that are present can be contained, and the group as a whole can function *with* the staff group rather than *against* it. A mix is particularly hard to manage if a few young people are present who are prone to violent or disruptive behaviour and the others are barely managing their own similar tendencies. Contagion and imitation of unacceptable behaviour may well follow.

We suggest that the potential for contagion and imitation is a to-be-expected feature of group living, and that staff need to be alert to the potential for such events and develop skills in forestalling and dealing with them. We also suggest that it is important, anywhere, to pay attention to the mix of young people and the consequent mix of strengths, vulnerabilities, and disruptive tendencies.

Some children and young people are hard to help or manage in 'ordinary' Children's Homes

In the Homes we came to know, there were some young people whom staff members felt they could neither work with nor help. These young people could not be protected from self-harm or from being harmed by people outside the Home. If they were in an ongoing chaotic state and out of control much of the time, they repeatedly caused damage within the Home, or were at risk through constantly running away or being out at night. Some young people behaved in ways which led to disturbance or distress in the other young people. Some showed signs of mental illness. The Homes in the study, it should be remembered, were 'ordinary' Children's Homes. It does not follow that the young people just referred to cannot be helped or managed in a group care setting of some kind, providing that it has been designed with their needs in mind. The general point which can be made is that care needs to be taken in devising care settings appropriate to the needs of particularly disturbed or difficult-to-manage young people.

Work with individual young people can be thought of as occurring on three 'fronts': (a) exercising control over the young person as needed, including physical constraint if necessary; (b) working at the frontier of each young person's needs; and (c) engaging in reparative work when this is indicated

Thinking in terms of these three 'fronts' emerged from noting what staff actually did in response to the very different young people with whom they worked (see Chapter 5). We believe that this way of formulating the directions or 'fronts' for work with individual young people will prove to be more generally applicable, but this needs testing in a wider range of group care settings. We predict that the relative emphasis on the different fronts will depend on the specialised functions of care settings and the kind of young person being looked after.

Diverse routes towards working with individual young people are available in Children's Homes, and all need to be used and exploited

These routes include reserving time for one-to-one work; exchanging briefly with a young person in the course of daily events; working in and through the group of young people; and working with others in the young person's network on his or her behalf. We believe that these routes are intrinsic to residential group care and will be found elsewhere.

Characteristics of good practice can be named which transcend the specifics of any particular care setting

Practice, whether good or poor, occurs within the task areas or arenas of working with individual children, with the mix of children, with the larger organisation, with people and organisations in wider networks (including the networks of each child), and within the staff team itself. To these should be added establishing structures, procedures, and customs within the Home facilitative of work within the first two task areas or arenas. We believe that this classification is so near to events themselves that they are likely to be useful generally.

In any arena, good practice involves such matters as:

- noticing what is going on, so that a worker does not fail to register, for example, that a child is under particular stress, that a change in a young person's family circumstances either closes or opens opportunities for him or her, and so on;
- placing plausible and justifiable meanings on a young person's be-haviour rather than operating on stereotypes or superficial catch-phrases which do no more than put a name to the behaviour;
- setting goals in all the arenas of the staff's work, and noticing when a changing situation requires a shift in goals or in the focus of the work or in the kind of work undertaken; and
- being aware of one's own feelings, so that, for instance, one knows one is becoming stressed, resentful, etc., in ways which interfere with clear thinking or with practice.

This is an abbreviated formulation of features of good practice which needs to be spelled out (as was done in Chapter 12) to be of practical use. Other ways of categorising and describing good practice are undoubtedly possible, though we suggest that the points we have made would have to find a place in alternative formulations. It would, of course, be interesting to examine how different formulations compare with one another.

Practice consists both of working purposefully on the basis of well-thought-out plans, and intervening intuitively and spontaneously in response to immediate, unpredictable situations

Working purposefully involves the successive steps of setting goals, making plans, taking action, reflecting on consequences, and then revis-ing goals or plans as indicated. In addition, however, life in a Children's

Home presents many opportunities for helpful interactions with individual children or the group which cannot be predicted or planned for ahead of time. 'Intuitive' responses can be exactly right for the child and the circumstances.

We found the 'think-work', which precedes both planned interventions and intuitive responses, to be extremely important. Interventions of whatever kind need to be based on an understanding of each child, and of the state of the group as a whole. Such understandings need to be as full and as reality-based as can be achieved. This can only be achieved if time is reserved for thinking out what is the case for each child and each mix. Staff members need to be open to revising their views about individual children or the whole group.

The points just made apply also to working with own organisations and network members—for example, neighbours, teachers, and others.

Staff members are bound to make practice errors from time to time, some of which are more important and harder to retrieve than others

Errors of omission and commission have been detailed towards the end of Chapter 12, where the issue of the retrieval of errors is also discussed.

We think it reasonable to assume that practice errors will occur from time to time in any residential care setting, given the complexity of the task. We suggest that anticipating the likely nature of errors and appreciating ways of retrieving them will be generally useful to care staff.

Errors, and poor practice, are more likely to occur and be maintained if a staff group which is highly cohesive and turned inwards, keeps rigid boundaries between itself and outsiders

Staff groups can be so turned inwards, so mutually reliant only on one another, that there is a danger of inappropriate attitudes or behaviours becoming established and maintained through conscious or unconscious collusion. This is an important general point, for it names conditions under which serious harm can come to young people.

Relationships between a staff group and its own higher management crucially influence staff morale

Relationships marked by conflict, mistrust, or mutual withdrawal, can lead to staff members becoming so disheartened, or so preoccupied with their problems with managers, that they lose energy and zest for the task.

Some people are well-placed, by personality or temperament, to look after children in group-care settings, or to learn to do so. Others are not well-placed

Staff members who can best cope with the job and sustain themselves in it are reasonably self-confident and relaxed, personally courageous in the face of difficult and challenging situations, sensitive to others' moods and needs, and capable of sticking with a situation rather than running away from it or avoiding it. While staff members cannot be paragons who never make mistakes, it is a great help if they are in touch with their own feelings and have some control over whether and how they express their feelings in behaviour, and are able to reflect on their own actions and learn from successive experiences encountered in day-to-day work. Beyond this, a member of staff needs genuinely to like young people and to be committed to their welfare and personal development, even when liking a particular young person is difficult.

Personal characteristics which make a person unfit to work in a Children's Home include a need to exercise power and control over others, a need to make use of the job for personal emotional gratification, a high anxiety level which makes it hard to confront and stay with difficult situations, a defensive posture and a tendency towards self-justification, insecurity to the point of having to flee from difficult situations or to counter-attack immediately if attacked (physically, or otherwise) by a young person, or being unable to tolerate a young person's pain.

It follows from the above that staff selection is of crucial importance and that decisions should not be made on technical grounds alone, such as years of experience or professional qualifications.

A very broad knowledge base is useful to care workers, which does not exactly coincide with any academic discipline

The knowledge base needed by residential care staff draws selectively from a number of diverse disciplines which, taken together, assist residential workers to make sense of situations arising in the group care of children and adolescents.

Such a conglomerated knowledge base would emphasise the following:

- *From personality dynamics and human development*: the impact of different forms of early trauma on the current behaviour of children and young people, and the dynamic of developing, on the basis of earlier experience, characteristic assumptions about what self and others are like, which are brought into any new living environment, together with associated behaviours; an understanding of how people protect themselves from emotional pain, in order to be alert to this in young people and also in themselves.
- *From social and clinical psychology*: appreciating features of interpersonal interactions, including the ways in which one young person may cue others into behaving in ways consistent with their characteristic 'image of self and surroundings'; understanding the positive and negative potentials of group living (in particular, processes of contagion and imitation).

- *From the fields of organisation and network dynamics*: a sense of how organisations work, especially with regard to the location of decision-making power, the flow of information, and the kinds of information held by differently positioned members of the organisation; an understanding of how networks of people and organisations function.
- *From the fields of cultural and social anthropology*: understandings about culture-consonance and culture-dissonance.

The practice skills needed by care workers include understanding and being able to work with individual children, with pairs and trios, and with the group as a whole

Direct practice skills needed by residential workers include being able to listen to and observe individual young people and the group as a whole, carefully and closely; being alert to early warning signs that some problem is about to erupt for a particular young person or for the group; developing as full and as accurate an understanding of individual children and young people as possible, basing such understandings on what actually can be seen and heard and on plausible inferences as to the meaning of what is seen and heard (avoiding basing 'understanding' on own predilections and needs); being ready to revise initial understandings on the basis of subsequent experience; devising appropriate plans for individual young people and being prepared to revise them in the light of changing circumstances; seeing and using opportunities for benefiting young people in among daily events; learning the skills involved in providing 'reparative' experiences for young people; seeing and using opportunities for benefiting young people through group interactions; being aware of one's own feelings and emotional reactions to events, and taking them into account without always or necessarily expressing them in behaviour; learning and using acceptable means for controlling young people, in circumstances where physical constraint is needed; and staying in touch with evolving situations, either with respect to individual young people or the group of young people, such that the work done is adapted to changing circumstances.

Interpersonal and group-management skills are also relevant to working within one's own staff group, working effectively with network members across the boundary of the Home; and working effectively with own management—learning to take initiatives with own management, and avoiding unnecessary conflict or adversarial confrontations.

Particular values need to be in place, and shared by those working in care-providing organisations, and attention needs to be paid to how values are expressed in both practice and policy

Many, probably most, residential care workers would express or accept a general statement of values which emphasises having the welfare of each young person in mind and seeking to benefit him or her. How this is put into practice is crucial, for some ways of behaving with young people are in line with this overall value and others are not. Assumptions about how to respond to a young person who has misbehaved, for example, may vary. Some workers might respond very punitively, believing this to be in the young person's best interests, while others take great care to respond in an understanding way, while at the same time, calling to the young person's attention the consequences of his or her behaviour. We have made the point that consonance or dissonance between espoused values and values-in-action crucially influence quality of care. This must be the case wherever adults look after children and young people.

Some factors likely to interfere with the effective functioning of Homes are not located in the Homes themselves but in the larger organisation or networks of organisations

Those in the larger organisation who are not doing direct work in Homes but are nevertheless responsible for the quality of the work, are bound to try to establish means of assuring quality. This is commonly done by establishing guidelines and mounting inspections. We suggest that this needs to be done with great care, and that a commonly seen, though understandable, error on the part of managers is to try to control every detail of direct work through more, and more detailed, directives and guidelines. This approach to quality control can interfere with staff flexibility and creativity. For the field of residential care, generally, different approaches to assuring quality of care need to be devised and evaluated for their full consequences.

Problems which often occurred in our sample of Homes, and ought to be borne in mind in case they occur elsewhere, had their source in imbalances in the location of decision-making power and of information relevant to decisions, lack of clarity as to jurisdiction, and differences in opinion about priorities. (See the final section in Chapter 7.)

Force-field analyses are useful in assisting key members of care-providing organisations to examine their own functioning and to identify actions which could be taken to improve practice and outcomes for individual children

In presenting findings relevant to the quality of practice and the quality of outcomes for individual children, we made use of prose descriptions and also presented the same information in diagram form, using force-field diagrams, after Kurt Lewin (see Chapters 13 and 14).

An amalgamated force-field diagram depicting forces which assist or hinder good practice was used in a dissemination exercise with members of care-providing organisations. Meetings were held with people from different levels of the same organisation, all concerned with the care of children and young people—senior and middle managers, line-managers, councillors, direct care workers, training officers, and field social workers. Those present were invited to inspect and discuss the force field, and to consider which factors pertained to their own situation, which of the helping factors could be strengthened and which new helping factors could be introduced, and which of the hindering factors could be removed or weakened. This allowed those present to see for themselves the actions they could take, given the particularities of their own situation and their own organisation.

This procedure was effective, providing senior managers show commitment to it; but less effective if people in the lower echelons are left to themselves. We suggest that it is a helpful device for helping practitioners and managers to see the relevance of research findings to the particular world in which they are operating.

A CONCLUDING COMMENT

Throughout this book we have portrayed the complexity of the world of staff when working in local authority Children's Homes in England. In this chapter we have given thought to the general relevance and applicability of this work. We have made a series of assertions which refer to aspects of residential care and to the contexts in which it occurs, and have suggested that some assertions are generally applicable, and that others need to be tested for relevance to particular situations and care settings.

The set of assertions name key areas which are challenging to staff who work in residential care settings, and to others in their larger organisations and networks. We believe them to be important for everyone involved in the provision of 'social care' for children and young people. We have concentrated on front-line workers in Children's Homes and how they think and operate. However, work with and on behalf of young people extends widely, up and down organisation hierarchies and across agency boundaries. Front-line practice cannot be understood without looking also at organisational and network dynamics. We believe that what has been learned is of interest not only to those providing direct care, but to policy-makers, inspectors, educators and trainers, health care and housing professionals, and to the police and courts.

The following points deserve special attention.

1. *Front-line staff need regularly scheduled, ongoing opportunities to learn from their own experience.* Staff members need time, as a group, to reflect on the work they have been doing, the goals they have been pursuing and, above all, the consequences of the actions they have been taking. Examining consequences against goals and actions enables learning about

the realistic—or otherwise—character of the goals and the appropriateness—or otherwise—of the plan and the actions taken so far. Concrete instances of practice need to be examined, which argues for relatively frequent and regularly timetabled opportunities for the whole staff group to discuss their work. An independent consultant or facilitator is essential since someone outside the staff culture can call attention to matters which might otherwise be taken for granted in a close-knit staff group. Meetings need to be protected from interruption. Organisational structures and procedures need to be provided to protect staff time for think-work and reflection.

2. *Maximum use needs to be made, by those who formulate plans and make decisions, of the information and understandings which staff members hold.* Residential staff are in a position to know whether a prospective admission is likely to fit into the current mix, or not; whether events in a young person's life, or work currently being done with him or her, have implications for the timing of a move elsewhere; whether a new procedure or policy under consideration by management, and meant to solve some particular problem, is likely to generate others. To make certain that such information is taken into account, effective communication channels, upward through the organisational hierarchy, need to be put in place, and/ or shared decision-making provided for. On the whole, this is a management responsibility to organise and structure. In follow-on work, undertaken after our research had been completed, we found that meetings attended by members occupying different positions in the care-providing organisation (top and middle managers, front-line workers, field social workers, training officers, those responsible for placements and transfers) were effective in facilitating communication and sharing points of view.

3. *Front-line staff need to be protected from unnecessary distractions, preoccupations and stress.* Residential work with children and young people can never be stress-free. However, some stressors could be avoided—for example: rumours concerning the future of the Home; staff members' worries about young people who really cannot be managed in 'ordinary' Children's Homes or who adversely affect the experience of others; and concerns that managers will not support members of staff during investigations following allegations made against them by young people or parents. Such stressors, especially if they pile up, distract and preoccupy staff. Staff have less energy for thinking about and working with the young people in their care.

4. *People and organisations in the wider network involved in the care, education, or control of young people need to work together in an integrated way.* A challenge for the future of residential care is to find ways to facilitate all those concerned with it to work together in an integrated way. Each professional group in a care network, each layer of agency or Department

staff, and residential care workers themselves, needs to start from the same point and share the same goal: that of working towards improving the quality of the lives of young people who live in residential Children's Homes. Consensus with respect to the overall goal is important, but it is not enough in itself. All concerned need also to identify operational goals and develop related practices, in their own sphere of work, which are in line with the shared goal. They need to take realistic account of their specific responsibilities and work contexts. Working in an integrated manner requires each to understand the demands placed on the others. Each needs to understand the impact of his or her own actions on others. It is by no means easy to work in an integrated way on behalf of young people when each organisation, each organisational unit, and often each person, necessarily has different responsibilities and priorities. It is to be expected that it will be difficult to maintain conflict-free, integrated efforts at all times. Yet this is what everyone concerned needs to strive for if maximum benefit is to accrue to young people being looked after in residential settings.

REFERENCES AND FURTHER READING

Ainsworth, F. & Fulcher, L. C. (Eds) (1981). *Group Care for Children: Concepts and Issues*. London: Tavistock.

Argyle, M. (1969). *Social Interaction*. London: Tavistock Publications.

Baldwin, N. (1990). *The Power to Care in Children's Homes*. Aldershot: Avebury.

Bebbington, A. & Miles, J. (1989). 'The background of children who enter Local Authority care.' *British Journal of Social Work*, **19**(5): 349–368.

Beedell, C. (1970). *Residential Life with Children*. London: Routledge & Kegan Paul.

Beedell, C. (1977). 'Working with individuals in the residential context.' *Social Work Today*, **8**(26): 11–16.

Berridge, D. (1985). *Children's Homes*. London: Basil Blackwell.

Berridge, D. & Brodie, I. (1997). *Children's Homes Revisited*. London: Jessica Kingsley.

Berry, J. (1975). *Daily Experience of Residential Life*. London: Routledge & Kegan Paul.

Biehal, N., Clayden, J., Stein, M., & Wade, J. (1995). *Moving On: Young People and Leaving Care Schemes*. London: HMSO.

Blatt, E. (1990). 'Staff supervision and the prevention of institutional child abuse and neglect.' *Journal of Child and Youth Care*, **4**(6): 73–80.

Boalt-Boëthius, S. (1983). *Autonomy, Coping and Defense in Small Work Groups*. Stockholm: University of Stockholm, Department of Psychology.

Brown, A. & Clough, R. (Eds) (1989). *Groups and Groupings: Life and Work in Day and Residential Centres*. London: Tavistock/Routledge.

Brown, E., Bullock, R., Hobson, C. & Little, M. (1998 forthcoming). *Making Residential Care Work: Structure and Culture in Children's Homes*. Aldershot: Ashgate.

Bullock, R., Little, M. & Millham, S. (1988 forthcoming). *Secure Treatment Outcomes: the Care Careers of very Difficult Adolescents*. Aldershot: Ashgate.

Cartwright, D. & Zander, A. (Eds) (1960). *Group Dynamics: Research and Theory* (2nd edition). Evanston, Illinois: Row, Peterson & Co.

Case, C. (1977). *Culture: The Human Plan*. Washington, D.C.: University Press of America.

CCETSW (1992a). *Setting Quality Standards for Residential Child Care: A Practical Way Forward*. London: Central Council for Education and Training in Social Work.

CCETSW (1992b). *Residential Child Care in the Diploma in Social Work*. London: Central Council for Education and Training in Social Work.

Children Act 1989, Chapter 41. London: HMSO.

Department of Health and Social Services (Northern Ireland) (1986). *Report of the Committee of Inquiry into Children's Homes and Hostels*, London: HMSO.

Department of Health (1991a). *Inspecting for Quality: Guidance on Practice for Inspection Units in Social Services Departments and Other Agencies. Policy, Issues and Recommendations.* London: HMSO.

Department of Health (1991b). *The Children Act 1989, Guidance and Regulations, Volume 4, Residential Care.* London: HMSO.

Department of Health (1991c). *Children in the Public Care: A Review of Residential Child Care.* London: HMSO (The Utting Report).

Department of Health (1992). *Choosing with Care—The Report of the Committee of Inquiry into the Selection, Development and Management of Staff in Children's Homes.* London: HMSO (The Warner Report).

Douglas, T. (1986). *Group Living: The Application of Group Dynamics in Residential Settings.* London: Tavistock.

Farmer, E. & Pollock, S. (1998 forthcoming). *Caring for Sexually Abused and Abusing Children away from Home.* Chichester: Wiley.

Fisher, M., Marsh, P., & Phillips, D. with Sainsbury, E. (1986). *In and out of Care: The Experiences of Children, Parents and Social Workers.* London: Batsford in association with British Agencies for Adoption and Fostering.

Fulcher, L. C. & Ainsworth, F. (1985). *Group Care Practice with Children.* London: Tavistock.

Gibbs, I. & Sinclair, I. (1988 forthcoming). 'Private and local authority children's homes: a comparison'. *J. of Adolescence.*

Golan, N. (1981). *Passing through Transitions: a Guide for Practitioners.* London: Collier Macmillan.

Handy, C. B. (1985). *Understanding Organizations* (3rd edition). Harmondsworth: Penguin.

Hardwick, P. J. (1991). 'Families and the professional network: an attempted classification of professional network actions which can hinder change.' *Journal of Family Therapy*, **13**(2) May: 187–206.

Hills, D. & Child, G. (1998 forthcoming). *Evaluating Residential Child Care Training: Towards Qualified Leadership.* Chichester: Wiley.

Howe, E. (1992). *The Quality of Care. A Report of the Residential Staffs Inquiry.* Local Government Management Board on behalf of the National Joint Council for Local Authorities' Administrative, Professional, Technical and Clerical Services.

Jaques, E. (1974). 'Social systems as a defense against persecutory and depressive anxiety'. Chapter 11 in G. S. Gibbard, J. J. Hartman & R. D. Mann (Eds) *Analysis of Groups.* San Francisco: Jossey-Bass.

Kahan, B. (1994). *Growing up in Groups.* London: HMSO.

Knapp, M. (1989). *Measuring Child Care Outcomes.* PSSRU Discussion Paper 630, Canterbury: University of Kent.

Krueger, R. A. (1988). *Focus Groups: A Practical Guide for Applied Research.* London: Sage.

Levy, A. & Kahan, B. (1991). *The Pindown Experience and the Protection of Children: Report of the Staffordshire Child Care Inquiry.* Staffordshire County Council.

Lewin, K. (1935). *A Dynamic Theory of Personality: Selected Papers.* New York: Jessica Kingsley.

Lewin, K. (1951). *Field Theory in Social Science: Selected Theoretical Papers.* New York: Harper & Bros.

Lewin, K. (1966). 'Group decision and social change.' In E. E. Maccoby, T. M. Newcomb, & E. L. Hartley (Eds) *Readings in Social Psychology* (3rd edition). London: Methuen, pp. 197-211.

Little, M. with S. Kelly (1995). *A Life without Problems? The Achievements of a Therapeutic Community*. Aldershot: Ashgate.

Manning, N. (1980). 'Collective disturbance in institutions: a sociological view of crisis and collapse.' *International Journal of Therapeutic Communities*, **1**(3): 147–158.

Marrow, A. F. (1969). *The Practical Theorist: The Life and Work of Kurt Lewin*. New York: Basic Books.

Marsh, P. (1990). 'Changing practice in child care—the Children Act 1989.' *Adoption and Fostering*, **14**(4): 27–30.

Marsh, P. & Triseliotis, J. (Eds) (1993). *Prevention and Reunification in Child Care*. London: Batsford.

McDavid, J. W. & Harari, H. (1968). *Social Psychology: Individuals, Groups, Societies*. New York: Harper & Row.

Menzies Lyth, I. (1988). *Containing Anxieties in Institutions: Selected Essays*, Volume 1, London: Free Association Books.

Miles, M. B. & Huberman, A. M. (1984). *Qualitative Data Analysis: A Sourcebook of New Methods*. London: Sage.

Millham, S., Bullock, R., Hosie, K., & Haak, M. (1981). *Issues of Control in Residential Child-Care*. London: HMSO.

Millham, S., Bullock, R., Hosie, K., & Haak, M. (1986). *Lost in Care: The Problem of Maintaining Links between Children in Care and their Families*. London: Gower.

Morgan, D. L. (1988). *Focus Groups as Qualitative Research*. London: Sage.

National Children's Bureau (1990). *Working with the Children Act 1989*. London: National Children's Bureau.

National Children's Bureau (1991). *Residential Care and the Children Act 1989: A Resource Pack for Staff in Residential Child Care Settings*. London: National Children's Bureau.

Newcomb, T. M. & Hartley, E. L. (Eds) (1947). *Readings in Social Psychology*. New York: Holt.

Nitsun, M. (1991). 'The Anti-Group: destructive forces in the group and their therapeutic potential.' *Group Analysis*, **24**(1): 7–20.

Olweus, D. (1994). 'Bullying at school: basic facts and effects of a school based intervention program.' *Journal of Child Psychology and Psychiatry*, **35**(7): 1171–1190.

O'Hagan, K. (1993) *Emotional and Psychological Abuse of Children*. Buckingham: Open University Press.

Packman, J. & Jordan, B. (1991). 'The Children Act: looking forward, looking back.' *British Journal of Social Work*, **21**(4): 315–327.

Parker, R., Ward, H., Jackson, S., Aldgate, J., & Wedge, P. (Eds) (1991). *Looking after Children: Assessing Outcomes in Child Care*. London: HMSO.

Parker, R. (1988). Residential care for children.' In I. Sinclair (Ed.) *Residential Care: The Research Reviewed*. London: HMSO.

Parkes, C. M. & Stevenson-Hinde, J. (1982). *The Place of Attachment in Human Behaviour*. London: Tavistock.

Peterson, C., Maier, S., & Seligman, M. E. P. (1993). *Learned Helplessness: A Theory for the Age of Personal Control*. New York: Oxford University Press.

Philpot, T. (Ed.) (1989). *The Residential Opportunity? The Wagner Report and After*. Wallington, Surrey: Reed Business Publishing/Community Care.

Redl, F. & Wineman, D. (1957). *The Aggressive Child*. New York: The Free Press.

Redl, F. (1966). 'The concept of a "therapeutic milieu"'. 'Group emotion and leadership' and 'The phenomenon of contagion and "Shock Effect"'. In F. Redl, *When We Deal with Children: Selected Writings*. New York: The Free Press.

Roberts, J. P. (1980). 'Destructive processes in a therapeutic community.' *International Journal of Therapeutic Communities*, 1(3): 159–170.

Rose, M. (1990). *Healing Hurt Minds: The Peper Harow Experience*. London: Tavistock/Routledge.

Rosenfeld, A. & Wasserman, S. (1990). *Healing the Heart: A Therapeutic Approach to Disturbed Children in Group Care*. Washington, D.C.: Child Welfare League of America.

Sanford, N. (1981). 'A model for Action Research.' In P. Reason & J. Rowan (Eds) *Human Inquiry: A Sourcebook of New Paradigm Research*. New York: Wiley.

Schein, E. (1990a). 'Organizational culture.' *American Psychologist*, February: 109–119.

Schein, E. (1990b). *Organization Culture and Leadership: A Dynamic View*. San Francisco: Jossey-Bass.

Seligman, M. E. P. (1975). *Helplessness: On Depression, Development, and Death*. San Francisco: W. H. Freeman.

Shealy C. N. (1995). 'From Boys Town to Oliver Twist: separating fact from fiction in welfare reform and out-of-home placement of children and youth.' *American Psychologist*, August: 565–580.

Shorter Oxford English Dictionary (3rd edition), 1955.

Sinclair, I. & Gibbs, I. (1998 forthcoming). *Children's Homes: A Study in Diversity*. Chichester: Wiley.

Social Services Inspectorate and the Department of Health (1994). *Standards for Residential Services: A Handbook for Social Services Managers and Inspectors, Users of the Services and their Families*. London: HMSO.

Stein, M. & Carey, C. (1976). *Leaving Care*. London: Blackwell.

Strauss, A. & Corbin, J. (1990). *Basics of Qualitative Research: Grounded Theory Procedures and Techniques*. London: Sage.

Tizard, J., Sinclair, I., & Clarke, R. (Eds) (1975). *Varieties of Residential Care Experience*. London: Routledge & Kegan Paul.

Trieschman, A. E., Whittaker, J. K., & Brendtro, L. K. (1969). *The Other 23 Hours*. Chicago: Aldine.

Wade, J. & Biehal, N., with Clayden, J. & Stein, M. (1998). *Going Missing: Responding to the Needs of Young People*. Social Work Research and Development Unit, University of York. Report to the Department of Health.

Wagner, G. (1988). *Residential Care: A Positive Choice*. London: HMSO.

Ward, H. (Ed.) (1995). *Looking After Children, Research into Practice. The Second Report of the Department of Health on Assessing Outcomes in Child Care*. London: HMSO.

Waterhouse, L. (1989). 'In defence of residential care.' In S. Morgan & P. Righton (Eds) *Child Care: Concerns and Conflicts*. London: Hodder & Stoughton in association with the Open University.

Wheelan, S. A., Peptone, E. A. & Abt, V. (Eds) (1990). *Advances in Field Theory*. London: Sage.

Whitaker, D. S. (1987). 'Groupwork understandings and skills applied to intervening in personal networks.' *Journal of Social Work Practice*, 93–112.

Whitaker, D. S. (1992). 'Transposing learnings from group psychotherapy to work groups.' 15th S. H. Foulkes Annual Lecture. *Group Analysis*, 25(2): 131–149.

Whitaker, D.S. & Archer, L. (1992). *The Impact of a Serious Fire on the Peper Harow Community.* Unpublished research report, University of York: Department of Social Policy and Social Work.

Whitaker, D. S. & Cook, J. (1984). *The Experience of Residential Care from the Perspectives of Childlren, Parents, and Care-Givers.* Unpublished research report, University of York: Department of Social Policy and Social Work.

White, R., Carr, P., & Lowe, N. (1990). *A Guide to the Children Act 1989.* London: Butterworth.

Whyte, W. F. (1991). *Participatory Action Research,* London: Sage.

INDEX

Action Research, 7, 133–4
  as described by Lewin, 134
  as presented to staff, 134, 151–2
  as elaborated for purposes of
      analysing practice, 134
  diagram showing steps in, 135
  staff reactions to, 136–9
  as a structure to guide goal-setting,
      planning, and taking action,
      139–40
  as a template for understanding
      practice, 140–4
Argyle, M., 3, 239

Baldwin, N., 95, 238
Biehal, N., Clayden, J., Stein, M., and
  Wade, J., 206, 238

Case, C., 218, 238
CCETSW (Central Council for
  Education and Training in Social
  Work), 95, 238
Children see Young people
Children Act 1989, 103, 105, 154,
  238
Children Act 1989, Volume 4 of
  Guidance and Regulations, 53,
  154, 239
Constructive group situations, 67–70
Containing and controlling, 52–4
  examples of, 60
  good practice in relation to, 168
Corrective emotional experiences see
  Reparative experiences
Crucial emotional experiences see
  Reparative experiences
Culture
  consonance and dissonance, 117–19
  definition and components of, 2–3
  and Group Dynamics, 4–5

salient features of, in Children's
    Homes, 208–18
totalities or Gestalten, 218–20

Demographic information
  about Homes, 10–13
  about staff, 10–11
  about the location of Homes, 11
Destructive group situations, 70–73
'Disconfirming experiences' see
    Reparative experiences

Education Services: Authorities,
    schools, Education Welfare
    Officers, teachers, 108–10

Field social workers, 91–94
Force-field analyses
  description of, 180–1
  use of, for improving outcomes for
      young people, 199–206
  use of, for improving practice,
      182–94
Frontiers
  good practice in relation to working
      at, 168–9
  young persons', 54–6

Goals
  dropped or interrupted, 138–9
  overall, 182
  set by others in the organisation,
      145–6
  set by staff, 136–7
  strategies for achieving, 182–93
Good patches and bad patches
  inevitability of oscillations between, 46
  mixed character of, 42
  triggers for, 43–6
  also see Ups and downs

Generalising to other Homes,
    elsewhere, 223–37
Group dynamics
    and culture, 4–5
    definition and components of, 3–4
    salient features of, in Children's
        Homes, 208–18

Heads of Homes *see* Unit managers
Health Services: Authorities, hospitals,
    general practitioners, 107–8
Homes in the study, descriptions of,
    11–13

Inappropriate placements, 87–9
    types of, 87–8
Individual young people, working
    with, 47–65
    approaches to, 48–50
        through one-to-one work, 48–9
        through brief exchanges, 49–50
        through working with groups of
            young people, 50, 67–70
        through working with others, 50–2
        Examples of, 50–2, 55, 59, 60, 61,
            62, 63–4, 144, 146–8, 148–9,
            155–6, 156–7, 158, 160, 160–1,
            163–4
    'fronts' for, 52–60
        containing and controlling, 52–4
        providing reparative experiences,
            56–9
        working at the 'frontier' of young
            persons' needs, 54–5
        working simultaneously on
            different fronts, 59–60
    setting goals, 48
    slow progress and set-backs, 60–2
        break-throughs, 61
        constraints on work, 63–4
        young people with whom staff
            feel they cannot work, 62–3

Knapp, M., 206, 239

Lewin, K.
    and action research cycles, 134
    and force-field diagrams, 180, 239
    and the concept of life-space, 23
Life space
    diagram of, 24

of staff, 23–24
Line-manager, role and pivotal
    position of, 94–6

McDavid, J.W., and Harari, H., 23, 240
Milham, S., Bullock, R., Hosie, K., &
    Haak, M., 53, 240
Mix of young people, 18
    changes in the mix, 80
    character of favourable and
        unfavourable mixes, 78–80
Mix of young people, working with
    the, 66–80
    avoiding difficult mixes, 73
    avoiding escalating difficult
        situations, 76–5
    examples of, 67–8, 70–2, 74, 75, 76,
        77, 156, 157–8, 159, 160–2, 164–5
    good practice in working with the
        mix, 171–3
    repairing the consequences of
        difficult group situations, 75–6
    responding to early warning signs, 74

Neighbours, 113–14, 162–3
Networks, a Home's, 113–19
    component parts of
        Inspection Teams, 116
        local schools, 116
        neighbours, 113–14
        other Departments in own
            organisation, 114–16
        the general public, 116–17
    cultural consonances and
        dissonances between members
        of, 117–19
    see also Networks, young persons',
        formal parts of
Networks, young persons'
    examples of, 102–3, 104, 109, 113,
        115, 162–3
    formal parts of, 107–12
    informal parts of, 102–07
    staff as members of, 112–13
    working with, 102–13
        good practice in, 173–5
Newcomb, T.M., and Hartley, E.I., 134,
    240

Officers-in-charge, *see* Unit managers
Organisation, the larger

and communication problems, 82–4
and differences in priorities 99–100
examples of, 82, 83, 84–5, 96. 88–9,
    89, 90, 90–1,92, 92–3, 94, 96, 97,
    159–60
good practice with reference to,
    175–6
imbalances between the location of
    decision-making power and of
    information in, 98–9
and impact of decisions made by
    managers, 86–7
and impact of restructuring, 96
key figures in, 81
and lack of clarity with respect to
    jurisdiction, 99
and relationships with field social
    workers, 92–4
and support or otherwise from
    managers, 84–6
and tensions around inspections,
    90–2
and tensions around placements,
    87–9
and tensions around staff selection,
    89–90
working with and being managed
    by, 82–100
Outcomes for individual young
    people, 195–207
actions to improve, 205–06
assessing, times
    for longer-term outcomes, 197–8
    for 'point-of-departure' outcomes,
       196
    for 'way-station' outcomes, 196
consolidated and unconsolidated
    positive, 197
definitions of good, poor, and
    uncertain, 199
factors which support or hinder
    good, 199–204
judged against individual start-state,
    196
points made in the literature
    concerning, 206–07

Parents, foster parents, and relatives,
    103–6
Parker, R., Ward, H., Jackson, S.,
    Aldgate, J., & Wedge, P., 206, 240

Police, the courts, legal procedures,
    110–12
Practice
    arenas in which practice occurs, 148
    characteristics of good, 167–77
    definition of, 153
    errors and their retrieval, 177–8
    examples of good practice, 50–2,
       155–6, 156–7, 157–8, 158, 159,
       159–60, 160, 160–2, 162–3, 163–4,
       164–5
    examples of poor practice, 74, 75
    factors which support or hinder
       good practice, 179–94
    general definitions of good and
       poor, 154
    also see Tasks
Purposes, of the book, 1
    rationale for, 1
    also see Work, purposeful

Quality of Homes, 208–22
    criteria for judging, 221
    features related to, 208–18
    staff-perpetrated abuse and possible
       dynamics, 220–1
    timing of 'readings' of, 221–2

Redl, F., & Wineman, D., 80, 240
Reparative experiences
    definition of, 56
    example of, 146–8
    process of, 57–8
Reparative work, good practice in
    relation to, 169–70
Research
    data-analysis methods, 6–8, 22–3,
       31–2, 47, 66–7
    design requirements, 1
    dissemination and follow-on
       activities, 8–9
    partnership character of, 2
    plan, 5–7
    Project Coordination Group, 7
    Project Workers' Team, 7
Rewards and stresses, 31- 46
    anticipatory stress, 40–1
    failing to manage stress, 130–1
    how rewards compensate for stress, 41
    how stressors combine and persist,
       38–40

Rewards and stresses (*cont.*)
  managing stress, 128–30
  methods for ascertaining, 31–32
  and relation to ups and downs,
    41–2
  sources of rewards, 32–4
  sources of stress, 34–8

Schein, E., 3, 241
Set-backs and reversals, 61–2
  example, 62
Staff groups, viability and non-
  viability, *see* Viability
Staff members
  demographic information about,
    10–11
  induction of, 127–8
  knowledge base needed by, 232–3
  personal qualities needed by, 231–2
  practice skills needed by, 233–4
  selection of, 127
Stresses, *See* Rewards and stresses

Tasks
  categories of, 25–6
  examples in day-to-day work, 19–22
  method for classifying, 22–3
  pile-up of, 28–30
  table showing, 26
Theory
  of action research cycles, 134
  classification of approaches to
    working with young people,
    48–52
  cultural consonances and
    dissonances, 117–19
  culture and group dynamics, 2–5
  of force-fields, 180
  'fronts' for working with individual
    young people, 52–60
  imbalances between the location of
    decision-making power and of
    information in organisations,
    98–9
  Lewin's concepts of life-space, 23

Unit managers
  leadership style of, 209–10
  as newcomers to a staff, 121, 123–4

Ups and downs, 32, 41–3
  see also Good patches and bad
    patches

Viability of staff groups
  and change, 127–8
  definition, of, 120
  examples of failure: 124, 125, 126,
    128
  examples of success: 121–2, 122–3,
    123–4, 126, 127, 129, 130
  failures in maintaining viability,
    124–5
  good practice in, 175
  managing stress, 128–30
  recovering from low morale, 125–6
  team-building exercises, 125–6
  threats to, 131–2
  working to maintain, 121–32

Work
  issues concerning, 150–151
  purposeful, 133–152
Working with and being managed by
  the larger organisation, *see*
  Organisation, the larger
Working with individual young
  people, *see* Individual young
  people
Working with the mix of young
  people, *see* Mix of young people
Working with people and
  organisations in wider networks,
  see Networks
Working within own staff group to
  maintain viability, *see* Viability of
  staff groups

Young people
  care career, 17–18
  circumstances and backgrounds, 13–14
  circumstances around coming to live
    in the Homes, 14–15
  emotional and physical state of,
    15–16
  life stage of, 17
  personal characteristics of, 16–17
  relationships with parents, 17
  schooling, 18